# POWER
# SCREENWRITING

## The 12 Stages
## of
## Story Development

Michael Chase Walker

ifilm publishing

LONE EAGLE PUBLISHING COMPANY, LLC™
1024 N. Orange Dr.
Hollywood, CA 90038
Phone 323.308.3400 or 800.815.0503
A division of IFILM® Corporation, www.hcdonline.com

Printed in the United States of America
10 9 8 7 6 5 4 3 2

Cover design by Lindsay Albert
Book design by Carla Green

Library of Congress Cataloging-in-Publication Data
Walker, Michael Chase
    Power screenwriting : the 12 steps of story development / Michael Chase Walker.
        p.  cm.
    ISBN 1-58065-041-4
    1. Motion picture authorship.  I. Title.

    PN1996.W225 2002
    808.2'3--dc21                                    2001050213

Books may be purchased in bulk at special discounts for promotional or educational purposes. Special editions can be created to specifications. Inquiries for sales and distribution, textbook adoption, foreign language translation, editorial, and rights and permissions inquiries should be addressed to: Jeff Black, Lone Eagle Publishing, 1024 N. Orange Drive, Hollywood, CA 90038 or send e-mail to info@ifilm.com.

Distributed to the trade by National Book Network, 800-462-6420.
IFILM® and Lone Eagle Publishing Company™ are registered trademarks.

# CONTENTS

# WHY I WRITE

I've spent the better part of my life reading, learning, developing and telling stories of one kind or another. Whether through the boundless reaches of my childhood imagination, or in the wiles and wilderness of Millbrook, New York—under the auspices of Dr. Timothy Leary—where I devoured the ancient religious texts of the Old and New Testaments, the Koran, the Bhagavad-Gita, the Chinese Book of Changes, the Egyptian and the Tibetan Books of the Dead; or my six years devoted entirely to Sanskrit literature and Eastern Philosophy. My one constant and abiding desire has been to experience, learn and convey the universal and transcendent power of myth.

From 1975 to the present, this obsession has been largely directed towards the screen with efforts such as (chronologically): *The Ramayana, The Last Unicorn, The Gladiator, Earthman's Burden, The Alamo, V: The Series, The Wayside School, The Michael Rockefeller Story, Pinocchio's Christmas, Sir Gawain and the Green Knight, The Flight of Dragons, Mount Analog, Christmas in Camelot, Wee Geordie, Cupid, Sleepy Hollow, Catch a Fire, After Man, Folktale, Lizzie Borden, The Song of Solomon, Love and Anarchy, The Beast Is Dead, The Mask of the Red Paw, Cupid and Psyche, The Arrow and the Lamp, The Court Jester, Siddhartha, Seven Years in Tibet, Supernatural, An American Tragedy, Mister Death and the Red-Headed Woman, The Sorcerer's Apprentice, Witches, Circus Gallacticus* and *The Poet and the Tsar,* for which I have served in a variety of writing and/or producing capacities at TriStar Pictures, Amblin, DreamWorks, Warner Bros., Marble

Arch Productions, New World Productions, Vanguard Films, Howard Grossman Productions and Rankin Bass Productions.

As a network executive at CBS Entertainment, I conceived, developed and supervised production for the shows that would become *Pee Wee's Playhouse, Galaxy High School* and *Wildfire,* as well as supervising over seventy hours of animated and live-action television programs.

My switch from producing to writing came in 1988 after tiring of the inconstant variables in getting a film off the ground. I had been languishing in development for an agonizing two years when Sydney Pollack, the legendary film director whose offices I shared at the then-fledgling TriStar Pictures, took me aside one day and told me bluntly, "Producers don't get films made, Michael. Actors, writers and directors do." It was the best thing he could have said to me. After some ten years of seeing one project after another fail because of the weakness of a writer's script, I'd had it! I never wanted to ever have to depend on another writer again.

While working in New York around Christmas that year, a film producer and very good friend, John H. Williams of Vanguard Films (*Shrek, Seven Years in Tibet*), suggested I make a change. My thirteen-year marriage was on the rocks, my career at a crossroads and the television program I was consulting on was a soul-crushing disaster.

"Michael, you're one of the best storytellers I know. Why aren't you writing screenplays?" he asked.

I had dabbled in it and even earned some supplementary income writing animated movies and television shows for Hanna-Barbera (*Dinosaurs*), Filmation (*He-Man* and *She-Ra*) and World Event Productions (*Voltron*), but the prospect of becoming a full-time screenwriter seemed a big stretch. First of all, I was far too extroverted to sit in a room for umpteen hours a day banging away at a typewriter. (Yes, we wrote on typewriters way back then!) I'd always been a good salesman, a shmoozer, a pitch man, an enthusiastic "idea guy," but I thought mustering the discipline, craft and intellectual weight that writing would require was way out of my league. But John responded with something else in mind, or rather in his jacket pocket: a fully paid tuition to Robert McKee's "Story Structure Seminar." "Merry Christmas," he said, handing over my ticket. I'll never forget that moment, or his act of shrewd generosity. My entire life was about to change.

Robert McKee's enthusiasm for film and literature, along with his passionate insights into the craft of screenwriting, jolted me out of my lethargy like a proverbial Saul on the road to Development Hell. After ten years in the entertainment industry—with some successes and many disappointments—my own passion and integrity had dwindled, along with a thousand cherished dreams. To hear McKee speak with such conviction was more inspiring than anything else I'd heard in my entire time working in Hollywood. Here was a teacher, writer and former actor, speaking and even singing, about truth, philosophy, love and the great movies that had changed his life. It was a far cry from the producers and studio executives I was used to, whose primary passion was having their BMWs detailed over lunch.

Yet I cannot and will not fault them, for I had also fallen victim to the same vacuous Hollywood syndrome. My reluctance to write my own stories, or hone my own story-crafting skills, while relying on others to do it for me, was exactly what was wrong with the studio system and, ultimately, with me.

I've always had an innate talent and sense to recognize the type of book, story or concept that could make a terrific film. Over my fifteen years in the business I've watched a hundred of them become other people's movies, either because I couldn't get the material up to speed, or because the project was too ambitious for its time. In the end I had no one to blame but myself. If I wasn't taking the time to craft my own ideas into screenplay form and prove they were achievable to myself, then why should I expect others to spend the time and money developing them? The nexus of failure was in my own lethargy.

To repent for my years of empty-headedness, I spent between eight to fourteen hours of every day of the next eleven years devoted entirely to the craft of screenwriting. I watched at least ten films a week, attended every seminar, and pored over every book I could find on the subject. I went back and read and reread the masters of literature, myth and theater, from the entire works of Joseph Campbell to Charles Dickens, Vladamir Nabokov, Anais Nin, Ernest Hemingway, Henry Miller, Plato, Aristotle, Alexander Pushkin, Molière, Paddy Chayevsky, Clifford Odets, Horace Walpole, Josh Logan, Harold Clurman, Sanford Meisner and Stanislavsky. Through it all I weathered different countries, seven homes, divorce, a bankruptcy, destitution, isolation, alienation from friends and family, abject solitude and even a few moments of personal insanity in furtherance of my goal—to see the world through an original mind and to be able to put it down on paper. The result is this book, fifteen screenplays (including *Catch a Fire: The Bob Marley Story, The Mask of the Red Paw, Folktale, Sleepy Hollow, Seven Years in Tibet, Love and Anarchy, The Poet and the Tsar, The Song of Solomon, The Sorcerer's Apprentice* and *The Arrow and the Lamp*), various independent development deals and a five year lecture course at the College of Santa Fe, where I taught Screenwriting, Story Development and The History of Animation.

*"All art is magick!"*

*—Aleister Crowley*

At the time, I thought I was doing what was necessary to become a screenwriter. I never realized that with every word I worried, every sentence I scrutinized, every storyline and plot twist I wrestled with, some ineffable force was purging, cleansing, rectifying me, absolving me of the cynic, the supercilious "showman," the "pitch" man, and forging in me the substance of an artist, mythmaker and teacher.

And yet that is exactly the transformational power of our stories. Virginia Woolf once wrote, "Love is a story we tell ourselves, about someone else." To which I would I add, as is life itself, a story! Whether it is the Buddhist musing of the "Emperor who dreams he is a butterfly only to ponder if he is a butterfly dreaming he is an emperor," or the ancient Mayan proverb, "We are but a dream, dreaming," or, as the ancient Jewish saying reminds us, "We do not see the world the way it is, we see it the way we are." It is all, everything, a wonderful, terrible, marvelous, story!

The magical power of the writer then, is the ability to change the story, for himself first and then for the rest of his or her tribe. Its transcendent experience is not just for those who observe it on the screen, but for those fortunate enough to be called to the "Calling" itself.

This book is not only for those who intend to write for the movies. It is for all artists, seekers, thinkers, philosophers, raconteurs and mythmakers. The archetypes herein are the foundations of consciousness, psychology and human evolution. Not only will they provide the essential tools and inspiration to the modern storyteller, but perhaps they will enhance the overall transformational experience of movie-goers and movie makers around the globe.

Michael Chase Walker
Santa Fe, New Mexico

# ACKNOWLEDGMENTS

I would like to acknowledge my extreme debt and gratitude to the lectures, wisdom and genius of John Truby. I had the good fortune of stumbling across a selection of Truby's Story Structure tapes tucked away in a producer's drawer, while pulling double duty writing chores on *Sleepy Hollow* and *Seven Years in Tibet* back in 1993. I can honestly say that listening to these tapes not only started the unraveling of the great mystery of the cinema, but changed my whole way of seeing the world forever. It is my sincere hope that this book may inspire other screenwriters as profoundly as he inspired me.

I would also like to acknowledge the many other individuals who have made my life's journey, and specifically this book, possible. They are numerous and far-reaching in their specific contributions either by guiding, goading, instructing, observing, obstructing or facilitating my incremental enlightenment. Each is magnanimous in their own right; whether as collaborator, mentor, friend, ally or even dark antagonist, I am very proud to have known them all.

Dan Blatt, Martin Starger, Sydney Pollack, Jeffrey B. Walker, Edward L. Rissien, Gary Hendler, John Calley, Jack Rapke, Paul Flaherty, John Feltheimer, Chris Columbus, Anthea Sylbert, Willie Hunt, Mark Zander, Peter S. Beagle, Maggie Fields, Mark Gesarch, Linda Palmer, Gary Abrahams, Kit Thomas, Mo Siegel, Barry Glasser, Paul Lazarus, Arthur Nadel, Lou Scheimer, Margaret Loesch, David and Zev Braun, Sydney Beckerman, Christopher Lee, Lou Weitzman, Charles Hirschhorn, Steve Tolkin, Paul Reubens, Howard Grossman, Syd Iwanter, Richard Gilbert

"The secret to great storytelling, as to living a full and rich life, is to learn to appreciate your opponents and villains as much as your heroes and allies. Try as you may to hate, separate or deny them unduly, ultimately they are only a reflection of your self."

*—Anonymous*

Abramson, Alan Berger, John Burnham, Bob Crestani, Phil Hartman, Bruce Wasserman, Judy Price, Candy Monteiro, Fredda Rose, Guy and Jacqui Magar, Donna Ostroff, Mike Young, Peter Rosenthal, Steve Oaks, Tony Lani, Kathleen Courtney, Nancy Coyne, Carol Scott, Doug Wood, David Sheehan, Arthur Rankin, Buzz Potamkin, Danny Goldberg, Flint Dille, Christian Miller, Robert Rhoades, John Parkinson, Temple Mathews, Bill and Marisa Berry, Rich Vokulich, Brad Waisbren, Howard Grossman, Harris Tulchin, Miguel and Debby Grunstein, and Rudy Langlis.

Jonathan Wacks, Joelle Collier, Gene Youngblood, Danny Rubin, Chris Orbaker, Deborah Fort, Carole Evans, Randy Man and the students and staff of the Moving Image Arts Department at The College of Santa Fe.

To Lauren Rossini, Mirabai Starr, Liz Rhymland, Corinne Lebrun and Jane Crawford who gave their precious time, skill, comments, criticisms and editorial wisdom. I dedicate these immortal words of Von Goethe to you: "Das Ewig-Weibliche Zieht uns Hinan."

To Jane Janssen, my former wife and child bride. Though the winds of change have blown between us, thirteen years and a beautiful son are deserving enough.

To my son Joshua, whose ancient wisdom, artistic, psychological and musical prowess along with his ferocious integrity are a constant and abiding inspiration to me. I am blessed to walk with you on the journey.

To my mother Patricia Frye, who deserved so much more than she ever bargained for. To my father, Jack Walker, whose humor and advice I miss terribly. To my "other mother" Phyliss Altman, who has always kept her heart, hearth and home fires radiating with warmth and graciousness. To my friend and patron, Dr. Jacquelyne Doyle, without whom this book would not be possible.

And finally to John and Lacey Ford Williams, who befriended and supported me and my talent, work and craftsmanship through a dozen different unwieldy incarnations. You saw in me worth, vision and talent that I scarcely saw in myself, and for that I will be eternally grateful.

"The more successful the villain the more successful the picture."

–Alfred Hitchcock

# FADE IN:

Writing for motion pictures is now more popular than ever, and with the record breaking fees paid for finished screenplays it is no great wonder why. How-to manuals, monthly magazines, seminars, tapes, software and writers boot camps have proliferated so that an aspiring screenwriter has more assistance than ever before to guide him through the elaborate turns of creative storytelling. Unfortunately, there is a type of lottery mentality that accompanies this new gold rush, and many of the popular techniques being offered are more directed towards exploiting these "get rich quick" abstractions. The truth is, the odds of writing and selling a screenplay are probably just as great as winning the state lottery or the next Publisher's Clearing House Sweepstakes. Yet, with the emphasis directed towards the big bucks sale, the aspiring screenwriter may be deprived of one of the greatest transformational processes known to man: the craft of spinning a well-told story.

The best and most enduring stories have always solved problems. From the earliest cave pictures of horned rhinoceros found in Lascaux, to those of reborn Osiris on the temple walls of Luxor—every story is an attempt to communicate the storyteller's view of the world's problems and how to remedy them. Our earliest myths sought to explain the natural events of earth while those of the Middle Ages concerned one's duty to God, the Church and the prevailing monarchy. The birth of sentimental love in the 11th century brought about the romance literature of the 18th and 19th centuries with their dire warnings about society's repressive hold over human desire. These haunting, ghostly tales told how people's lives could be ruined by paying either too much, or not enough, attention to love's beckoning.

Today, we ponder the impact of technology on our intuitive selves and we worry about integrity in an age of mindless talk shows and lottery fever. We are concerned with international and national terrorism, racial violence, legislated morality, governmental encroachment on personal liberties, mindless conformity, repressed sexuality and the disintegration of the traditional family unit. With the dearth of provocative problem-solving myths in these arenas, we can actually witness our confusion playing themselves out in real life tragedies, such as the bombing of the World Trade Center, the O.J. Simpson trial, The Clinton/Lewinsky scandals, or even the election debacle of the year 2000.

"The truth will find us out," so to speak. Yet it is not the writer's task to merely chime in with the prevailing cacophony and regurgitate these scandals into the latest Movie-of-the-Week; it is the writer's task to try to shed new light and meaning on these explosive social issues, much like the ancient court viziers and magicians would decipher dreams and the stars. Just as our private dreams reveal our innermost fears and subconscious emotional blocks, our national scandals and urban dramas portray mankind's collective unconscious in catharsis. We wrestle with anxieties about our own xenophobia and the future of our society, species and planet by going to movies that play out those fears for us: *Star Wars* enchants us and *Close Encounters, Alien* and *Blade Runner* appear to shed further light on the subject and we accept these fanciful musings until *Contact* and *A.I.* arrive to further our thinking in more contemporary ways. In this way, we inch forward through the power of our own myth-making and story telling. The better the storyteller applies his craft, hopefully, the more civilization advances in its intellectual, emotional and inter-personal growth.

The screenwriter today must strive to be a prophet, shaman, truth-teller, mystic, hero and outlaw. He or she must be a non-conforming, independent "free" thinker. As Quentin Tarantino quips in his cameo appearance in the movie *Sleep with Me*, "It's about being subversive!"

Sigmund Freud suggests the heroic dilemma in his book, *Sexuality and the Psychology of Love*, "*Since the beginning of civilization, man has had but one choice, to conform or not to conform. If he conforms he is a dead man. His life is over, his life's decisions predetermined by the society he joins with. If he chooses not to conform, he buys himself one more choice, to become outlaw or hero.*"

While the outlaw proclaims his individuality by striking out against conformist society and its rigid hypocrisy, he winds up unwittingly joining an even greater nation of sheep, either in prison, or with a more harshly defined sub-culture of criminals. The modern hero, on the other hand, first determines what is deficient within himself and then elects to change, usually leaving us a chronicle how others might do the same.

As Joseph Campbell writes in the last paragraph of *The Hero with a Thousand Faces*, "*The modern hero, the modern individual who dares to heed the call and seek the mansion of that presence with whom it is our whole destiny to be atoned, cannot, indeed, must not, wait for his community to cast off its slough of pride, fear, rationalized avarice, and sanctified misunderstanding. 'Live,' Nietzsche says, 'as though the day were here.' It is not society that is to guide the creative hero, but precisely the reverse.*"

The mythic movie hero is usually someone who is acting in a way that is off-kilter. He or she goes about life wounded in some capacity and that flaw affects everyone and everything around him. When an inciting incident occurs and presents the challenge of a lifetime, the hero must strive to correct his way of acting, and make the necessary changes in time, in order to defeat his opponent and achieve his goal. This is the general plot of the well-told story: *Someone wants something very, very badly, but must change in order to defeat his opponent and obtain his desire.*

In the movie *Witness* (written by William Kelly, Pamela Wallace and Earl Wallace), Harrison Ford plays John Book, a self-righteous, "holier-than-thou" cop. He behaves this way in reaction to the corruption of his fellow detectives. When he is assigned to protect an innocent Amish boy, he is faced with the challenge of a lifetime. He must change from being a man "of the gun of the hand" to being a witness to the power of true righteousness over violence and corruption. As John Book states in the motion picture's riveting climax, "What are you going to do, Paul? Kill him, kill her, kill me? When does it all stop?"

In the end, and through the exciting climax of this motion picture, we all become witnesses to the power of true righteousness over corruption when we witness the peace-loving Amish community disarm the corrupt police officer, Paul Schaeffer, by the overwhelming presence of their moral integrity.

In the film *Moonstruck* (written by John Patrick Shanley), Cher plays Loretta Castorini, a frumpy bookkeeper about to marry Johnny Cammareri—not because she loves him, but because she feels cursed. When she meets his younger brother, Ronny, a tragically wounded, ogre-like baker, she is faced with the challenge of a lifetime. Loretta must eschew her silly belief systems about marriage and accept passionate love, with all of its terrifying mystery. In the end she summons the courage to trust her emotions again and finds true romance.

Of course, not all film heroes change: James Bond, Ace Ventura, Batman and other action figures are too busy *effecting change,* by saving the world or making us laugh, to undergo personal transformation. However, in the film stories we turn to time and time again, be it *Casablanca, Witness, Moonstruck, Chinatown* or *In the Line of Fire,* the hero solves a personal problem and undergoes a change that endears him to us forever. We are grateful for their experience because most of us do not have the time in our busy lives to pursue self-transformation. Instead, we go to the movies. We pay movie stars a lot of money to show us *how* to change. The lay movie audience must pay the bills, feed the insurance companies, serve its families and provide for its children. These normal everyday distractions obstruct them from the hard, introspective work of determining their purpose in life. Of all the folks who toil to make one motion picture—from the star to the producer to the director—the person most likely to undergo a deep transformational experience is the writer. The true storyteller spends a lifetime pondering the issues he writes about—passionately arguing his point of view, before devoting months, if not years, to putting it down on paper.

Since the dawn of time (another tale we tell ourselves) stories have shaped our lives, belief systems and civilizations. The power of these stories, created and recorded for thousands of years, is as alive today as when they were first handed down. The archetypal Greek gods are as commonly evoked in the offices of Jungian psychologists today as they were during the great mystery plays of ancient Eleusis over three thousand years ago. The sky deity Jehovah is as demanding and judgmental today as when he first guided Moses on Mount Zion. So-called sophisticated societies still go to war over sentiments formed thousands of years ago by zealous writers and prophets. We may question their sanity, but these ancient myths are proof that a well-told story can last for millennia.

For what are *One Flew Over the Cuckoo's Nest*, *Cool Hand Luke* and *Dead Poets Society* if not brilliant restructurings of the dying god myths and messiah tales of ancient Sumeria, Judea and early Christianity? The power of a well-told story can inspire revolutions, renaissances, religions and inquisitions. They are transformational on both an individual and mass scale. The power of creating myths is one of humanity's greatest achievements and one of the most rewarding vocations we can create for ourselves.

This book is designed to inspire and guide the new mythmakers and creative heroes who not only have the courage to change their own lives, but to create the legends and movies that will in turn change the world. As Dostoevsky writes, "If we don't show what man is like, he will never change."

Michael Chase Walker
Santa Fe, New Mexico

# A WRITER IS BORN

You are about to embark upon a wondrous journey of self-discovery and enlightenment. You are standing before a strange new threshold, pleading for admittance to the grand temple's inner sanctum. Inside are the conscious thinkers of the past: Plato, Socrates, Homer, Freud, Jung, Nietzsche, Ortega Y Gassett, Steinbeck, Arendt, Joyce, Miller, Hawthorne, Nin, Melville. You are asking to join the great fraternity and sorority of the collective conscious.

Will you be allowed in?

What are your credentials? Your papers, please?

We're sorry, but entry is not permissible in your present state. We require rebirth. We are asking you to take birth in the realm of true being, of non-denominational awareness. We are asking you to lay yourself bare before your own inner genius without pretense, rank or material classification.

Welcome. You made it. You are now an orphan/wanderer/hero facing the great journey before you. You are now free to make mistakes on your own terms. There will be no punishment, gold stars or grades. It is entirely up to you. You are free to wile away the hours conversing with the flowers, cavorting with the trees; free from any form of the Protestant, Jewish, capitalist, corporate work ethic. You are now a free soul poet, set loose to explore the moral universe that is yours and yours alone to define. Where do you start? What will you do? What is your destiny?

> "God has stolen the mind of the poet and replaced it with his own."
>
> *—Heraclitus*

Don't worry, many of our mentor/guides have set up excellent guideposts. They really want you to succeed. All they ask is that you commit yourself to the truth.

There is an ancient African proverb about the gods of antiquity deciding where they will hide the truth, for, if too easily found, humans won't appreciate it. At first they decide to hide it under a rock, but think better of it in case the fox finds it and steals it away. Then, they consider placing it in a tree, but then quickly change their minds when they think the monkey might discover it and rip it to shreds. Next, they choose a mountain top, until one of them points out that the eagle might snatch it up and spirit it away. In the end, they decide to place it in man's heart for he will rarely, if ever, look for it there.

William James, the father of American psychology states, "Genius is the ability to see things differently than others." So the hallmark of the mythmaker is to develop a second sight into the true nature of things. For this you must stop taking the world at face value. Forget everything you have been taught by others. You must seek your own view of the world. (Isn't this exactly what the historians have done?)

Have you noticed how few of those around you have formed an original opinion of their own? They just seem to go along with what they've been told. Are you frustrated by the way your friends profess one thing and then shrink away when asked to practice it? You will no longer be able to behave this way. You must find your own original voice and back it up with hard choices. It is no longer permissible for you *not* to have a well-formed opinion. We are asking you to commit yourself to your own truth and to the life of a truth seeker/teller. When your ideas are your own, you will care about them profoundly. This commitment to see the truth and tell it like it is the first goal of the storyteller/screenwriter.

The truth is not found in a certain set of circumscribed facts, but in the commitment of the truth-seeker. It lies in the murky realms between right and wrong, morality and immorality, and in most cases it is the opposite of what you have been taught. Don't look to find it in the society around you: your friends, family, the

"Well, my art of midwifery is in most respect like theirs, but differs, in that I attend writers, not women, and I look after their souls when they are in labor, and not after their bodies: and the triumph of my art is in thoroughly examining whether the thought which the mind of the young writer brings forth is a false idol or a noble and true birth."

*—Plato*

church and other organized religions for these will only persuade you to their view of the world. Remember you are a newborn hero and must turn all such preconceived notions and ideas inside out and find that the truth, your truth, lies within you.

What's that? Ralph Waldo speaks to us again.

*"To be great is to be misunderstood."*

Ah yes, thank you.

Now do we bequeath to you the great invincible sword and shield of knowing, the second great mystery revealed—

Failure is success, and success is failure.

You are forthwith absolved and forever encouraged to wallow in your own mistakes. From this day forward you will learn to love your mistakes, to nurture them, bask in them, yearn for them and grow in them because they are yours and yours alone. You will never again blame them on someone else; no one else has earned the right to claim your mistakes. Let them make their own. Your mistakes are yours to keep. You will own up to them, because from them will come your greatest movie heroes and most dastardly villains. Listen to them; they will tell you who they are. They are you.

Being free of the failure/success cycle is the next step. Just because our society and all of its dutiful citizens measure success in terms of capital gain doesn't mean that you have to. Your parents, friends and family may encourage you to forget about writing and get a real job, or tell you that you can do both. They will cite many examples of so and so, and how they achieved success, and you may sometimes even convince yourself they are right. Forget about it. They are wrong.

The artist/writer/hero must cast off the shackles of the success/failure mind-set that moves the world. You are a free spirit now and this freedom means that you must wrest your life back on your own terms. *You must have time for yourself.* You must have time to work out your problems and those of the world. This is the third step to emancipation—to acquire the artist/hero's sentiment.

"A foolish consistency is the hobgoblin of little minds, adored by statesmen and philosophers and divines. With consistency a great soul had little to do...but I say, speak what you think today in hard words and tomorrow speak what tomorrow thinks in hard words again, though it contradicts everything you said today."

*—Ralph Waldo Emerson*

Doomsayers urged Henry Miller to consider a job as a night watchman, as William Faulkner had once been so employed. "Let Faulkner make his own mistakes," Miller retorted, "I have my own to make."

*"I have no money, no resources, no hope.*
*I am the happiest man alive."*

—Henry Miller, *Tropic of Capricorn*

*"A real artist will let his wife starve and his children go barefoot before abandoning his art."*

—George Bernard Shaw

*"Firstly, you're either a revolutionary or you're not,*
*and if you're not you might as well be an artist as anything else.*
*Secondly, if you can't be an artist, you might as well*
*be a revolutionary..."*

—Tom Stoppard

"There is indeed one element in human destiny, that not blindness itself can controvert. Whatever else we are intended to do, we are not intended to succeed; failure is the fate allotted. Our business is to continue to fail in good spirits."

*–Robert Louis Stevenson*

The point here is that by giving credence to one's self—one's words, one's ideas, taking the initial leap of faith—the artist forms a sacred pact with his art: *Truth is more important than money. Art is more powerful than economics.*

As our society does not support the truth seeker, our first task is to show that the hero does not need society's support. If you don't have the required faith in yourself, if you're not up to the task, then no amount of time or financial endowment can give it to you. Here is where you must put it all on the line.

Picture Harrison Ford in *Indiana Jones and The Last Crusade* (written by Willard Huyck and Gloria Katz, based on characters by George Lucas). Indy is teetering over a cavernous abyss, about to take the great Leap of Faith. He hesitates, falters, but then summons the courage to take the first step, and instantly a bridge appears beneath him. He needed to take the first step before he could see it. Writing is like that. You need to take the initial step of believing you have something to say, and to hell with the doom-sayers. The rest will follow; the bridge will appear.

After my divorce, I was surrounded by family members urging me to get a job. I was a single parent raising my seven-year-old son on my own. One by one they argued, "You can't afford to pursue your career as a screenwriter. It isn't fair to your son. You need to get a job and write in your spare time!" I considered their views. They were right. I had exactly $1.35 to my name, and no other income in sight. To add to my troubles, I had to leave the house I was living in within two weeks. The prospect of being a homeless, penniless, single father was very real. "You're right!" I answered, "but if I don't do this now, I'll never do it and if I never do it, I might as well put a gun to my head. My life will have meant nothing. Not to myself. Not to anyone. I'd sooner be dead."

Two days later I received an unsolicited check for thousands of dollars from a film producer who wanted me to ready my affairs—he was sending me on assignment to the West Indies to write the screenplay *Catch A Fire: The Bob Marley Story*. This low point in my life instantly became one of the richest and most rewarding adventures of my career. And it began by saying "nay" to the nay-sayers.

Somehow, saying "no" to those who want you to "stop this nonsense and get a 'real' job," is what the Universe asks of you, to see if you possess the "right stuff" and are able to act on it. The lesson for me was never to underestimate the power of my own art to solve any problem, even my most pressing financial ones.

Our society is an extremely superficial one and often measures a person's worth by how active they are socially. Nietzsche explains this as the residual morality of the aristocratic/slave cultures of the past. A person is judged "good" or "evil" by his ability to contribute and "pay" his way. Our modern value system is formed by this simplistic judgment alone: *money is good, poverty is evil*. This philosophy only serves as an extension of slavery. It is what keeps the rich, rich, and keeps the poor helplessly oppressed.

While driving through the South of France, I was struck by the number of centuries-old castles lined up like gas stations along a busy trade route. These bastions of ancient aristocracy once thrived through robbery, theft and the wholesale murder of innocent peasants and merchant caravans migrating to the sea. This seemed a fitting parable for our modern society as well. The robber barons still prey on the lowly, but rather than bludgeon them with clubs and swords, they use the enticements of television and magazine advertisements to manipulate the masses. Today, the average guy barely stands a chance. He works all day to buy things on credit, paying others to do the work he cannot do, because he's too busy working and acquiring what Madison Avenue says he needs to be a "responsible" citizen. All the while, he thinks he is happy because he has an insurance policy, a house, a family and a decent car. He never quite understands, except in moments of his personal despair, that *his life is not his own!*

"Behold! Human beings living in an underground den...like ourselves...they see only their own shadows, or the shadows of one another, which the fire throws on the opposite wall of the cave."

*–Plato*

Forget about the world, it will do very nicely without you for the time being. The cogs of the commercial machine will keep on turning perpetually and fools will happily rush in to take your place on the assembly lines should you choose to abstain. But what we don't have enough of—will never have enough of—are creative heroes. The hero breaks the chain of slavery and pursues a life of freedom. Every writer must choose to be free and every story he or she tells will ultimately be about that personal journey from slavery to freedom, or vice versa.

In the movie *Ordinary People* (written by Alvin Sargent), we see a family mired in the socially adept, affluent world of suburban Chicago—their lives, emotions, houses, lawns and schools appear to be in picture perfect order. When a beloved son is drowned in a raging storm at sea, the Jarrett family is forced to reexamine their values. Through the heroic journey of the surviving son, Conrad, the family is released from a type of emotionally bleak, living death, and reborn as a collection of individuals who must now face life in all of its random shifts and progressions.

Our stories are wake up calls to humanity. The writer is committed to awakening himself and then sounding the trumpet for others to follow. The decision to write is not a vocation, but a calling—an opportunity for the creative individual to alert himself to a better way of living, seeing and existing. The writer's journey is therefore every bit the hero's journey.

There is a Sanskrit proverb about three blind men regarding an elephant. The first one holding the trunk describes the creature as long and round with holes on the end. The second, rubbing its side describes it as immensely wide with thick leathery skin. The third blind man, fumbling with the tail, exclaims that the beast is thin and hairy. All of them are right, and yet they are wrong. They do not see the elephant for what he truly is, but only from their own imperfect perspective. Today's writer/hero needs to develop the eyes to see the wholeness of things.

"We do not see the world the way it is, we see it the way we are."

—*Traditional Jewish Proverb*

# THE TOOLS OF CRAFT

*Tools: Anything used to do work or effect some result*

In order to write the wrongs of the world, you will need to gather the necessary tools. Unlike the painter, who must amass (at considerable expense): canvas, gesso, oils, acrylics, easels, palette and brushes, the writer requires little more than a pen and paper. This is especially amazing when you consider the millions of dollars the studios spend each year on writers. From a sheer economic point of view there is no greater margin of profit. If only it were that easy. It is the writer's talent that is really is being acquired—and the price of that talent is escalating all the time.

Apart from pen and paper, what other tools does a writer need? Unfortunately, they cannot be acquired at the local supply store. The screenwriter's tools are acquired by knowing, defining, assimilating and applying the instruments of craft:

Ideas
Themes
Premises
Paradigms
Knowledge of Structure: External and Internal
The World of Story
Psychology
Foreshadowing
Character
Dialogue
Genre

Archetypes
Reference and Research
Time
Format
Discipline

as well as other material utensils such as a word processor, screenwriting software, desk, dictionary, thesaurus and so on.

With the talent and craft to apply these tools, the screenwriter can be as powerful as any film studio in the world. Motion picture production companies spend years and many millions of dollars developing the stories, articles, plays and ideas that will become movies. The writer needs only pen, paper, a good idea and the skill to achieve it.

Mastering these seemingly simple tools is another thing all together. In order to apply their lessons, you must first understand their meaning. A vague notion of premise will lead you to a vague premise. A misinterpretation of theme will lead you to an unclear theme. It is the task of the novice writer to know the correct definition, meaning and application of each tool. Because the screenwriter's tools are so often abused, even by other writers, it is important for you to learn their individual functions for yourself and not rely merely on "industry speak."

In my classes at the College of Santa Fe, I lecture for hours on the difference between theme and premise. Still, it takes months of concentrated effort before my students learn to apply them correctly.

The most important tool any filmmaker can acquire is the skill of screen story development. Whether you choose to be a screenwriter, director, cinematographer, film editor, producer or actor, you should know that careers have been made and destroyed on this ability alone.

# DEVELOPMENT

*The first step in a movement or composition in which a theme or themes are developed.*

You are writing a script for a major studio and you're on your seventeenth draft after a full three years on the same project and there is no end in sight. Secretly everyone has given up on the project (even you), but no one has the courage to pull the plug because they need the gig. You wonder what you ever did to get into this position. You swear you will never do it again. In Hollywood, Hell is always just around the corner. Your next assignment, in fact. There is no way out. You have hit the dreaded bottom of Development Hell and you must abandon all hope.

You pick yourself up. You tell your agent you're through. You turn down the rewrite payment promised as a part of your deal. Fifty, seventy-five, maybe even a hundred thousand dollars or more. You feel good, though. You've redeemed yourself. You're going off to your parents' cabin in the woods to write the one screenplay you've been promising yourself for a lifetime. You don't care whether it sells or not. This is one from the heart and that's all that matters. Eight months later, you finish it. You're happy. You give it to your agent because you're proud of it. You say, "Read it, I don't care if it sells." They read it. They love it. They sell it at auction for $500,000 or better. You're on top of the world. Everyone loves you. Everyone wants you for their next project. They're throwing outrageous numbers at you—money you've never even dreamed of. You're flattered, dazzled, bamboozled. You make the rounds. You meet the snarling minions. You hear their praise, and then, rather depressingly, you hear their projects. You hate them, but you must choose one, because, hey, who knows? You tell yourself it has potential. You convince yourself you can fix it. Seventeen drafts and three years later you're right back where you started: Development Hell again.

And this is a *best case* scenario for most screenwriters. It's what is in store for you, if you don't remember...

> *"Hollywood is a place you can be encouraged to death."*
> —F. Scott Fitzgerald

"Writing is an exploration, you learn as you go."

–E.L. Doctorow

A good way to avoid development hell is to learn and internalize the steps of development faithfully. Do not be like the amateur, who thinks of an idea and immediately writes a screenplay. This may bring you some success in the beginning, but you will burn out in the long run. Take time to know your craft. Research and development are the real joys of screenwriting. Learn to relish them.

The following is a list of the stages of the development process. While the stages can be approached chronologically, they don't have to be. Developing a motion picture is an organic process more akin to knitting than to building a house. It requires stitching, back-stitching, shoring up, tightening and then letting go. So, if you're unsure of stage three, go to stage four. Work it, problem solve, sketch the template of how you want your story to move, imagine the world of your story, feel the anticipation of the audience as they watch it unfold on-screen. Now go back to your theme, and ask yourself what the story is really about. In this way you will develop a complete motion picture drama.

Each step of the development process leads into the next. Each question brings an answer and each answer provokes another question. It is the constant process of agitation and revelation that leads to a remarkable achievement.

# THE TWELVE STAGES
# OF DEVELOPMENT

1.  Determine the central theme and expand it into three acts
    with a beginning, a middle and an end.
2.  Draft a three-act template to determine an overall strategy.
3.  Develop the premise.
4.  Determine the proper external structure.
5.  Develop the internal structure.
6.  Develop the five character relationships.
7.  Write a working treatment.
8.  Define and create the world of story.
9.  Select the genre(s).
10. Research.
11. Design the image system.
12. Break the story down scene by scene. Now, go to script!

# THE FIRST STAGE
## Determining Theme

*Find the central theme and expand it into three acts*

*THEME: A short subject from which variations are developed.*
—American College Dictionary

Every screenplay is the living proof of a theme. Theme can be defined as what the story is really about. It is what you will ask yourself with every movie you write, as well as every movie you see. *What is the story really about?* It is the subjective storyline behind all the action, dialogue and exposition unfolding on-screen. By carefully examining every movie you see for its underlying theme, you will remove yourself from the experience of the lay movie audience.

*You will no longer see movies as others do.* From now on, you will determine, judge and examine films for what they are saying and how effectively they say it. It will take a lot of practice. Once you're on track, you will notice how every frame of a good film echoes the theme—from the visuals, to the characters, dialogue and practically every word spoken or unspoken throughout the course of the story. A good screenplay is an entire symphony of purpose, emotion and meaning fused by and fueled by the theme.

*Theme is the wellspring from which the writer draws all characters, dialogue, subtext, description, action, locations and transitions. Everything that happens in a screenplay is a direct by-product of the writer's theme.*

When an architect sees a building, he sees more than an interesting facade. He looks at the overall design, construction and the craftsmanship. He determines for himself whether it works or not. Your goal should be to become an architect of film—try to examine films with a growing and concise criterion as to how the writer worked within the chosen theme. Did the director, art director, production designer and actors prove it? Did they even get it? If they did, it is a good movie; if not, then it is a failure. It is that simple. It doesn't matter whether you agree with the writer's theme or not, it only matters that the finished film proves the point.

Watch movies and look for their themes, for the story behind the story. Become expert in determining *what* they are saying and *how* they proved it in three acts. Note when the dialogue, visuals, music and action relate to the theme. This will go a long way in helping you determine what will go into your own stories. It is here where you can begin mastering the art of storytelling.

"When I finally discover what I'm writing about, I tape it to my typewriter."

*–Arthur Miller*

To develop original themes you must call upon your most subversive insights. How honest are you willing to be with yourself? How good are you at facing your own problems, mistakes and weaknesses? What is most meaningful to you? Try to go beyond the safe, obvious complaints. You need to identify and comprehend the real problems of the world. Joseph Campbell once wrote that every world disturbance—from a child's temper tantrum to the outbreak of world war—is caused by a restriction of consciousness. What is your weakness? Pinpoint the root cause of your own problem and then engineer its solution. Don't waste your time on "disease of the month" topics unless you can bring a fresh approach to them. If you're going to take on a subject like drugs, do so with laser sharp insight as to what the real problems are, and not just the ones fabricated by the friendly automatons down at D.A.R.E.

Recently, the movies *Blow* (written by Nick Cassavetes and David McKenna, based on the book by Bruce Porter) and *Traffic* (written by Stephen Gaghan, based on the miniseries *Traffik*, written by Simon Moore) took on the socially loaded subject of drugs and drug dealing with decidedly mixed results. *Traffic's*

Academy Award®-winning screenwriter, Stephen Gaghan, applied passion and considerable personal experience in adapting this Channel Four television documentary into a stirring indictment against America's failed drug policies. *Blow* on the other hand, succeeded only in being a hodge-podge, morality tale of cliché after cliché, with very little to distinguish itself—other than managing to make one of the finest young actors in the world today (Johnny Depp), look ridiculous in a stunning array of bad hairpieces.

Peter Jennings' television exposé, titled *Pot of Gold*, had more compelling and contemporary insights into the real problems of illegal drug trafficking than either of the aforementioned movie efforts combined. The point is that the screenwriter must not only scrutinize society's injustices and hypocritical values, but must be willing to sacrifice his own hand-me-down prejudices and come up with something truly new.

The films of Quentin Tarantino are excellent examples of subversive themes in action. His screenplays—*Reservoir Dogs, True Romance* and *Pulp Fiction*—all take ironic, controversial and subversive stances and play them out to astonishing conclusion.

In *Reservoir Dogs* (written by Quentin Tarantino), we are immediately invited into a circle of thieves planning a heist and given a harsh, humorous and highly personal view of their personalities, backgrounds, relationships and ethics. They are ruthless, professional and seasoned criminals about to walk head-on into a set-up that will cost them their lives and freedom. To add to their difficulties, a sadistic psychopath and an undercover cop are operating covertly among them. As the story unfolds, we get to see how each of them reacts according to their own code of ethics. So the entire edge-of-your-seat drama delivers a hard-hitting variation on the age-old maxim of *honor amongst thieves*. It is subversive and ironic because we don't normally think of hardened criminals possessing any personal code or ethic, so the sheer juxtaposition of these values becomes utterly fascinating.

In *True Romance* (written by Quentin Tarantino), we are introduced to two social misfits: a delusional comic book salesman with a borderline personality disorder and a flighty call girl hired to entertain him on his birthday. They surprise us by doing what we least expect from such outcasts—they fall in passionate romantic love and pledge undying fealty to one another. Once again the surprising, subversive theme of *romance amongst misfits* creates a subversive hook that compels us to root for them as they fight to create a life for together, free from oppressive Mafioso and pseudo-Rasta pimps.

Finally, in *Pulp Fiction* (written by Roger Avary and Quentin Tarantino), an Academy Award®-winning screenplay, Tarantino and Avary achieve the apex of subversive storytelling. Here we meet an entire repertoire of hit men, crime-bosses, drug-dealers, has-been boxers and underworld wannabes, and are given glaring insights into what it takes to survive and ultimately escape their ruthless existence. It is no coincidence that the film's only successful characters, Butch (Bruce Willis) and Jules (Samuel Jackson), are endowed with the virtues of valor and philosophy respectively, and it is their adherence to these qualities that leads to their salvation. Once again the contrast of *valor* and *philosophy* from characters we presume to be devoid of any virtue, makes for compelling, tragic, and often hysterically funny conflicts and resolutions.

Now consider the body of work of David Webb Peoples, to my mind one of the greatest thematic screenwriters of our time. *Blade Runner, Hero, Unforgiven* and *Twelve Monkeys* are just four of his produced screenplays. Peoples is a master of creating stories that depict society's compulsion to rationalize its need for violence.

In the movie *Blade Runner*, Harrison Ford plays sanctioned killer Rick Deckard, a futuristic cop recruited to kill renegade replicants who have come to Earth seeking to extend their lives. After tracking them down and killing them off, one by one, he confronts their outlaw leader, Batty, played by Rutger Hauer. In the film's harrowing conclusion, Batty winds up saving Deckard's life, and proving that all life is sacred—whether it is born or manufactured. Not only is this theme apparent by Batty's compassionate bettering of Deckard's wanton morality, but it is actualized, as Deckard escapes to freedom with the beautiful replicant,

Rachel. (That is, he escapes in the original film release version. Ridley Scott's Director's Cut relegates this final escape to the editing room floor.)

*Blade Runner's* theme is clearly stated and proved by the maxim, *all life is sacred.* And because this story has a beginning, middle and end we see it realized by following the protagonist's actions through three ironically fortified acts, which might also be stated as:

**To kill any form of life/leads to/reverence for all life.**

Let's look at another one of People's masterpieces, the movie *Unforgiven.* We leave the oppressive world of the future and are now in the small frontier civilization of Big Whiskey, where society is just defining its laws for what kind of violence is permissible (rational justice). From the opening scene we watch, hear and see the whores, barkeep and town sheriff pleading their reasons for retribution and revenge. What is masterful about this Academy Award®-nominated screenplay is that each of the plaintiffs—in their own way, according to their own truth—is being honest. Each plaintiff's need for violence is justified. We hear the constant refrain, "He's got it coming! They got it coming!"

Now Peoples introduces William Munney, a renowned killer of women and children. He has been converted through the love of a good woman, yet has little personal insight into either his conversion or his own past rationale for murder and mayhem. In fact, he makes no excuses. He is the very personification of an irrational killer. He is likable, heroic even, precisely because he makes no attempt to rationalize his past. In the end, he becomes the screenwriter's perfect mouthpiece for the countertheme, "We *all* got it coming, kid!"

William Munney is the perfect protagonist to prove the writer's theme. Violence is never rational no matter how we try to make it so; *it is inherently irrational.* And because this is a Western mythic drama, with a beginning, middle and end, the writer's theme is proven in three acts:

**Rational violence/leads to/irrational violence.**

Another example of strong thematic screenwriting is *Moonstruck*, John Patrick Shanley's masterpiece about the silly, superstitious nature of mankind's mating rituals. His story brilliantly proves the theme: *Romantic Love is not a reason for living, or even a preventative from dying. It is a* part *of living; to live is to embrace life and love beyond superstition, and with passion.*

Listen as Ronny Cammareri (Nicolas Cage) expresses the writer's belief when he says, "We're not perfect, Loretta. Snowflakes are perfect. We are not here to make anyone perfect. We are here to love all the wrong people and die!" And because this is a romantic comedy, the writer's theme is expressed with a beginning, middle and an end.

**To choose passion over ritual and superstition/ leads to/ true love and fulfillment.**

Another example of strong thematic construction is how in the movie *Witness*, John Book, a self-righteous detective, is shown dragging an Amish mother and her son through the streets of crime-riddled Philadelphia in search of suspects. He is so convinced of his own righteousness, he thinks nothing of subjecting these gentlefolk to the seamiest side of the city's underworld.

He then goes on a journey to a type of heavenly kingdom, where he must dwell amongst people of true righteousness; there he learns that self-righteousness is no substitute for true righteousness and that truth and honor are always more powerful than corruption and violence. Because this is a mythic drama proven in three acts—the theme is:

**True righteousness/ conquers/ violence and corruption.**

Of course, these are my interpretations, and you may challenge or apply them as you wish. Your work is to start mining the depths of life's multi-faceted truths lurking behind everything you do, behind every person you meet and behind every single thing you hear. All of life is crying out for you to be conscious of the infallible truth, your truth, in every moment of existence.

Some films, in lieu of a specific theme, will explore a parable, or and ancient anecdote. Neal Jordan's *The Crying Game,* is inspired by the Hindu book of fables, *The Hitopadesha,* which explores the infallibility of dharma, karma and one's true nature. The theme of *The Crying Game* in three acts might be defined as:

### The search for truth/leads to/the discovery that one's true nature is inescapable.

You may recall the parable of the scorpion and the tortoise told by Jodie, the British soldier kidnapped by the IRA (Forest Whitaker): A scorpion asks a tortoise for a ride across a river and the tortoise refuses saying, "Are you nuts? We'll get half way across and you'll sting me." To which the scorpion reasons, "Don't be ridiculous. We'd both drown if I did that." The tortoise acquiesces until half way across the river, when the scorpion stings him. The tortoise cries out, "But why? Now we'll both drown!" The scorpion can only shrug his shoulders and answer, "Because it's my nature." And this parable becomes all the more poignant with the "sting" Stephen Rea receives from the hermaphroditic Jaye Davidson in the film's denouement.

> "The sole secret and purpose of Christ, my dear, is to drink of life's undying essence."
>
> —*Henry Miller*

*The Usual Suspects* (written by Christopher McQuarrie), is another example of a story developed around a parable. In this case it is G.K. Chesterton's declaration, "The greatest lie the Devil ever told was to convince the world he didn't exist." This paradox resonates throughout the picture and is even quoted twice by the diabolical Keyser Soze as he devises his own disappearance from a world hot on his trail.

*The Legend of Bagger Vance* (written by Steven Pressfield and Jeremy Levin), is a misguided effort to dramatize the mystical precepts of the Hindu scripture *The Bhagavad Gita* for Western audiences. Matt Damon's character is named Rannulph Junah (R. Junah = Arjuna) and Will Smith's mysticism-spouting caddie is Bagger Vance (Bhagavan)—derivations of their Sanskrit counterparts in the "Song of God" (Bhagavan meaning God, Gita meaning song). The problem is that the film is such a mish-mash of jumbled "isms," it would take a real Sanskrit scholar to decipher what it is actually trying to say. If there is a lesson to be had, it is to the pretentious screenwriter who aspires to greatness, always remember—when adapting foreign books of wisdom make sure you understand what is being said before trying to explain it to others.

*Where do you get your ideas?* This is the most commonly asked question, and if you have to ask, you've probably already missed the point. The storyteller is constantly barraged with ideas culled from everyday life. He is the proverbial honeybee extracting the nectar of truth from life's every passing moment. *The goal is not so much for more ideas, but to determine which ones to write about.* Which of your ideas offers the greatest chance of success and personal reward? Which theme will create the kind of characters and conflict that will attract actors, directors, financing and an audience? You will not have the time in your life to turn every idea and inspiration into a screenplay, so you have to develop an internal sense of what you are capable of and match it with the marketplace.

> "Love the art in yourself and not yourself in the arts."
>
> —*Stanislavsky*

In the beginning, your eyes will be bigger than your stomach in that your knowledge and craft will not be equal to your ideas. You are among one of the most sophisticated media generations in history. Since early childhood you have been bombarded with pre-established images and regurgitated values produced by the most powerful technologies and media companies in the world. (Compare this situation to less than eighty years ago when G.K. Chesterton and J.R.R. Tolkien were hotly protesting the inclusion of illustrations in children's books.)

You have seen much more than you can possibly achieve with the little bit of practice you've had. To realize your vision on film you will have to apply yourself to craft. On a scale of one to ten, your sophistication level may be as high 8.5, but your craftsmanship cannot yet do it justice.

Writing is an organic process and requires years to develop. Every screenplay you write feeds into the next with growing clarity and skill. There are no short cuts. You're not fooling anybody, or pulling the wool over anybody's eyes, especially your own. It is an exacting and arduous process. No one will be able to appreciate your ideas, your theme or your brilliance, unless you put in the work. You're going to have to work very, very hard, while accepting the looming possibility that your hard work may not sell. So you may as well make sure you benefit from the journey. The joy is in the doing, the reward is the process itself. So it is time to begin. You're a hero now, or had you forgotten? There is no turning back from the magical world of journey.

"The beginning is the most important part of the work."

—*Plato*

# THE SECOND STAGE
## Drawing the Three Act Template

*The set of all inflected forms of a single root or theme.*

Constantly on alert to the true meaning of things, to what is being said beyond what is spoken, seeing the hidden truth behind the facade, the writer/hero extracts the essence of life and applies it to his craft by holding up a mirror image.

*We must externalize the unseen.* This is the painter examining the blank canvas before him. What size is it? Where to start? How many coats of gesso does the canvas require? Screenwriting is a medium that demands precise structuring. You must create in a defined arena. That arena calls for roughly two hours of filming at approximately one minute per page. Ideally, 120 minutes equals 120 pages, or two hours of film.

The rule of thumb breakdown at one minute per page is:

*The Beginning* is thirty pages long and provides time to introduce the theme, premise, inciting incident, main characters, problems, desires, relationships, genre and the world of story.

*The Middle* is sixty pages in length and leads the central theme, premise, main and opposing characters into confrontation and extreme conflict.

*The End* is also thirty pages in duration and reveals the completion and consequence of the second act build up, while also offering a glimpse of what the world might be like when the main character's problems have been solved and the writer's theme has been proven.

Try to determine the themes beneath what you are currently writing. If you are between projects, you might scan newspaper articles or poems and try to determine their underlying values. You will need to practice this and then expand your findings into three separate acts that introduce your story's elements and characters, prompt them towards confrontation, extreme conflict and resolution, finally impacting the world of story.

There is a wonderful scene in Michael Tolkin's *The Player*, where Peter Gallagher plays a "wunderkind" executive trying to impress his new studio bosses. At one point he challenges his fellow colleagues to randomly pick and read any newspaper headline, which he then deftly turns into a compelling movie concept. Although it is meant to be facetious, the ability to discern important themes in everyday life and then break them down into simple thematic constructions is an invaluable tool every writer should master.

Draw the three-act template and determine whether the theme has the potential to develop into three acts. Do not be persuaded by the current trend of screenwriters who counsel writing ninety-minute screenplays. While it is true that many of today's movies are not actually two hours (120 pages) in length, most have been edited down to that length. If you don't develop the skill to write full-length screenplays now, it is doubtful you can go back and learn to. Remember, screenwriting is for the long distance runner, not the sprinter. You have to be in it for the long haul.

Some screenwriting theorists proclaim the obsolescence of the three-act structure, arguing that it is a convention of the stage and does not apply to film. This is not completely correct. Other screenwriting teachers expound on three-act structure as the end-all and be-all of screenwriting. This is overly simplistic and can result in the writer hitting all the precise marks—like an actor on a stage—without ever finding the dynamic "inner spine" of the story. *The three-act structure is no more, or less, than the application of Aristotle's maxim; "A whole is that which has a beginning, middle and an end."* It is not an invention of the theater, but a natural construction of mankind's oldest myths and stories.

The three-act structure is nothing more than the canvas on which you will plan your work of art. It is the proving ground of theme, whether you apply it to ten minute productions or three-hour epics. *Your story must have a beginning, middle and an end.* It doesn't matter how or when you segue from one act to the other in the beginning. Your craft will demand that you smooth these edges and link the sequencing in future drafts, just as a painter paints over any penciled guidelines. To start, you need to take your central theme and configure it into a beginning, middle and an end.

At this stage, while formulating your thesis with a beginning and end value, you may use a generic "leads to" in the middle to indicate the action of your second act. When your end value is clear and reflecting the ironic growth from your first act value, you can then go back and determine the specific way in which the first one "leads to" the end value.

Let's say you are keen with the observation of how a person's pathological lying has destroyed the lives of those around him. You've noticed how your own weakness and backsliding from the truth has caused you difficulty at times. You have witnessed how one small, casual lie can lead to disaster and you want to tell a story about this. You will take the first value of *lying* and go to the end point *disaster* and apply it to the template of three acts.

**A lie, no matter how small/leads to/disaster.**
**1st Act//2nd Act/3rd Act**

From here, you should examine the logical growth and development of your theme into a full-fledged story. From the end value of *disaster* you can invent all types of scenarios: war, pestilence, suicide, nuclear holocaust, or perhaps the painful breakup of a family—all caused by one person's casual dishonesty. Such a tale can take place anywhere: the military, the Centers for Disease Control, an apartment, a space ship or even a haunted island in the Adriatic. You can conceive of a story with a beginning, middle and end and determine the individual plot points of how one *value* leads to another and another and another to its ultimate conclusion.

In the beginning you'll want to look for sufficient irony in your thematic construction. The themes you choose should evoke action, conflict, growth and, most of all, *contrasting values*. For example, the description small (lie) contrasts with disaster (big), which implies something large and overwhelming. Your job is to then dramatize how the interconnectedness of humanity depends on the truthfulness of every individual, and how one selfish, ignorant, misguided half-truth can have a devastating effect on us all.

> *"You cannot pick a flower without troubling a star."*
> —Frederick Thompson

"If you want to send a message, send a telegram."

*–Sam Cohn*

Your talent for determining values and themes will assist you in finding the underlying meaning behind all things. What did your boyfriend mean when he said he couldn't live without you? Does this imply he would kill himself, or you, if you left him? Is obsessive love real love, or just another kind of addiction? How much of what we call love is really fear of loneliness? Once again you will expand the theme to include a beginning, middle and end and postulate a theory.

### Obsessive love/leads to/murder.
### 1st Act/2nd Act/3rd Act

Note the presence of ironic construction: love and murder are at opposite ends and yet they are linked together. Just imagine the endless stories you can create from this theme (or watch any of the countless film noir movies, like *Body Heat, Double Indemnity* or *Blood Simple*). Such a potent combination of conflicting ironic values makes for unlimited variation of stories.

Finding a theme is not the same as developing a moral (as in Aesop's Fables). We solve problems; we do not send messages.

For an excellent example of the difference between proving a powerful theme and sending a message, watch Stanley Kubrick's masterpiece, *2001: A Space Odyssey*, then view its disappointing sequel, *2010: The Year We Make Contact* directed by Peter Hyams. Enough said.

## CREATIVE ENGINEERING: Thematic Problem Solving and the Art of Story Development

A good exercise for developing your skills as a creative engineer is to select a poem or article and develop it into a short story. Practicing and perfecting this ability will eventually enable to turn any single sentence into a full-length motion picture.

For demonstration purposes I've randomly selected a poem by Edwin Arlington Robinson entitled *Richard Cory*. I first heard the poem in a song by Paul Simon and Art Garfunkle in the mid-sixties. Aside from the fact that the poem itself is in the public domain, its timeless examination of social values lends itself to a modern retelling for cinema.

By following the steps of development we will come as close to creating a motion picture story as possible. Step-by-step through the development process I have included examples from a wide assortment of films that best illustrate these stages. If you have not seen the movies, you may want to rent and watch them as you proceed. If you've already seen them, it is a good idea to watch them again, this time with these specific traits in mind. Try to put aside your personal bias if the films referenced are not on your list of favorite films. It may offend your sophisticated sensibilities to watch *The Sound of Music, Mary Poppins* or *Beauty and the Beast,* but there is cinematic gold to be found for those who can put their egos aside and become children again.

Remember, we are looking for very specific details in character development and plot development—important developments that may have slipped past you before you became a screenwriter. To begin, be mindful of what the poem is really saying, and to your emotional reaction as it unfolds.

### RICHARD CORY
#### by Edwin Arlington Robinson

*Whenever Richard Cory went downtown,*
*We people on the pavement looked at him;*
*He was a gentleman from sole to crown,*
*Clean favored and imperially slim.*
*And he was always quietly arrayed,*
*And he was always human when he talked;*
*But still he fluttered pulses when he said,*
*"Good morning," and he glittered when he walked.*
*And he was rich—yes, richer than a king—*
*And admirably schooled in every grace:*
*In fine, we thought that he was everything*
*To make us wish we were in his place.*
*So on we worked, and waited for the light,*
*And went without the meat, and cursed the bread;*
*And Richard Cory, one calm summer night,*
*Went home and put a bullet through his head.*

Now imagine that you have been selected, along with a handful of other writers, to develop this poem into a full-length motion picture. Jeffrey Katzenberg of DreamWorks SKG has just purchased the film rights and he wants to hear *your* take on it. The job is yours if you can convince him that you can adapt it into an exciting two-hour motion picture. Your agent has set up an appointment in one week. Where do you start? What's the first question you ask yourself?

*What's the story really about?*

You are correct if you immediately probed for the theme of the piece. How else will you know if you are up to the task? How else will you know if this is something you can use to bring your unique talents, perception and craft to achieve on paper? Integrity is required. If you're just doing it for the money, you will be found out. You will fail, and much worse, you may not be given the opportunity a second time. The studios, producers, directors and movie stars do not want to waste their time. They don't care if the rent is due, or that you need to pay Aunt Martha's hospital bills. They want to know, and rightfully so, that you can turn this into a compelling motion picture screenplay. They will not look favorably upon you if you take the job and then make only a half-hearted attempt at writing it. They want blood (and they'll happily spill yours). This is a business, not a charity.

Conversely, you will want to determine whether this is something you can pour yourself into. With the money at stake, you can readily convince yourself that it is, but your writer's/hero's voice will not (should not) allow you to do it for the money alone. You are going to tear your hair out doing the best job you can, and if your heart and head aren't into it then you will probably fail. Moreover, if you do fail, you will not be called again.

Every prospective work-for-hire is a potential Faustian dilemma—while you may get the pay-off in the short term, if you sell yourself out too often, you can destroy your craft. Hollywood is legendary for its burn-outs and cynical hacks—writers who sell out for the quick buck and wind up writing cartoons or one-liners for Wrestlemania. If you're in for the long haul, you need to protect your talent. *If you're going to write movies, you must develop the really big ideas and the craft for writing them.*

"There is more truth in art than in all the history books in the world"

—Charlie Chaplin

What is the theme of *Richard Cory*? What is the poem really about?

The poem paints a haunting portrait of a man who has everything in a world where people project onto him everything they wish to possess for themselves. Sound familiar? How many times have you wished to be somebody else? This is an ageless, timeless problem, isn't it?

So, ultimately, the story is about our perceptions being different than reality. Richard Cory is perceived to be better off and yet he kills himself. Why? Because status and material possessions do not necessarily make for a happy life. There are many dramatic values implied here: Ambition, envy, wealth, false perception, delusion, disillusionment, suicide, pretense, misery, scandal, judgment, class struggle.

An age-old maxim comes to mind—*Never judge a man until you've walked a mile in his shoes.*

We can now select from any of the above values to configure our first act theme. I have selected false perception, because it is how I interpret what the poem is really about. By adding the generic "leads to," I have loosely formulated my second act dynamic. Later, I will need to complicate the plot with confrontation and extreme conflict, but for now this will suit the purpose of engineering my second and third act values.

### False perception/leads to/

Now to decide the third act value. The poem ends with Richard Cory's suicide, which connotes a type of dissolution—where the illusion of false perception is dispelled. By applying the end value of suicide I can come up with the final conclusion.

### False perception/leads to/suicide.

"Truth is more important than fact."

–Alexander Pushkin

So let's critique the theory. In what ways could a person's false perception lead to suicide? Easily, if someone lived their whole life modeled after somebody else, they might wind up empty, vacuous and devoid of authenticity. This could lead to a type of despondency, which could then lead to death. The theme is logically sound and dramatically possible, but is it dramatic enough? An experienced dramatist can easily read this as a tragedy and a somewhat predictable one at that.

*Now* ask yourself, do you really want to spend the next ten months writing a moribund and predictable tragedy? Maybe, but tragedies are a "hard sell" and fairly depressing for everybody, especially the writer. So my preference would be to go back and reconfigure the problem, and turn it into something I can really care about.

At this point you may need to depart from the chronological events, themes and facts of your source material. While this may cause you some concern, your first obligation is to yourself and to your vision. This departure is known as creative or poetic license. While it is possible to be true to the underlying material and accomplish your goal, the real job is to make the material your own. If this is not possible, perhaps you should reconsider in favor of something more personal to you. If you still have doubts, re-read the chapter on Development Hell and proceed duly fore-warned.

What really intrigues me about the theme and story of *Richard Cory* is the opportunity to dramatize how human beings project their best and worst on to others and wind up living their lives based on this false perception.

We delight in success stories where the underdog achieves his heart's desire and we imagine ourselves doing the same. Or, we watch the scandalous antics of the rich and famous and delight in seeing them get their just desserts. Humans tend to live their lives based on how others perceive them and how they are perceived in return. But is this authentic? I would like to show how this flawed thinking leads to a type of living death and how personal fulfill-ment comes from living more authentic lives. If I can reformulate my hypothesis, I have a chance of coming up with a solution I care strongly about. I can try dropping in the value of personal fulfillment as my ending.

**False perception/leads to/personal fulfillment.**

But this is like saying "Ignorance is bliss" and I definitely don't want to spend my next ten months promoting ignorance. So how do I solve the problem of false perception? By dramatically prov-ing what happens when the bubble of false perception bursts. What value do I have then? Disillusionment? Now I can apply this to the theme and look at its outcome.

**Disillusionment/leads to/personal fulfillment.**

*—or—*

**False perception, dispelled/leads to/personal fulfillment and happiness.**

It works! This shows a logical growth from beginning to end and postulates a theory I can believe in. Having now developed an initial theme and expressed it in three acts, there is a story with a very real problem that affects everyone. Now I'll have to tell a story that proves it, which leads to the next stage: Drawing the three-act template.

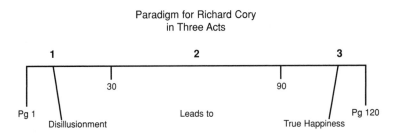

Paradigm for Richard Cory
in Three Acts

The first act deals with dramatization of the particulars of false perception and disillusionment. The second act will chart the character's journey from disillusionment to self-discovery and the third act will determine the outcome of personal fulfillment and true happiness.

Now I can start to see where the pieces will fit within a two-hour movie. By glancing at the template, I can draw a map of where I need to start and where I need to go for my final resolution. This allows me to pinpoint certain time references and page numbers where I will need to introduce new information, conflicts and complications to my protagonist's quest. I will need to bring all of my talent, craft and experience to developing, defining and dramatizing the story of one person's journey from false perception and disillusionment to personal fulfillment and true happiness. This will be also be a personal journey. One in which I will participate with all the emotion, determination and conflict of my main character.

Do not even think of going on a writing journey without taking yourself along. Call upon the times that your own false perceptions and self-doubts have lead you astray. You will need to become a method actor for the roles you create, and this will require that you while draw upon your personal life experiences. Doing so will make your characters come alive and give you a reason to write a story with great meaning and emotional impact.

Your main character should be able to prove the story's theme. The main character is a living window into the values, conflicts, personality and challenges dictated by the theme, and is known as the protagonist.

## THE PROTAGONIST:
### The main character in a play or film

The protagonist is the embodiment of your theme in action. A character through whom your audience will actually experience the very real problems, desires, conflicts, and the quest for transformation. It is this series of desire/plan/action/conflict and outcome that will form the internal spine of your plot. It is vitally important to understand that plot is not something external to your main character, it is your main character.

The critically acclaimed *Memento* (written and directed by Christopher Nolan) is an excellent example of how the protagonist's past, his weaknesses, desires and objectives are perfectly integrated into the seamless unfolding of the plot. Although the film turns conventional narrative structure upside down, or rather, back to front, end to start, it is a crowning example of the Aristotelian notion that "character is plot."

Applying this to our adaptation of *Richard Cory*, the plot is formulated through a series of dramatic progressions that begin with false perception and disillusionment and "leads to" personal fulfillment and true happiness. Turning back to the source material, the poem mentions only Richard Cory by name. If I choose to make him the protagonist, I will weave one type of story—the story of a wealthy and powerful man who ultimately kills himself. Since I have previously discarded this scenario for the obvious reasons, I am faced with creating a new protagonist. The poem is told through the writer's point of view, and this suggests another character. I can easily imagine this unnamed someone as a young person who looks up to Richard Cory and someone who ideally embodies the problem I wish to solve, which is one of false perception. The choice of an as yet unidentified young person as my new protagonist fits well with my theme. It is about a young person who idolizes a wealthy man for all the wrong reasons. Now I can play around with the potential plot in a freestyle "imagineering" process called "what if?"

*What if* a young person falsely perceives [idolizes] a very wealthy man named Richard Cory?

*What if* Richard Cory commits suicide?

*What if* the shock of such a suicide causes a young person's hopes, ambitions and dreams to derail?

*What if,* due to such a derailment, the young person rebels?

*What if,* in rebellion, he hits rock bottom and learns a shocking truth about himself?

*What if* that shocking truth causes him to reprioritize his values?

*What if,* by reprioritizing his values, a young person finds he needs to change?

*What if,* by changing, a young person arrives at a difficult decision?

*What if* that difficult decision will determine the quality of his life forever?

*What if* the consequences of that choice will effect everyone in the community?

By asking *what if,* I can see a premise or objective storyline emerge from my theme. This premise will conform to the three-act requirement of beginning, middle and end, and will align with my theme. Do these elements fulfill the basic requirement of a well-told story? Let's see: *Someone wants something very, very badly, but must change in order to defeat an opponent and obtain a strongly held desire.*

We're partially there, but there are more questions we still need to answer.

What does our protagonist want?

Who or what will oppose him?

What changes will he need to make in order to get what he wants?

The purpose of probing the theme and applying it to a three-act template is to gradually determine the objective storyline or premise.

# THE THIRD STAGE
## Determining the Premise

*A proposition, from one of several, in which*
*a conclusion is drawn.*

Premise is the external plot line, or the objective storyline and determines how the plot, the nature of conflict and universe of your characters will interact. It is very important that the premise be solidly organized in the beginning so that a.) you will stick to your own story, and more importantly perhaps for everyone else concerned, b.) so you can Keep It Simple, Sweetheart (K.I.S.S.).

Movie premises have more in common with short stories than they do with long form novels. The only way to prevent wandering too far off and getting lost is to carefully work through the premise phase. The DreamWorks film, *Evolution* (written by Don Jakoby, David Diamond and David Weisman), is an unfortunate example of a story and script that wanders off course so violently that it has no alternative but to end up nowhere. The finished product is an embarrassing mess, resembling something spewed out by an obnoxious, pre-adolescent class clown. The scatalogical humor and infantile characterizations destroy what had the potential to have been an intelligent, well-crafted retooling of the popular *Ghostbusters* formula. As it stands, it is perfect example of what happens when screenwriters don't take their own stories seriously.

> *"A comedian can only last till he either takes himself serious*
> *or his audience takes him serious."*
> —Will Rogers

Writing is a world where all things are possible. It is very easy to get lost. With a thousand different possible scenarios, how will you be able to choose the right one? The premise is the screenwriter's map. It is the sell-through guideline that ties the writer to his own material. A screenplay is the result of some nineteen-thousand-word decisions culled from millions of alternatives. Each choice has an effect on your plot. You will not find your way unless you have a clear map. Your map is your theme translated into three acts, then clearly transposed to a well-defined premise. The premise will contain and guide you through the forest of possibilities.

In order to develop a proper premise, you will first need to design a dramatic event that intervenes in the main character's life and starts the action rolling. This dramatic event is called:

## THE INCITING INCIDENT: An occurrence or event that prompts the protagonist into action

Just as the subjective storyline (theme) is transformed into the objective storyline (premise) by asking *"what if?"* the inciting incident is determined by asking the question: *When?*

The inciting incident is an essential event that spurs your hero into action and usually occurs within the first thirty minutes of the film. A good way to create this important step in your story is to become expert at identifying inciting incidents in other motion pictures. The inciting incident should be a very distinct plot point—a highly dramatic intervention that propels your main character out of the first act into the second act with great momentum. It is a critical step in all stories and applies to whatever external structure you will eventually choose.

Some examples of movie premises with their inciting incidents are:

*When* a beloved general is *betrayed* by Caesar's son and sentenced to die, he escapes and plots his revenge by becoming the most honored gladiator in all of Rome, where he wins the hearts of the people, *defeats* the treacherous emperor and restores Rome as a republic. *Gladiator*

*When* a romantic, but hopelessly blocked, playwright meets the love of his life, their love affair leads him to *overcome* all the hindrances of 16th century living, to create and produce a play which truly conveys what love is really like. *Romeo and Juliet*, *Shakespeare in Love*

*When* an abused street prodigy is sentenced to undergo psychological counseling, his emotional sparring with his brooding therapist *purges* him of his self-sabotaging patterns in time to pursue the woman of his dreams, as well as a bright future for himself. *Good Will Hunting*

*When* the beloved child at an orphanage *rebels* against his kindly mentor's views on abortion, he moves to an apple orchard, where he discovers that the rules of the outside world are even more randomly cruel and oppressive than anything at the orphanage. This leads him to fulfill his destiny and return to the orphanage as his mentor's successor. *The Cider House Rules*

*When* a fabled and noble warrior seeks to hang up his sword and *retire* with the woman he loves, duty, vengeance and destiny pull him back into the fray, where he meets the disciple of his dreams, and it is this conceit that ultimately costs him his life. *Crouching Tiger, Hidden Dragon*

*When* a self-righteous detective must *protect* an eyewitness to a brutal murder, a young Amish boy, he takes shelter amongst the Amish community and learns that true righteousness is more powerful than corruption and violence. *Witness*

*When* a band of prostitutes in a corrupt western town *hire* a merciless killer in an effort to obtain rational justice, they succeed only in bringing murder and mayhem down around them— because violence, no matter how justified, is always irrational. *Unforgiven*

*When* a dowdy bookkeeper *invites* her fiancé's estranged brother to her wedding, she reluctantly falls in love with him and learns to choose passion over superstition. *Moonstruck*

*When* a troubled young man *visits* a psychiatrist after hospitalization for a suicide attempt, his search for self-control leads to the unraveling of his mother's desperate need to control everyone, and forces her to leave the home. *Ordinary People*

*When* a repressed mute woman *marries* an uptight New Zealand farmer, she finds true love when she meets his primitive foreman who awakens her repressed emotions. *The Piano*

*When* a sanctioned killer is *recruited* to destroy renegade replicants, he confronts their leader who ends up saving his life, causing him to revere all life, regardless of its origin. *Blade Runner*

*When* a cynical bar owner is *reunited* with the woman who spurned him, he is faced with caring, feeling and loving again, and ultimately must choose between love and honor. *Casablanca*

*When* an eccentric inventor is *imprisoned* by an enchanted beast, his daughter offers herself as the beast's prisoner and gradually teaches him the power of selfless love, thereby dispelling an enchantress's curse. *Beauty and the Beast*

*When* an urchin "street rat" *releases* a powerful genie, his efforts to marry the Sultan's daughter lead him to find his own inner worth and save the kingdom from an evil Sorcerer. *Aladdin*

Notice how the word "When" connects with a specific event? Well, that specific event is the inciting incident. There is an art to thinking this way, but the process of seeing themes and developing them into premises is really what the screenwriter does. We are mediums and specialized translators of the unseen to the seen. We are highly skilled—and sometimes somewhat subversive—observers who, through our craftsmanship, make the non-manifest, manifest. We take the big ideas and transpose them to two hours of living drama. Or we take small conflicts and magnify them to earth-shattering proportions. The ability to do this does not come overnight; it will develop in accordance to the time you spend cultivating it.

What you are experiencing right now, as you tear your brains out trying to differentiate theme from premise, is the chasm between the way you were taught to think and the way you must train yourself to think as a storyteller. There is nothing wrong with you if you don't get it at first. This is a profession and craft requiring years of self-discipline and practice. Be mindful that these steps are not inherently chronological. You may be researching one theme and come up with a more interesting premise. Or your newly formed premise may lead to a more powerful theme. At any point, you may return to an earlier stage of development, or skip to a later one. The only requirement is that you have a well-formed answer to all Twelve Stages before going to script.

In developing *Richard Cory*, we've advanced through the previous stages and now must design the movie premise and an inciting incident.

What dramatic event might cause a falsely perceiving young man to become disillusioned? The answer is in Richard Cory's suicide. Which allows us to formulate the following working premise:

*When* a young man's idol (Richard Cory) *commits suicide*, he becomes disillusioned and rebels. In defiance of his previous values, he becomes self-destructive and soon crashes and burns. Down and out, he discovers a truth about himself and this spurs him on to re-examine his life and find personal fulfillment.

Let's look at how this breaks down.

The Beginning:
*When* a young man's idol (Richard Cory) *commits suicide*, he becomes disillusioned and rebels.

The Middle:
In defiance of his previous values, he soon crashes and burns.

The End:
This spurs him on to re-examine his life and find personal fulfillment.

Stating the premise in three phases allows us to see an orderly sequence of events illustrating one man's decline and slow rise from false perception to disillusionment to discarding all values to self-discovery and personal fulfillment. By developing your theme into a working premise and by expressing it in one sentence, you will come to an objective storyline.

The objective storyline can be stated in a group of concise sentences. It is how the audience watches the theme in action. *Theme is what the story is really about. Premise is how the theme is proven.*

This aspect of screenwriting is akin to creative engineering. Your success will come from a keen perception of universal problems and engineering their solution through dramatic conflict. We now have a subjective and objective storyline: a theme, a premise, a main character and an inciting incident. Next, we need to choose an external structure that will best suit the premise: The fourth stage of development. Before you can do this, you should evaluate your premise and ensure that it is a story you want to tell.

## EVALUATION

The professional screenwriter will now determine whether the story he or she has developed is worthy of the time and energy. When evaluating your premise, be careful not to delude yourself, be very honest and be as objective as possible. Remember the age-old saying: the doctor who treats himself as a patient has a fool for client. In other words, you will only be fooling yourself.

Some general questions you might ask yourself are:

Is this story big enough for the big screen? (It doesn't always have to be, and that's okay. But you should at least ponder its potential.)

Can the story be told in a way that fulfills the utmost emotional demand for dramatic conflict?

Will the story sell, not only to a studio, director and star, but ultimately to an audience?

Whatever your answer, you need to make an informed decision and you need to know about the tool of *high concept.*

## HIGH CONCEPT:
## A general notion; the immediate object of an idea that promises quick and easy comprehension

The premise is often confused with what is generally referred to as high concept. Some purists scoff at the studios' demand for a clear and concise statement of what the story is about. This is naïvely unrealistic, because a large part of the screenwriter's job is to take a dramatic storyline and condense it into a two-hour format. So whether the studio demands it or not, you will want to practice working your story into a clearly stated premise in the beginning. This is preferable to getting halfway through a full-length script and realizing it isn't working. A good way to evaluate high concept is by asking: What's the big idea? Does your story have a really big idea at the core of its theme and premise?

Here are a few examples of the big idea behind some very successful movies:

A terrible, ugly, and lonely ogre rescues a beautiful princess, only to discover she is the girl of his dreams. *Shrek*

A computer hacker is designated to be the messiah of a futuristic reality where machines have imprisoned humankind. *The Matrix.*

A drug czar's daughter becomes an addict and this forces a government to reexamine its failed policies. *Traffic.*

An unemployed, working-class single mom with big hair, lots of cleavage and never-say-die street smarts outwits high-priced lawyers and investigators to win a huge class action lawsuit. *Erin Brockovich*

Ghosts hire an exorcist to rid their house of humans. *Beetlejuice.*

Children befriend an extra-terrestrial and protect him from the government. *E.T.*

Extra-terrestrials communicate with a mixed variety of human beings and orchestrate man's first contact with an advanced alien civilization. *Close Encounters of the Third Kind.*

A nebbishy bank clerk finds a Nordic mask that gives him superhuman powers. *The Mask.*

A brilliant geneticist creates an amusement park for hybrid dinosaurs, who then escape and run amok. *Jurassic Park*

A Great White Shark appears in a New England tourist town and starts munching on the local economy. *Jaws*

An isolated space ship picks up a strange alien breed that devours the crew. *Alien*

Two of humanity's most inept individuals find a briefcase full of money and inadvertently foil a crime. *Dumb and Dumber*

Two musicians join an all-girl band in order to elude the Mob. *Some Like It Hot*

A little boy is left alone for the holidays and proves himself a formidable opponent to two hapless burglars. *Home Alone*

Note how each of the above descriptions expresses the really big idea of each story? So, apart from theme and premise you should also begin looking for the big idea behind your premise. If you can design that idea to be immediately comprehensible, for as wide an audience as possible, you are on your way to developing a high concept movie. If your story misses the mark, keep trying to determine the big idea behind the story and make it as easy to grasp as possible.

Some concepts are so ingrained in the popular culture that they do not require much to sell them. *The Beverly Hillbillies, Mission Impossible, Josie and the Pussycats, The Brady Bunch* and *Charlie's Angels* are examples of big budget films that all relied heavily on their presold marquee value—with somewhat mixed results.

There is nothing wrong with high concept. It is a tool, nothing more, nothing less. If you can develop your premise into a high concept vehicle, more power to you. You may well find riches beyond your wildest dreams—but high concept should not be the only goal of storytelling. *No matter how high your concept is, it will never replace the desirability of a well-told story.* Make no mistake about it, the studios want high concept stories. In lieu of this, they will opt for well-told, compelling films. Regardless of whether your premise is high concept or not, it still should be constructed neatly with a beginning, middle and an end. The next chapters are devoted to the timeless structures available to every storyteller, which will lead us to the fourth stage of development.

# THE FOURTH STAGE
## External Structure

*A mode of building, construction or organization;*
*an arrangement of parts, elements or constituents.*

Three-act structure is an important tool of development, but it is only a partial component of a screenplay's foundation. In reality, a screenplay has two structures: internal and external, subjective and objective. We will now deal with the elements of determining the proper external structure for your story.

*"...the reality is that the single most important thing contributed by the screenwriter is the structure."*

*—William Goldman*

### STRUCTURAL ARCHETYPES: THE HERO MYTH
**An invented story or belief that is built up in response to the collective wishes of a group.**

The hero myth is a highly developed, time-honored and impeccably structured means for telling a certain type of story. It is a neatly assembled arrangement of events so powerful, the sheer use of it will communicate to your audiences the very nature of the conflict ahead. Establishing such a common ground with your audience is an invaluable tool because it means you won't have to spend valuable screen time doing so. The hero myth communicates on an archetypal level. It cries out from the nether regions of our psyches, "Watch me! Stay with me! Join with me in the perils that lie in wait ahead and be transformed!"

The mythic structure is so integral to the way we tell our stories, its very nature determines why we have a beginning, middle and an end in the first place. Our earliest myths comes from ancient Sumer and many of them chronicle the plight of a Queen/Goddess Inanna, sometimes worshipped as a fertility goddess, who, in a drought-plagued provincial world descends to the Netherworld in search of her lost lover/husband/brother. In this world beyond life, she faces judgment, purgation, and baptism by fire where she finds herself stripped bare and exposed to her true unfettered nature. From this rebirth, she triumphs over Ereshkigal, Queen of the Netherworld, and rescues her lost masculine half. The two ascend as one divine couple: male and female united, and together they restore the provincial world with rain, food and abundance. From the primal origins of the myth, we see the orderly construction of all myths with a beginning, middle and end.

### Three Worlds = Three Acts

Each act represents three separate worlds and six progressive states-of-being for the hero.

1. *The Provincial World*, wherefrom the hero departs.

2. *The Magical World of Journey*, where the hero is challenged, purged, dies and is reborn.

3. *The Return World*, where the hero becomes monarch or visionary and returns to the provincial world to restore order and guide it into the future.

A template of the mythic journey looks like this.

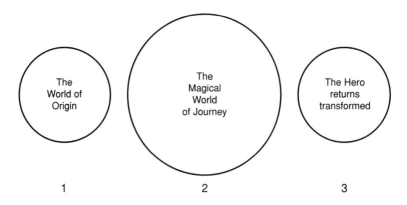

| The World of Origin | The Magical World of Journey | The Hero returns transformed |

1        2        3

From the oldest Sumerian myths to *The Matrix*, we see the prototype of the mythic journey developed, enhanced and reinvented thousands and thousands of times through the legends, stories and religions of every culture on earth. In every instance, each cultural myth indicates a specific problem their society must have solved: drought, slavery, the conquest of death, or even the restoration of man's soul.

From Virgil's *The Aeneid* to David Mamet's *The Verdict*, the mythic hero's quest is structured the same way. The hero starts off in a provincial world, where his people are suffering and he is incomplete. He then crosses a threshold into a magical world of journey. It does not literally have to be a fairytale world with ogres, dragons, witches or bald midgets. We describe it as magical because this is where your hero becomes a magician: a whole and truly empowered human being.

The mythic journey through the underworld is the hero's metamorphosis from chrysalis to butterfly. It can take place on a trek from New York to California, the inner depths of Hell, or the outer reaches of space. What is most important, regardless of the location, is to show the hero confronted with an inner and outer challenge that strips him bare of all pretense and allows him to emerge as a fully realized magician. He is now empowered to restore the world of origin (the return world) to its rightful condition. *The Myth is not just a physical journey from world to world, but a metaphorical one that we all experience from birth to death.*

Carol Pearson describes these phases of transformation in her excellent book *The Hero Within*, which I have, for the purposes of film structure, translated to:

1. Orphan
2. Wanderer
3. Warrior
4. Innocent/Apprentice
5. Magician
6. Wizard

We leave our familial nests as orphans, to wander and develop our physical, mental, and social skills, where we become warriors in the marketplace. As this grows tiresome, we yearn to know our inner selves better, and become innocents again where we explore more authentic ways of living and relating. Here we develop into apprentice magicians of our better natures, as though guided by a great wise man or guru and practice becoming wise souls (wizards) before passing beyond. The six phases of growth can be charted through three worlds: the world of origin; the magic world of journey and finally, the world of return. The beauty of the mythic structure is that it tracks the hero's inner growth through an outward journey to symbolic perfection.

These are not just formulas, but principles that have worked since time immemorial. You will see them applied in as many diverse tales as *The Cider House Rules, The Matrix, Witness, The Verdict, The Sound of Music, The Wizard of Oz, Chinatown* and *The Silence of the Lambs.* Yet no one comes out of *The Verdict* exclaiming, "Hey, that was just like *The Wizard of Oz!*"

We apply these structures to more quickly communicate to our audience on an archetypal level. If your work deteriorates into formula, you are not doing your job. You must make these principles your own, master them and apply them for different results.

## THE ELEMENTS OF MYTHIC STRUCTURE:
## A single component or constituent of the whole piece

### The Miraculous Birth

From the earliest tribal stories, the mythmaker has been faced with the difficult challenge of distinguishing the hero from the rest of the tribe. Since everyone knew everything about everyone else, storytellers needed to find a hero who possessed distinct qualities from the others. They couldn't just have anyone wandering off to find their destiny—someone needed to stay back and attend the day-to-day business of survival. So our earliest heroes were assigned a mysterious origin in order to show that they were in some way unique. Initially these heroes were gods, later they became specially gifted characters who were either born that way or earned the distinction through some sort of fantastic trial. The point is the hero is not like everyone else on the surface, because we only become heroes when we set ourselves apart from the rest of the tribe.

While the others tend to their chores, the hero lounges drowsily on grassy knolls, pondering the meaning of the universe or imagining greatness for himself beyond what life has dealt. Outwardly he may be a dreamer, or even a wastrel, but inwardly he is uniquely qualified by the virtue of this separateness. This dreamlike sense of yearning is what we all know is our destiny. *The hero seeks greatness beyond conformity, and a destiny beyond the norm.*

### The Orphan

When a hero starts his life as an orphan, it is to show he has nothing to lose. He is unattached and unencumbered by family ties and social obligations, so he is usually portrayed as an orphan to indicate that he is not saddled with the normal attachments the rest of us have. This sense of not belonging is a part of all of us. It connotes loneliness, a separateness, a yearning to be something that is not yet realized. The orphan/hero's initial problem is that he is not content to join the rest of his tribe, but looks for a greater purpose beyond it. The orphan/hero today is created by giving your main character a single and footloose status. He may be divorced, widowed, abandoned, handicapped or a maverick. It doesn't matter. The point is that the heroes or heroines must be free to seek their destiny and reclaim their birthright.

Computer hacker Thomas Anderson/Neo (Keanu Reeves) is every bit the orphan in *The Matrix*, as is Homer Wells (Tobey Maguire) in *The Cider House Rules*.

Paul Newman as Frank Galvin in *The Verdict* is just as orphaned as Judy Garland's Dorothy in *The Wizard of Oz*.

As John Book in *Witness*, Harrison Ford is every bit the orphaned hero, as is Will Hunting as played by Matt Damon in *Good Will Hunting*. And Jodie Foster as Clarice Starling in *The Silence of the Lambs* is just as orphaned as Ford's John Book.

Jake Gittes, as played by Jack Nicholson in Robert Towne's *Chinatown*, is orphaned from his time and culture, in part due to his cynical disregard for the politics and corruption of Los Angeles in the 1930s.

*The task is not to descend into a world of clichés, but to truly understand the archetypal values your character represents.* Your hero does not literally have to be a dirty faced waif from the local orphanage in order to be an orphan. He just needs be detached enough from ordinary responsibilities to be able to leave the provincial world and enter the world of journey. If your hero is at first ensnared by everyday life, you will have to create an inciting incident powerful enough to wrench him from his mundane chores and allow him to follow the call of adventure.

In George Lucas' *Star Wars*, Luke Skywalker is an orphan living a contented life with his aunt and uncle until the Empire destroys his family and farm. This inciting incident spurs him onward to find Obi-Wan Kenobi and his destiny as a Jedi Warrior.

### The Talisman

The orphan/hero possesses a mysterious object from birth. It is usually a birthmark, a medallion, a bag of baubles or sometimes even an animal familiar, like Toto in *The Wizard of Oz*. While the ruby slippers might seem like a more obvious talisman, and are indeed objects of power, they are reduced in their significance because they were bestowed upon Dorothy *after* she ventures into Oz.

Toto is a more classic talisman or animal familiar because he has been Dorothy's life long companion, and is pivotal in both her departure from and return to Kansas. Toto's importance as an animal familiar is established right from the beginning of the film where saving him from imminent danger is Dorothy's both primary and near-final objective. It is saving Toto from the hands of Mrs. Gulch that prompts Dorothy to search for a place somewhere that is "trouble free" and it is Toto's lunging after the cat that prevents Dorothy's return to Kansas in the wizard's balloon. Furthermore, it is Toto's imperilment that reveals Kansas as a bleak and dire place where the rich have power over the meek, and since it is Dorothy's quest to prove that when seeking ideal utopias there is no place like home, Toto becomes an essential living object of power that best represents Dorothy's quest.

The hero clings to this talisman for sentimental reasons, but rarely knows of its latent powers. The talisman, like its human counterpart, has an obscure meaning that reveals itself throughout the world of journey. The talisman is a physical symbol of the hero's impending destiny and will reveal its true nature as the hero advances towards the goal. In some instances, the weakening or loss of a talisman will signify a type of momentary derailment of the hero's journey, such as the death of Tinker Bell in *Peter Pan*, or the diminishment of E.T.'s heartlight. These magical figures, whether they are animate or inanimate, should be drawn to represent the inner most spiritual and psychological essence of the protagonist. To surround your hero with such archetypal totems is an art form worthy of the very best motion pictures and the very best storytellers.

### The World of Origin or Provincial World

The world of the orphan/hero is beset with some type of problem that only he or she can solve: drought, famine, tyrannical rule or foreign invasion. The homeland is suffering or threatened with extinction and it is the hero's calling to do something about it, but before he can, he must undergo an ordeal and change himself. In Disney's animated *Beauty and the Beast*, screenwriter Linda Woolverton distinguishes her heroine by making her an avid reader and, as such, she is intellectually "orphaned" from her community. Belle is not content to settle down "in this provincial life," but yearns for adventure, far off lands and true romance. Her separateness is shown in a beautifully choreographed sequence where she encounters the community at work. Her values, ideals and dreams are dramatically contrasted with those around her—further illustrating her individual destiny. In this instance, the obduracy of the provincial town will come into play later—when the people are enlisted by Gaston to storm the Beast's castle.

In *Thelma & Louise* (written by Callie Khouri), Thelma is married to an oppressive boob and, though she has a family, she is *orphaned* from her own authentic self. She is living with a philandering, abusive man who belittles her. From this world of origin, a simple weekend soiree with Louise quickly becomes a mythic quest of self-discovery, conflict and tragic emancipation.

When developing the provincial world of your hero, try to determine its contrasting value to the world of journey, thereby making the deficiencies of one world abundantly clear in the next. Hence the bleak, stark, black and white world of Kansas directly contrasts the richly vibrant and whimsical Technicolor Land of Oz.

The staid and routine conventions of a provincial French town in *Beauty and the Beast* contrast markedly with the humorous, magical, confounding castle of the Beast.

The world of cheap saloons, funeral parlors and Frank Galvin's low-rent offices of contrasts the opposing world of the Archdiocese, swank law firms, judges' chambers, and the gothic, imposing courtrooms in *The Verdict.*

The harsh, crime-riddled streets of Philadelphia contrast the sweeping, bucolic world of the Pennsylvania Amish in *Witness.*

The details of these worlds should be drawn from your story's theme. They should not be arbitrary contrivances, but well-conceived thematic visuals derived from contrasting values.

### The Next Element of the Myth is the Inciting Incident

This is an event from the outside that sets the hero off on his journey. It occurs within the first thirty minutes of the film. To determine the inciting incident of your story, you ask yourself the question, "When?"

Here are some more examples of well-known myths and their inciting incidents.

*When* the *threat* of a barbarian invasion falls upon a small Japanese farming community, the hero sets off on a quest to hire Samurai warriors to protect them. *The Seven Samurai.*

*When* Luke Skywalker returns to find the farm burned, his aunt and uncle *killed by Imperial Stormtroopers*, he joins Obi-Wan Kenobi in his effort to help Princess Leia and the rebel alliance. *Star Wars.*

*When* Belle's father is *imprisoned* by the horrible Beast, she offers herself instead, and proves herself the most likely person to show the Beast the power and meaning of selfless love. *Beauty and the Beast*

*When* a tornado *knocks* the runaway Dorothy unconscious, she travels to the enchanted Land of Oz in order to learn there is no place like home. *The Wizard of Oz.*

The inciting incident can come at any time and in any form. In the older myths the hero is either hand-selected by the community elders, or circumstances give him little choice but to heed the call. The inciting incident should always catch your hero and your audience by surprise. *Whatever you ultimately choose, the inciting incident should be portrayed as the first intervention of the hero's manifest destiny.*

### The First Threshold

We exit the provincial world through a doorway into the world of journey. This will be the first of several thresholds your hero crosses and is usually expressed by the value of surprise.

Your hero experiences the first revelation and now wonders, after a lifetime of dreaming, if he is suited for the momentous task at hand. The first threshold is immediately followed by doubt and vulnerability (the decline). It is important to stress the hero's predicament, because like yourself, there is no turning back from...

### The World of Journey

With this, we enter the middle act of our story. It is about sixty minutes on film, or sixty pages on paper. The rules of the story have now changed. While the hero suffers from the problems of his earlier existence, he is constantly forced to purge himself of these nagging fears and fatal flaws. Whoever he was in the previous world, it can not help him in this one and this matter takes on great urgency as he determines the need to gather allies quickly.

### The Inhabitants

In the world of journey, inhabitants are divided into two factions: they are either friends of the hero and share his goal inwardly and outwardly, or they are foes and owe their allegiance to the predominant ruler of the world of journey. The inhabitants of the world of journey are a wide variety of dragons, ogres, fairy folk, witches, wise men, ferrymen, guardians, trolls and imps. If you are creating a modern myth, you may want to draw on these archetypal creatures to create their modern equivalents. For instance, Joseph Campbell describes the dragons of ancient lore as creatures obsessed with the hoarding of women and gold—two commodities they could scarcely enjoy on their own. They collect them just for the hell of it. Campbell says we know of such creatures today; we call them "Jerks"!

In *The Cider House Rules* (written by John Irving), we are treated to an ingenious retelling of the ancient creation myths. The provincial world of the orphanage is a type of rustic heaven, where both birth and death are doled out by the benevolent Jehovah-like patriarch, Dr. Wilbur Larch (Michael Caine). He has many wise and attendant angels in the form of nurses who align with his daily chores of delivering or aborting fetuses, but his most beloved acolyte is his chosen heir-apparent, Homer Wells. (Refer to early biblical references to Lucifer, "the shining/falling star" beloved of God.)

Homer adores his father/mentor, but has his own views about abortion, and this contention draws him into conflict and rebellion against Dr. Larch. Homer's wanderlust causes him to leave the orphanage and dwell amongst the mortals for awhile. (Lucifer argued with God and refused to worship humans. Hence, evil is defined as that which denies love and respect to humankind). In the world of journey (the Cider House), Homer experiences the oppressive nature of man's laws. Justice in the material world is a confounding contrivance designed to oppress the poor, solely for its own vainglorious exertion of power, as evidenced by the redundant and arbitrary collection of prohibitions known as The Cider House Rules.

Along the way, Homer also experiences the love of a woman, the honor and horror of war, as well as incest, migrant farming and murder. In the end, he realizes that the natural disposition of life and death, as practiced by Dr. Larch, is far more compassionate and gentle than that of humans and their puny hypocritical regulations. Indeed, death need not always be selfish, cruel or born of ignorance (as shown by Delroy Lindo's self-sacrifice), but may be a responsible decision in the intelligent nurturing of all life. Homer returns to his rustic heaven, to take his destined place as Larch's (God's) successor, where he accepts the role of benevolent patriarch, "Goodnight, you Kings of New England, you Princes of Maine."

In *The Silence of the Lambs* (written by Ted Tally, based on the novel by Thomas Harris), the world of journey is the internal landscape of Clarice's haunted past, and the external hunt along the East Coast for Buffalo Bill. For Clarice to navigate both of these worlds, she must pass the incessant badgering of Hannibal Lecter's Sphinx-like riddles and grueling psychological examinations.

In *Witness*, John Book escapes the underworld of Philadelphia and enters the heavenly kingdom of the Pennsylvania Dutch. To stay there and heal himself he must purge himself of his self-righteousness and predilection for violence.

These modern films blend ancient archetypes and religious metaphors with contemporary situations and moral values to appeal to us on the deepest levels of our psyches.

### The Journey

At first, the world of journey is odd and unfamiliar, but along the way, the hero discovers that there is some inexplicable reason he has been called there. He has been delivered here for a purpose and the more information he gathers, the more this destiny becomes clear. Friends and foes discover the hero's talisman and recognize it as something prophesied long ago. They conclude that the hero must seek out the great wizard to explain it further.

Unfortunately, the wizard is not generally easily accessible. He is the archenemy of the powerful ruler of the world of journey. The wizard alone holds the key to breaking the evil lord's tyrannical rule. Thus, the wizard cannot be too readily available to just any stranger who comes a-calling; the hero must first prove himself worthy. This challenge to the hero will present itself in a series of trials he must undergo to prove to the wizard that he is the "chosen one." The hero's inner growth now escalates. Having already progressed from orphan to wanderer to warrior, he must now pursue his apprenticeship. He must be laid bare and purged of his flaws and self-doubts. For that to occur he will need magical training and guidance from the wizard. During his apprenticeship he learns the answer to many mysteries, but most of all, he learns that it is up to him to solve his own problems and those of worlds he must protect.

After the hero completes his apprenticeship, he sets off to battle against the evil ruler and is mercilessly attacked. Either he is betrayed, or his inner flaw resurfaces to sabotage his progress. The hero enters the world of death, where he must summon all of his inner strength, courage and skill to become a true magician. There, he learns that he will not die, but will survive to become a great ruler or a visionary leader—after he defeats his nemesis.

In the third world, the hero, with his talisman in full operation, marches into battle. By defeating the evil one he becomes a master (magician) in his own right and all mysteries are revealed. He learns that he was not an orphan after all, but instead a displaced foundling—spirited away as an infant to live in a world free of the political machinations of the evil one. This is where he learns that, in the dark reaches of the evil one's castle, there is a long lost brother or sister, or a beautiful princess whom he either joins or restores to the throne.

### The Return
The third world begins when the hero leaves the world of journey and returns to the provincial world. He is now a great wise man with the power and wisdom to solve the problems of the provincial world and to successfully guide it into the future.

## THE KEYS TO THE MYTHIC JOURNEY

### *The Beginning*
The orphan/hero, possessing only a birth object talisman, sets forth from the provincial world, and is either lured, carried away, or voluntarily proceeds (the inciting incident) through the threshold of adventure. *Here he confronts a guardian of the passage whom he must defeat or appease in order to proceed further through the world of journey.*

### *The Middle*
The hero wanders through the strange world encountering friends and foes, who either severely threaten or assist with magical aid. He learns that this world is polarized by two forces: good and evil. The good inhabitants look to the hero to depose the evil ruler, but to do that he must first seek out and find the great wizard.

The hero, as a wandering warrior, undergoes trial after trial and is stripped bare of all pretense and returned to innocence while preparing for his apprenticeship with the wizard. After training with the wizard, he masters the power of the talisman. He learns the real reason he has come to the world of journey and is sent into battle against the evil ruler.

Here he is attacked and utterly defeated, and sent to the underworld of the underworld, the world of death, where he must call upon his newfound powers to survive. He dies symbolically and is resurrected as a true magician. His destiny is now fully manifest, his talisman at full strength, he marches into battle.

### *The End*
The hero triumphs over the evil ruler, and there in the dark recesses of his castle, he finds his missing half—a princess or a long lost sibling. The hero either restores her to power or marries her, and at this time is presented with a great boon from the grateful inhabitants. The hero returns to the provincial world either as a great king or a wise man.

To determine whether your premise can be structured as a myth all you need to discern is whether your protagonist leaves a provincial community and physically or psychologically journeys to another. If there is a type of journey from one distinct world to another, with either a physical return or an implied one, you can easily assign the elements of myth. The mythic structure can be applied to any premise or theme for uniquely different results. It will serve you as much as you honor and understand it.

## MODERN APPLICATIONS OF MYTHIC STRUCTURE

The following examples show how mythic structure can be applied to all sorts of stories. The result doesn't have to be *The Hobbit* or *Alice in Wonderland* every time.

In the opening frame of *The Verdict*, we see Frank Galvin playing pinball in a bar at Christmas time. He is decidedly an orphan, with no familial connection to the provincial world. We also see that he is an ambulance chaser, and devoid of any personal integrity. He invades the funerals of strangers in order to solicit clients. He is an alcoholic. When his friend reminds him of a court date coming up in ten days (inciting incident), Frank Galvin enters the world of journey to win the case, while struggling with his deep lack of integrity. As a newly christened warrior, he encounters the inhabitants in this world: corrupt judges, slick attorneys, hypocritical doctors and opportunistic archbishops. As a warrior he must gather evidence, while trying to reconnect with the integrity he once possessed as an idealistic young attorney.

We learn that he was once a promising attorney with a deep sense of integrity, but that he was betrayed and framed for jury tampering. Presented with the opportunity to redeem himself, he goes into battle against Ed Concannon, the defending attorney (played by James Mason). Here, our hero is attacked and stripped bare of his inner flaws. He learns that evil only triumphs when good men succumb to hopelessness and do nothing. Though he is technically defeated by the terms of the prevailing establishment, his reclaimed sense of integrity inspires the jury to decide in his favor. He has become a true magician. In the last scene of the movie, we see Frank Galvin restored to wholeness. He is sober—drinking coffee—and reveals the inner strength to reject the advances of a lover who betrayed him. In other words, he has become a wizard, an emancipated human being.

This is an excellent example of mythic structure applied to the arena of modern-day Boston. Yet it employs all the elements of classic myth with surprisingly fresh results.

In the movie *Witness*, we enter into a heavenly world of simplicity, community and empathy that will become the world of journey for our hero. We see the Amish people and their graceful, simple ways aligned with the natural environment of amber grain and pristine farms. Through the eyes of a young Amish boy we enter the provincial world of Philadelphia, with its lack of community, transitory citizens and rampant corruption. We introduce our hero, John Book, a good cop surrounded by corruption. He is a lonely maverick, a displaced orphan whom his sister describes as "holier-than-thou." We see he is alone, and therefore wounded, by his self-righteous arrogance. When he must protect the Amish boy from the forces of corruption, the hero enters the heavenly kingdom and through his symbolic love affair with Rachel, and struggles with his own misguided sense of righteousness that maintains violence to be a necessary evil.

"The Sabbath was made for man and not man for the Sabbath."

—*Mark 2:27*

He is a man of the "gun of the hand" (the gun being the talisman) whose erratic actions as a warrior reveal his location to the evil powers searching for him. John Book goes through a series of trials and thresholds as he heals and constantly shifts back and forth from old beliefs to new ones. Finally, he is laid bare of all pretense, summoning his true magician self to conquer violence with the power of truth, as represented by the Amish elders who gather at the sound of the bell. We know that John Book has become a wise man, because he is the bridge between the two opposing themes when he says,

"What are you going to do, Paul? Kill him, kill me, kill him? When does it all stop? Enough! Enough!"

Deftly constructed, *Witness* is another example of the elements of mythic structure told with ever-fresh meaning and originality. If you're looking for the return world in *Witness*, we see it as John Book drives away and we are left with the question of what will become of him. We know he has changed. We know he will never be the same self-righteous person, for he has become a greater moral force than ever before.

The point is not to take these principles as rules set in concrete, but apply, adapt, rearrange and create through them. They are not meant to be taken literally or used as a paint-by-the-numbers arrangement; the tools of development are meant to free the writer's imagination, not to encumber it.

## THE OUTLAW MYTH:
### Structure versus Anti-structure

One of the most popular trends from today's generation of screenwriters is the not the hero myth at all, but the outlaw's journey. While these structures appear to be new and even anti-structural, they are as timeless as the hero's journey, but with diametrically opposed values.

The hero and outlaw take their cue from the same alienation and discontent with conformist society. Both are estranged from it and seek a more individual way of being in the world. While the hero is imbued with an altruistic sense that drives his every step, the outlaw is motivated by purely selfish reasons. The blatant immorality and ultra-violence of these of tales is sometimes shocking, but they remain exceedingly moral in that they seek to emphasize a personal code of ethics beyond all others.

Since the beginning of civilization, man has had but one choice: to conform or not to conform. If he conforms he is a dead man; his life is over; his life decisions predetermined by the society he aligns with. If he chooses not to conform, he buys himself one more choice: to become outlaw or hero.

For the mythmaker, both options are acceptable. The distinction is this: In hero myths, the hero leaves his provincial society to journey through a magic world and learns to shed his inner flaws and become a magician; after which he returns to the provincial world for the betterment of society at large.

In outlaw myths, the outlaw struggles to escape the criminal underworld while clinging to a single virtue, where he must redeem himself before escaping to a better life. Instead of being obstructed by a problem, the outlaw clings to a virtue. Instead of learning to become a magician, he struggles for redemption. In place of saving the world, he strives to be free of the underworld and achieve a balanced life for himself.

It is no wonder that the outlaw myth is so popular among young people, for just as the myth plays to a burning sense of destiny, the outlaw myth demands we stay true to ourselves and our own personal ethics, regardless of the situation. One of my favorite aphorisms is lifted from the grave marker of a deceased gunslinger buried in Boot Hill Cemetery in Tombstone, Arizona, and it reads:

"Be what you is, cuz, if you ain't what you is,
then you is what you ain't."

Hard to argue with logic like that.

The outlaw myth is rife with metaphorical allusions drawn from the myths of yesteryear—rather then a classic after-life environment inhabited by mythological terrors, we create cities, subcultures and strife-torn situations drawn from their ancient counterparts.

It is interesting to track the development of the outlaw tale back to its ancient roots. Before the concept of Hell as such came into being, the underworld was not so much an evil place as it was a mysterious and curious continuation of life. The early Greek plays and fables recount numerous legends like Orpheus, Demeter Persephone, and Cupid and Psyche where life after death are defied and even defeated. With the advent of Christianity and the Catholic Church, the afterlife became a darker and more fearsome place, especially for those who did not conform to the prevailing social mores of the time.

Today's outlaw tales have their direct origins in the classic Celtic story traditions known as "Imrams" or "Harrowings," where various legendary characters of literature, religion and myth were selected to go to hell with the specific purpose of retrieving a loved one or two.

One such tale was *The Harrowing of Jesus*, where the Son of God had to rescue all the heroes of the Old Testament who died off before he could cleanse them of their sins. In the peculiar world of Christian dogma the church had an interesting dilemma here, in that Christ died for all mankind's sins, and salvation required acknowledging this as fact. Thus, all the heroes of the Old Testament—who therefore lived and died before Christ arrived on the scene—were suffering in Hell. Very quickly, the holy fathers contrived to spin yarns of Jesus going to Hell and rescuing the like of Solomon, Abraham and good old Noah.

Another popular tale was *The Harrowing of St. Bartholomew*, commissioned by a wealthy noble who elected to memorialize his own adventures in rescuing his ancestors from the clutches of Satan's grasp. Soon afterwards, a literary trend was born, where other nobles, knights and status-conscious social climbers had to prove that their ancestors were free from the fiery reaches of Hell. This then is the origin of the outlaw archetype.

Today, the underworld is just as likely to be found in downtown Des Moines as it is in Dante's *Inferno*. And instead of the ever-conspiring Satan, we find manipulative crime bosses, such as *Pulp Fiction*'s Marsellus Wallace, plying their evil trades. Yet, wherever its whereabouts or inhabitants—be they devils, demons, hit men or drug dealers—the journey out is just as demanding, purging and harrowing as ever before.

## THE ELEMENTS OF THE OUTLAW MYTH

### *The Provincial World*

In the outlaw structure, the provincial world is rarely shown, but is referred to or evoked through an object of power or a talisman. The outlaw clings to the talisman as a fading reminder of what he once was before his fall from grace. Sometimes it is a photo of his mother, the house he grew up in or a memento from a previous life in the provincial world. In this way the outlaw myth refers to the provincial world by inference only and does not require spending a lot of time there initially. Although it is perfectly acceptable, it is not necessary to show how he became an outlaw in the first place. The focus of the outlaw story is his liberation from the criminal underworld. The emphasis is not on how he got there, but only that he wants to escape, and does.

In these instances, the outlaw is rarely an orphan, because he has already been living in the underworld for some time. In many ways he is the antithesis of his mythic counterpart who has been proven to have nothing to lose. It is an important characteristic of the outlaw to show that he has everything to lose should he abandon his life of crime.

The outlaw must be shown to have made his bed among the criminal element, and thereby has amassed a family, a girlfriend, a child and a small fortune along the way. These are boons from the King of the Underworld, and serve to anchor him in his present lifestyle. *Though we are repulsed by the unsavory nature of the criminal underworld, we endow the outlaw with status and wealth to show how much is a lot at stake for him should he decide to leave.*

The outlaw is a militant iconoclast and is in the underworld because he was unable to "fit" into the weak, hypocritical postures of the provincial world. Unfortunately, he now realizes that the underworld is even more rigidly conformist than the provincial world ever was.

We don't suspect it at first, but escape is exactly what he has in mind. It is a secret goal he guards from his most trusted allies, and even family members. Whether this underworld is ruled by the Mafia's Five Families, or by Pluto/Hades himself, the same immutable law has been applied since the beginning of time, "Once you're in, you're in. There is no getting out." It is as old as time, because the underworld is a metaphor for Death itself.

When we first meet the outlaw, we see he is uniquely possessed of a single virtue; a quality that endears him to the denizens of the underworld and for which he has been aptly rewarded. The outlaw can be capable of the most heinous acts—murder, kidnapping, burglary or drug-dealing. We will forgive him of almost anything, so long he wishes to escape and redeem himself. The outlaw's skill at what he does is beyond reproach. He is extremely professional, and this too, has earned him great status among the underworld elite. He is a "made man," a black knight of inscrutable honor, who has proved himself time and again through the grueling trials of criminal existence.

### The Inciting Incident

This dramatic event is as essential to the outlaw myth as it is to the hero's, but rather than serving as an act of destiny, here the inciting incident is a window of opportunity. It is his last chance. The law is closing in on him, or his sense of virtue is slowly dissipating. Whatever the reason, he determines he has one final score to make in a winner-take-all gambit. The inciting incident comes as his last chance to escape. Once he has made up his mind up to "get out" he must succeed or perish.

### The World of Journey

In the outlaw myth the world of journey is replaced with the underworld itself. The magical elements of the myth are replaced with hair-raising criminal obstacles, such as the last big score, betrayal, the police closing in or the death of a trusted ally. Since the hero is already in the underworld, the journey is his escape to a better life. The difference between the outlaw and the hero is that the outlaw endures the trials and tribulations in a last-ditch effort to redeem himself.

This is a treacherous world of darkness, where anything goes, any crime is justified and any deed sanctioned, so long as it is done in the name of the Lord of the Underworld. The supreme oath of all underworld figures is to serve the King of Outlaws. To serve him is to serve oneself. The only sin is to place one's self interest above that of the outlaw king. Once the outlaw decides to make his break, all the forces of hell will rain down upon him. Even though it is a lawless world, the one law the outlaw must never break is his personal code of ethics. No matter how severe his trials, or how closely he is compromised, the outlaw must preserve this code. If he doesn't, he will surely die. The moment he loses his virtue, he loses his chance at redemption—or even worse, the audience stops rooting for him.

### The Inhabitants

In the outlaw myth, the entire society is comprised of either friends or foes, but—because this is the underworld—the line between the two is very thin. Betrayal, deceit, fear and self-interest are everywhere. We do not know who can be trusted. When we experience the ease with which friends become foes and foes become friends, we are all the more anxious for our outlaw to get the job done and leave.

### The Final Threshold

The outlaw has now obtained the money that will sustain him in a better life. Yet before he can escape he must return for someone or something (a talisman) he has left behind. If it is a loved one, they are probably in the grasp of the underlord or the police. The outlaw could escape alone, but that would destroy his virtue, so instead, true to his code, he returns to their rescue.

This outcome of the final conflict will either lead to his redemption, death or imprisonment. If he does battle with the Lord of the Underworld, he must kill the Lord or win some boon in order to leave. It is by redeeming himself that the outlaw escapes the clutches of the Underworld. Through the transcendent power of redemption, he no longer belongs with the criminal element and is now a misfit there. Bloodied and beaten, he escapes his hellish existence to a new life that is truly his own.

### The World of Return

In the outlaw journey the return world is not the provincial society of the myth, but paradise itself. As a reward for his redeemed virtue he is finally free of all social obligations, criminal or provincial, and is left to a life of his own creation. It may be a mere shanty on the beach, but it is a better world then he has ever known. It is the only place he fits in; a place beyond rigid conformity and restraint. He elects to spend the remainder of his life there, chastened and resolved to a trouble-free existence, or at least until the outlaw cycle kicks in, as seen in our next step.

## THE OUTLAW CYCLE

Many film stories pick up the outlaw's journey after he has escaped the underworld. In these films, we find him in his island paradise, or his chateau in the South of France, or locked away in some forgotten prison cell. His expertise is needed by the very authorities who pursued or imprisoned him, only now they offer him a pardon. Sometimes this is a set-up, and he knows it. Other times the real culprit is a former protégé who is intimately familiar with his old technique. What *is* clear is that if he doesn't submit he will be framed with a new batch of crimes. At this point the outlaw's journey begins again. Will he maintain his virtue and redeem himself, or will he be outwitted by the younger, more cunning and ruthless outlaws who follow in his footsteps?

## MODERN APPLICATIONS OF THE OUTLAW MYTH

In three of Quentin Tarantino's scripts, *Reservoir Dogs, True Romance* and *Pulp Fiction*, we see outlaws conflicted by integrity, romance and philosophy in worlds where these virtues are not supposed to exist—and this makes them heroic in spite of themselves. They can murder, cheat, rob, lie, steal or deal heroin, but we are still fascinated by their steadfast resolve to remain virtuous to themselves. Although the outlaw does not always get what he wants, and his story ends in tragedy more often than it does in success, we care about the outlaw and his future.

In *Reservoir Dogs,* we watch Mr. White (Harvey Keitel) mistakenly protect an undercover cop at all cost, clinging to his belief that he is a trusted accomplice. When he discovers he is wrong, he personally assassinates him, remaining true to his own value system to the very end. *Honor amongst thieves.*

In *True Romance,* we see a psychopath and a prostitute, clinging to their virtuous love while fighting to make the last score, and freeing themselves from all those who would oppress them. *Love amongst outcasts.*

In *Pulp Fiction,* we watch the efforts of two outlaws (played by Bruce Willis [Butch] and Samuel Jackson [Jules]), clinging to their personal virtues of valor and philosophy respectively, as they redeem themselves and earn their escape from the underworld. At the same time, we follow lesser equipped criminals like Vince Vega (John Travolta), "Honey Bunny" and "Ringo" (played by Amanda Plumber and Tim Roth), and the band of preppy "wanna-bes" whose lack of personal ethics lead to the swift recriminations of outlaw life.

In *Married to the Mob* we follow the dangerously funny adventures of a housewife as she aspires for personal freedom outside the sub-culture of a modern mob family.

In the movie *Bound*, directed by the Wachowski brothers, we watch as two lesbian lovers redeem themselves through romantic commitment, as they team up to rip off their mob opponents of a final score and make a clean getaway.

In Michael Mann's stirring crime epic *Heat*, we follow an elite band of thieves as they seek their final score while under the scrutiny and relentless pursuit of Al Pacino and the police. In the end, Robert De Niro is defeated by Pacino when he breaks his own personal vow to "never get involved with anything [he] can't walk away from in thirty seconds." In this case, it is the beautiful Amy Brenneman whom De Niro returns for, and she has shown herself to be well-worth the risk.

In the thriller *Memento*, we watch, spellbound, as insurance detective Leonard Shelly (Guy Pearce) desperately tries to deal with his lack of short term memory, while tracking down the men who raped and murdered his wife. In the end he discovers it doesn't matter who or what the facts are, or even if he's killed the wrong guy, he just likes the renewed sense of purpose in his life. This story is laid out in the linear fashion of most outlaw structures, with the added innovation of turning the story on its end and telling it in from finish to start. And for this deftly told story, it works brilliantly!

Though they sometimes appear anti-structural, these outlaw myths adhere to a very precise structure. Their originality comes from reworking these time honored archetypal principles.

To work with anti-structure it is important to understand the original elements of the outlaw structure before departing from them. The amateur eschews structure in a misguided attempt to

**OUTLAW MYTH FILMS**
*Absolute Power, Atlantic City, Barbarosa, Bound, Butch Cassidy and the Sundance Kid, Cattle Annie and Little Britches, The Dirty Dozen, The Gray Fox, The Gunfighter, Heat, Kiss of Death, Married to the Mob, Memento, The Outlaw Josie Wales, One-Eyed Jacks, The Rock, Rocky, The Secret Invasion, The Usual Suspects, To Catch a Thief, Thief, The Wild Bunch, Young Guns*

be "original," whereas experienced writers know the elements of structure before departing from them.

The next radical departure from the hero and outlaw structure involves a type of inversion process. No longer do we see our heroes in defiance of, or leaving, a provincial world, but entering into one after they have elsewhere redeemed themselves or transformed into magicians. This innovation is called the inverted myth.

## THE INVERTED MYTH

As the mythmaker's quest to tell different types of stories grew, we stopped tracking the hero's journey into other worlds, and started imagining what would happen if the hero, after being empowered, chanced upon a provincial world mired down in political factionalism and strife. This structure has three variations, the first being:

### The Messiah Story

In the messiah story, the hero appears in the provincial world as a stranger with wondrous experience and remarkable powers. He possesses an inner truth that is at odds with everyone else in the provincial world. Though he may seem to be little more than an aimless, shiftless wanderer, he is the mythic orphan already metamorphosed as magician. His value is eloquently expressed by the great German mystic, Hermann Hesse, in his *Journey to the East*, "He who travels far and wide often sees things far removed from those he's left behind. Yet when he speaks of them in fields at home he is disbelieved, for obdurate people don't believe in what they don't distinctly feel and see for themselves."

## THE ELEMENTS OF THE MESSIAH STORY

### The Provincial World

In the messiah story the provincial world is an advanced society ruled by three tiers of political power: the prevailing authorities, the marginal powers and the oppressed insurgent rebels. It is important to show these three divisions of external authority, because the messiah story is a powerful allegory about individual (spiritual) power versus political hegemony. The messiah tale takes the unique view that though there are many levels to the distribution of power, they are all corrupt because they call for some type of subjugation of the individual. Spiritual power seeks not to oppress, control, or to enslave, but to liberate. It upholds the spiritual kingdom of the individual to be greater than any system of government devised by man. As the messiah tale exposes and attacks all such contrived institutions, it is important to show the visiting magician in conflict with all three.

The messiah tale predates Christianity by eons. The myth of the dying God is chronicled in ancient Sumeria and the Levant in its legends of Attis, Dammuzi, Mithra, Dionysis and Bacchus, where it evolved through the Greeks and into the early Hebrew prophecies before finally being enveloped into the early Gnostic and Christian belief systems. The point is not to get hung up in the specifics of any one messianic tradition, but to dramatize the conflict of intense personal philosophy versus all institutions of political power.

First and foremost of these institutions of power are the prevailing authorities—in the biblical context, these would be the Romans under Pontius Pilate.

### The Prevailing Authorities

In the messiah myth the provincial world is occupied by an elite foreign government, who seek not so much to enslave but to exploit those under them. Their overall aim is to maintain the status quo. Their power is absolute and this makes them completely apathetic to the personal aspirations of their subjects. They are so confident in their military might, that they may even dispense some political autonomy to marginal powers beneath them so long as it doesn't threaten or interfere with the export of riches.

### The Marginal Powers

The second tier of political power in the messiah tale is comprised the marginal powers who receive their influence from the prevailing authorities. They are to be characterized as exceedingly ambitious, unyielding, greedy and more overtly power hungry than even those from whom their power derives. These are the ubiquitous Jobsworths of Shakespearean note, the detail-driven bureaucrats who delight in the minutia of properly crossed t's and impeccably dotted i's.

We see examples of these deranged pencil-pushers everywhere from the 7/11 to the U.S. Post Office—but the clearest example can be found in Hitler's concentration camps, where the Nazi elite ruled absolutely, yet exercised their authority through a select group of cowed and vicious inmates chosen from the amongst the prison body. Ultimately it is this group that is most threatened by the arrival of the orphan/magician wanderer on to the scene.

### The Insurgent Rebels

Amongst the citizenry of the provincial town there is great unrest. A handful of dissidents seek to overthrow the foreign infidels and establish home rule. They are opposed to the prevailing authorities, and to the marginal powers as well. The insurgent rebels are likable, well-meaning and more noble than all the others, but nevertheless still aspire to have their will prevail over the populace. They've stopped believing in the people they seek to free and now seek only their share of the political pie. Thus, the tiny provincial world of the messiah structure is a highly charged political, volatile mixture where the least sign of disturbance could upset the very fragile balance of power. Into this precarious mixture wanders...

### The Orphan/ Magician/ Messiah

He has no political, personal agenda or allegiance. He is a loner, a maverick, a philosopher who speaks from his own experience—the truth of the pilgrim. He has seen much in his young years and knows it is in no one's interest, certainly not his own, to get involved in local or factional politics. He preaches naively, perhaps reluctantly, of the personal freedom he has known in his travels. He is an idealist—someone who has been touched by the kindness and barbarism of different lands and peoples. He is a champion of the poor and underprivileged, as these are the good souls who have fed and clothed him along the way—asking only for his blessing in return. He wanders about speaking this truth, never realizing he is about to become a pawn in the political game of much more cunning individuals than himself.

### Disciples and Adversaries

As the word spreads throughout the provincial world about the pilgrim's amazing insights and experiences, he attracts many curiosity seekers, fans and skeptics. He greets them all with the same openness and warmth, as if each were a different land, a different experience of their own. He does not judge them, as others might, but welcomes them equally into the fold, extending to them whatever he can in sage advice and hard-earned wisdom. He does not realize the magnitude of his gift, nor does he see himself as offering anything more than a personal truth. He never senses, until it is too late, that his message of spiritual empowerment is exactly what the common man has been yearning for.

As legends, stories and rumors of miracles spring up around him, the messiah dismisses them as little more than what is available to all who seek the "kingdom within themselves." He makes a mockery of those whose self-importance or political wrangling blinds them to the inherent worth of all mankind. As a result he offends as many as he endears. The power of his simple truth is very threatening, even dangerous, to those who seek to impose their authority on others. So, the more the people hunger for his message, the more the marginal authorities become increasingly alarmed.

Many of those self-same tales of wonder are manufactured and even amplified by self-interested parties who intend only to shake the various factions of power to their very core. They are less interested in the magician and his word, but rather in the momentary advantage he brings to those who associate with him. Eventually he becomes attractive to the insurgent rebels who quickly see him as a potential ally to their unpopular struggle.

### Betrayal, Persecution and Judgment

By now the messiah is a god to some, devil to others. And while he is much too powerful to attack directly, the marginal authorities set out to discredit him where he is most vulnerable— through the dubious collection of hangers-on and disciples who cling on to his afterglow.

There has been infighting and squabbling among them, each claiming to be closer, more enlightened, more favored by the magician than the others. To those disciples he disappoints, usually through some misconstrued, self-serving rationale, the messiah becomes expendable. The betrayer sees the messiah as a traitor to his zealous political cause, and maintains his own aspirations above the innocent grace of the magician's teachings. He elects to betray him as he feels he has been slighted. As a result, the Judas character plays right into the hands of the marginal powers who have been desperately searching for a way to bring the messiah down.

At this point there is a trial, where ludicrous, trumped-up charges are made. The magician is astonished by the spectacle his simple teachings have caused. He defends himself, but cannot and will not betray the truth he has come to know as his own. His personal message applies to aristocrat and plebeian alike. While spiritual empowerment is almost laughable to the prevailing authorities, it is a great threat to the marginal powers, who secretly envy him. So, they seek his humiliation and execution before all. The prevailing authority defers to the marginal ones. Sentence is pronounced: *The magician must die!*

A public humiliation follows, where disciples and skeptics all participate. The disciples are as eager to see the messiah's miraculous powers put to the test as much as the skeptics seek to have him exposed as a charlatan. But the magician is a true traveler and does not fear death, because he has lived and died many times, traversed many such thresholds in his journeys. He greets the transformation from life to death as he might any foreign land. He sees the next world as a better place than the one he is leaving.

*Death and Resurrection*

The martyred, crucified and slain magician is a metaphor for humankind's fear of individual or spiritual empowerment. You might say that the crucifix is no longer the symbols of a dying god's love for his creation, but of a prevailing establishment's warning against anyone who dares to claim their divinity. Indeed, how many of us have sacrificed our true magician selves in order to conform to society-at-large? The witnessing of the magician's demise shames even his harshest critics; compelling sinner and saint to ask, "Dear God, what have we done?"

While the skeptic walks away unrepentant, the disciple is inspired to change his life forever. In the end, the magician's death is no death at all, but a spiritual rebirth in the hearts and minds of millions. The one is sacrificed so that others can truly be spiritually free.

## MODERN APPLICATIONS OF THE MESSIAH STORY

In *One Flew Over the Cuckoo's Nest* (screenplay by Bo Goldman and Lawrence Hauben) Randall McMurphy is a brawling, whiskey-guzzling, free-spirited, ne'er-do-well, arrested on a charge of statutory rape. To get around pulling some hard time, he submits himself to the scrutiny of a local mental hospital. He is an orphan/wanderer/magician with a unique way of looking at the world. He is non-political. He has no agenda than to live his life pursuing the only freedoms he has ever known, which he describes as "fucking and fighting." He aims to get out of this latest imbroglio by using the charm and cunning that have served him so well in the past.

The provincial world of the mental hospital is one of absolute authority, ruled by the tightly wound Nurse Ratched. She welcomes Randall into the fold and perceives him to be of little threat to her domain. Her subjects are all docile, neurotic infants, who have long since given up any personal desire for freedom. Nurse Ratched, like all marginal tyrants, is highly delusional and possessive of the power she wields. Because McMurphy is a free spirit, he poses the greatest challenge to her egocentric control. As he

"It is a far, far better thing that I do than I have ever done. It is a far, far better place that I go to than I have ever known."

*—Charles Dickens, A Tale of Two Cities*

goes to work, performing miracles, dispensing freedom, and goading the others to free themselves, he is increasingly at odds with Nurse Ratched. There is a contest of wills. Whose reality is this? Who is truly insane: those who surrender their individuality, or those who seek to oppress it? Who amongst us is truly free, or sane, for that matter? It is clear now, the magician must atone; he will submit; he must be humiliated and defeated.

As Randall plans his personal flight to freedom, he lingers behind to bestow his greatest miracle on the tormented Billy Babbit, whom he delivers from the hell of sexual repression. And in the hours of his greatest accomplishment, Billy betrays the magician, Randall is delivered into the hands of the prevailing authorities, and condemned.

Now, the martyred magician, after receiving a frontal lobotomy, is subdued, quiet and defeated. While the skeptics resume their life of complacency, his greatest disciple, Chief Broom, emerges. Setting the magician's spirit free, the Chief carries the torch in his own flight to freedom. The magician's life has been sacrificed, so that others can be free.

In the movie *Cool Hand Luke* (based on the novel by Donn Pearce, screenplay by Donn Pearce and Frank Pierson) Paul Newman plays an aimless orphaned war hero sentenced to a prison camp for vandalizing parking meters. The provincial world of the prison camp is inhabited by hardened criminals, mental rejects and petty thieves. They are outlaws, but are also willing conformists in a world ruled by a smug warden and his sadistic prison guards. The prisoners spend their days in grueling slave labor, grateful for any scrap thrown their way. When Luke enters the fold, he is mistrusted and ostracized for his unwillingness to conform even to the society of prisoners. Luke is a true nonconformist, and his message of personal freedom is as great a threat to the inmates as it is to the guards. Gradually he wins the inmates over by showing them that freedom is ultimately a state of mind. By his example, he stands up to those who would enslave him and wins many converts along the way. As Luke goes about dispensing his miracles, he grows more and more powerful among the prisoners and a real threat to the marginal powers.

They seek to break his spirit at all cost. He must be humiliated and crushed as an example to all.

What follows is a public humiliation, and Luke feigns submission. But this is only in preparation for his final escape and greatest miracle of all. Extending his magnanimity to his closest disciple, George Kennedy, he reveals his plan. After the prison break, holed up in an abandoned church for hours of soul-searching despair, he is betrayed and delivered into the hands of the enemy, where he is promptly gunned down. We are left with a lasting impression of his fellow prisoners living through him, speculating about his final deliverance from all authoritarian domination.

For other examples of the messiah structure look at the films: *Dead Poets Society, Jean de Florette, Jesus of Montreal, Rebel Without a Cause, Spartacus, Stalag 17* and *A Tale of Two Cities.* These are powerful parables of man's struggle for spiritual and individual freedom at the expense of life itself.

The inverted myth continues in its progression to the:

## THE VENGEFUL MESSIAH, OR ANGEL OF DEATH STORY

In these dark, exacting and horrific tales, the orphan magician returns to the provincial world on a terrible mission, as the Angel of Death. He is now hell-bent on exacting retribution from those who wronged him in the first place. He is the martyred magician returned, not with the spirit of freedom, but of righteous indignation and vengeance.

There is no message of personal freedom here; the time for preaching and gentle parables is over. There is, quite simply, hell to pay! The avenging angel returns to expose corruption, hypocrisy and sin, to separate the good from the evil with the swift sword of judgment. There is no ambivalence allowed toward the Angel of Death; you are either friend or foe. No last minute conversions will be accepted. One must have demonstrated a commitment to the truth long before the Angel of Death appears on the scene.

A passage from the Hindu scripture, the Bhagavad Gita, expresses the value of the avenging godhead, as do most cultures and religions that take their cue from this universal sentiment. *"Wherever and whenever there is a decline in goodness and a predominance of evil, at that time do I manifest myself in order to deliver the righteous and destroy the miscreants."*

## THE ELEMENTS OF THE VENGEFUL MESSIAH MYTH

The provincial world is wholly corrupt and without a single virtue. It is not a real community bound by laws and ethical justice. It is a collusion of devils, a den of iniquity, a conspiracy of hypocrites and miscreants disguised as god-fearing, law-abiding citizens.

### The Prevailing Authorities

The provincial world is peopled by a stark collection of desperate men and women hiding from some dark secret or heinous crime they have committed in the name of progress. They are like the marginal powers who were responsible for putting the magician/messiah to death. They are a vicious, weak and conniving bunch of jackals, who have gotten away with murder. Desperate to get on with their meager lives, they convince themselves that what was done was unavoidable, and for the benefit of all. Their rationale, denial and machinations make them pathetic in our eyes, and hence all the more deserving of the devastation to come.

### The Orphan/Magician/ Avenging Angel

The vengeful messiah is the ghost of the slain magician returned. He is the messiah delivered from life, but not yet emancipated. He must accomplish one last deed before his spirit can be free. He appears on the scene not as a free spirit or benign traveler, but as a haunted, driven, mysterious stranger. There is something vaguely familiar about him, an air of mystery surrounds him that the corrupt citizens cannot quite place. It is with this quality of haunting, vague recognition that the avenging angel starts to tear at their fragile infrastructure.

At first, the Angel of Death appears to be cruel, and we are unsure about his intentions. Is he good or evil? He is swift, opin-

ionated, and ruthless. As he goes about befriending various outcasts, misfits and underdogs, he upsets the tenuous threads that
hold the community together, gradually exposing all the hypocrites for who they truly are. Bit by bit, we start to see the town
unravel. Although they scarcely realize what is happening before
it is too late, the martyred ghost begins to separate the righteous
from those who were directly responsible for his death. It is not
solely for revenge that the avenging angel returns, because
vengeance is not virtuous in itself; the Angel of Death has come to
restore the righteous. So his purpose must be shown to be
twofold.

The Dark Angel is both attractive and repulsive to the opposite
sex. We measure his goodness by the way the good and the down-
trodden are drawn to him. They have lost faith in the weak, sim-
pering manners of the town leaders. They look upon him as a real
man, a real woman. As a result, The Angel of Death causes familial and marital disharmony, liberating the good spouses and offspring from their contemptuous husbands, wives, fathers and
mothers. In this way the avenging hero pits good against evil,
father against mother, child against parent.

Note this passage from St. Matthew, revealing an aspect of the
gentle Jesus we rarely hear about. *"Do not think that I have come
to bring peace on earth; but a sword. For I have come to set a man
against his father and a daughter against her mother, and a daughter in law against her mother in law. And a man's foes will be those
of his own household. He who loves father or mother more than me
is not worthy of me; And he who loves son or daughter more than me
is not worthy of me; and he who does not take up his cross and follow me is not worthy of me. And he who finds his life will lose it, and
he who loses his life, for my sake, will find it* (Matthew 10:34;39).

Now a reverse humiliation takes place as the avenging angel
uses his power to expose, ridicule and embarrass the citizenry
with the truth about themselves. The terror escalates until the
town is uprooted, if not destroyed all together. In the end, the
martyred magician leaves, taking his rightful place in the beyond.
His true identity is revealed and the details of his execution are
revealed as the dark secret the town so desperately sought to con-

ceal. The evil doers have been vanquished and the good are elevated to power, and we, the audience, have been severely chastened along the way.

Excellent examples of the Angel of Death story are *Bad Day at Black Rock, Hang 'em High, High Plains Drifter, Pale Rider, Shane* and *Unforgiven*. For a remarkable examination of both the messiah story and avenging angel structure told back-to-back watch the brilliant French film series, *Jean de Florette* and *Manon des Sources* from beginning to end.

Poor examples of this structure are *The Crow*, and the Sharon Stone vehicle, *The Quick and the Dead*. By their glaring ignorance of the avenging angel archetype, these films quickly descend into one cliché after another as they neglect to endow the avenging angel with the twofold purpose of destroying the miscreants while delivering the righteous. In each case, The avenging angel comes off as either compromised and ineffectual (*The Quick and The Dead*), or just as despicable as the criminals who wronged him in the first place (*The Crow*).

The third variation of the inverted myth is...

## THE BLITHE ANGEL OR THE ANGEL OF MERCY

These are tales of joy, music, wonder and laughter. No longer do we have death, vengeance, political intrigue and retribution on our minds, but exactly the opposite.

The blithe angel is the liberating orphan/wanderer/magician come back as a divine rascal. He is on a mission of deliverance, not from evil, but from banality.

The blithe angel is the Hermetic trickster known in every culture as the maker of merriment, or the holy fool. He seeks not to destroy us but to lift our spirits high and to remind us to have a good time while we are here on Earth. He has all the magical/masterful qualities of the messiah and the Angel of Death, but very little awareness of who he really is. In fact the blithe angel often takes his considerable gifts for granted—freely dispensing them to one and all with little discernment. He shows us the folly of our staid and stodgy ways, not through martyrdom or wrath, but through mischief, music and gaiety.

## ELEMENTS OF THE BLITHE ANGEL MYTH

### The Provincial World

This is an idyllic world where the people, rulers, aristocrats and commoners are equal to each other. They share the blessings of their community as well as a common problem. The community is made up of stern, ritualistic, rule followers, who believe in law and order even when they seem to be overburdened by it. They cling to values without a lot of thought or deliberation on the matter: tradition, marriage, class, the "old ways," old time religion, and other foolish consistencies rank high on their list. They do things not because they enjoy doing them, but because "that's the way it's always been done, and who are we to change it?"

The prevailing authorities in the typical blithe angel myth are those of the well-intentioned town fathers. Rather than being decadent autocrats (as the appear in the messiah tales), these are well-known, and much beloved characters you would find in any town, the mayor, judge, the congressman, the librarian, the reverend. In this case, the marginal powers are the average everyday citizens, merchants and menial servants who prove themselves to be much more sensible than the elected officials.

The young people take the place of the insurgent rebels, but rather than pursuing the outright overthrow of the prevailing authorities, they express their restlessness through innocuous acts of defiance, either by breaking long established social taboos, or by crossing rigid class and racial lines. These young rebels love their parents and believe them to be well-meaning, but also wish they could lighten up and have a good time themselves once in a while. Admittedly, the prospect of this occurring without direct angelic intervention is clearly out of the question. And into this mix wanders...

### The Orphan/Wanderer/Magician as Blithe Spirit

Upon first arrival, this hapless, unassuming angel of mercy confronts the troubled community and is sufficiently put off by it. This is the last place on earth he would choose to settle down. The town is an easy mark for the kind of magic he freely dispenses:

whether it is his usual con job or any other light-hearted diversion. He can hardly work up a reason to stay in this sorry excuse for a town. They're not worth even cheating, he concludes, and swiftly attempts to depart. But he can't leave! The road is blocked, the train is down, or some other force majeure prevents him from exiting (the inciting incident). This is the first indication of the wandering angel's destiny. There is a reason he has been sent to this place, however reluctant he is to admit it.

### Disciples and Adversaries

The blithe angel is gradually befriended by some of the town's young people or other social outcasts who are won over by his magical, whimsical ways. They have secretly shared his philosophy for years, but never possessed the courage to act on it. They use the angel's encouragement to break all the rules as a testing ground for their own repressed desires. Either they want to sing, dance, marry someone from the wrong side of the tracks, start a woman's football league, hold a beauty pageant or some other frowned upon act of independence. The blithe angel encourages these acts of sedition with naive, blind and unabashed enthusiasm. "Follow your dreams," the angel sings. "Life is too short and sweet to live in the shadows of suppression. Live for the moment in love's sweet embrace and never worry about tomorrow. Let tomorrow take care of itself."

Of course, this flies in the face of the conventions of the prevailing authorities. Very soon, the rumors of the angel's words and miracles spread, earning him more and more disciples and adversaries as he goes along. All the while, the blithe angel grows wonderfully giddy about his accomplishments.

Because of his initial contempt for the townsfolk and the marginal powers it has been easy for the blithe angel to dispense, encourage and promote a sort of benign mayhem without taking responsibility for the results of his unbridled enthusiasm. And very soon too, do all those wild exhortations come home to roost, when tragedy befalls the angel's closest ally and he or she either winds up injured, in jail, or pregnant. This leads to a crackdown by the powers-that-be upon the young people, but most of all that foreign rabble-rouser.

### Betrayal and Judgment

The angel is brought to trial on trumped-up charges. We have never seen him so defeated. He blames himself for the predicament, for he never should have stayed so long. Like all the many other times and places he visited in the past, he should have gotten out while the going was good. During this period, the blithe angel's own Garden of Gethsemane, he seems to be in most need of his own special medicine. At this time it appears everything he ever stood for or warned against was wrong.

When the angel begins doubting his own message, it looks like fear, conformity and the status quo will triumph. As his trial before the community builds towards its inevitable conclusion and the situation appears hopeless, his chief disciple appears at the very last possible moment to testify on the angel's behalf.

He or she is the one most adversely affected by the angel's medicine. At first by enthusiastically supporting him and then later by rallying others to the cause. When tragedy strikes, the chief disciple becomes a perfect example of everything they were warned against and brings about the worst possible fate for himself and the blithe angel's cause. Either in a wheelchair, jail or maybe pregnant from an interracial affair, the chief disciple proclaims the angel's medicine as "more than worth the trouble" and, rather than condemn him for it, she or he outwardly proclaims it to be "the best experience" of his or her life. In the end, through the chief disciple's personal intervention, tragedy and testimony, the townsfolk and people of the community are forced to admit that they, too, have changed for the better in wake of the angel's visit.

At this point, the blithe angel demonstrates a display of miracles, converting even most hardened skeptics. The town revitalizes with joy, laughter, music and merriment. A mass coupling follows where the Angel creates marriages, friendships and alliances that once were impossible. In the end, the angel awaits word from above: will he be ordered on to his next mission, or will this be his final resting place?

## MODERN EXAMPLES OF THE BLITHE ANGEL MYTH

*The Bishop's Wife, Cold Comfort Farm, Down and Out in Beverly Hills, Groundhog Day, Hoosiers, Inherit the Wind, Footloose, Mary Poppins, The Music Man; Planes, Trains and Automobiles; The Rainmaker; Reuben, Reuben; To Wong Foo, Thanks for Everything, Julie Newmar* and *What About Bob?* are just some excellent examples of the blithe angel tale. It is an immensely popular structure and can be applied to any musical, comedy, or romantic fantasy. (The angel does not literally have to be an angel—as in *The Bishop's Wife, Chances Are, Heart and Soul, Heaven Can Wait* or *Oh God!*—but can be any free-spirited musician, con artist, poet or social misfit that shows up on the scene.)

An important detail is to make the opposing values between the angel and the provincial world very clear from the very beginning. Let it be shown without hesitancy that he possesses exactly the right medicine to cure this community, and, even if we don't see it at first, the community has the perfect formula for him.

The problem, therefore, is not one of "can he do it?" but instead, "will he?" For indeed, we know the magical angel can handle the big stuff—it's the smaller stuff of personal commitment and compassion that keep him on the move (*Groundhog Day*). When the blithe angel is touched, either by romantic love, as in *The Music Man*, or through the adoration of a child and loving family as in *What about Bob?*, then and only then, can his own healing begin to take place.

## REVIEW

We have progressed through mythic structure and its natural development into five structural variations: the hero myth; the outlaw myth; the messiah, avenging angel and blithe angel myths. Now let's return to our *Richard Cory* exercise and see if any of these structures can apply to our working premise.

*When* a young man's idol (Richard Cory) *commits suicide*, he becomes disillusioned and rebels. In defiance of his previous values he soon crashes and burns, when he discovers a truth about himself and this spurs him on to re-examine his life and find personal fulfillment.

Is this a myth? Does the main character go on a physical journey? If so, is it a hero, outlaw or an inverted myth?

Is the hero already an accomplished orphan magician, or must he journey to magician status?

Does he stumble into a provincial world from the outside, or does he rise from within?

Analyze the elements of your story and determine the appropriate structure. Does the premise indicate any of the previously mentioned structures?

The premise of *Richard Cory* most closely resembles the myth, but before we can accurately choose it for our film, we need to know of other available structures.

## THE WAY OF THE FAIRY TALE:
## A statement or account of something incredible

From the myth and its myriad mutations, the next development in the storyteller's craft was to condense the elements of the myth and confine it to a contained arena of conflict—the fairy tale kingdom. A graphic melding of the three worlds of myth to the more contained one of the fairy tale kingdom might look like this:

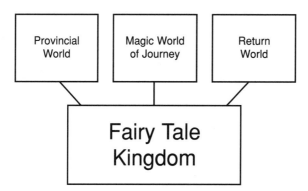

In the fairy tale we see all three worlds of the myth; the provincial world, the magical world of journey and the return world, all condensed into one world: the fairy tale kingdom. The difference between them is that in the fairy tale, the hero emerges from within the fairy tale kingdom itself, rather than wandering away from, or stumbling into it.

## ELEMENTS OF THE FAIRY TALE STRUCTURE

### The Fairy Tale Kingdom

There is a king, a queen, a castle, a village, and a community of craftspersons, commoners, farmers, merchants and culture of noble men and women. There also are outcasts in the form of ogres, dragons, witches, gnomes and fairy folk. In other words, it is a completely self-contained society, a universe in miniature. This can be the Little Italy of today, the summer camp of yesteryear or any small community in the future.

What we communicate through the fairy tale structure is the insular similarity of the human village in general. It conveys the subtle imperative that no matter how far you travel in distance or in time, human beings are basically the same everywhere you go. Whether it's the perpetually confounding antics of the Kalahari Bushmen, school teachers, bushwhackers, rebels and politicians of *The Gods Must Be Crazy*; the streetwalkers, pimps, hustlers, lawyers and businessmen of *Pretty Woman*; the flower merchants, grocers, morticians, plumbers and professors in *Moonstruck* or the Long Island compound, feuding Dons and extended Italian families of *The Godfather*, the fairy tale kingdom is the complete history and scope of human culture in a single glance. *The fairy tale structure gives the audience an immediate sense of the protagonist's world and his or her social standing in it.*

From the moment the fairy tale story opens, there is a wedding, a christening, a coronation, a tournament or festival in progress. This establishes an instantaneous familiarity with your audience. They will derive untold comfort in knowing, much like their own lives, that the action about to take place will do so within the ranks of the immediate world presented. Intuitively, they know to seek out the protagonist and focus their attention on the hero's quest against overwhelming odds.

### The Inhabitants

The fairy tale kingdom is peopled with denizens from all walks of life: nobles, merchants, farmers, laborers, as well as fairy tale figures of imaginary origins intermixing in the full spectrum of daily life.

These are extremely quaint communities where an individual's social status is immediately apparent simply upon meeting them for the first time. We can tell who's who with little or no introduction, and this is one of the great advantages of the fairy tale structure. You don't have to spend a great deal of time setting your story up.

### The Hero

The protagonist of the fairy tale usually starts off from either a very lowly position, or extremely high social status, because the most salient purpose of this structure is to chronicle the adventures of the lowly being uplifted, or the high and mighty being humbled.

These stories were born of a time of entrenched social oppression. As much as we know of these caste systems, it was virtually impossible for a person of low rank to marry or better themselves beyond the circumstances of their birth. In the Varna-Ashrama system of India, the four factions of society were priests, the military, the merchants and the laborers. Beyond these there were the devas, demigods and demons aligned at either end of the social spectrum and beyond these were the Chandalas, or dog-eaters, the demons, villains and "Untouchables." Those unfortunates who qualified as "Untouchables" were considered so inferior that they could not even touch a person of higher caste.

So, it was only natural that storyteller traditions within each class would fashion together fantastical tales of like-situated heroes and heroines who would do the unthinkable and raise themselves up to marry a king, find a pot of gold, kill a terrible giant, melt a witch or rescue a princess, thus magically winning favor well beyond their social standing.

Likewise, in feudal societies, it could prove extremely dangerous to openly remark, or even idly speculate, on the idiosyncrasies of a fatuous marquis or the unfortunate protuberances of an uncomely queen. How much more politically feasible (and safer) it was to allude to such tyrants as the frog prince, the Snow Queen or as an alm-greedy troll, rather than as their real life counterparts? Thus, we find in the archetypal regions of the fairy tale the perfect means for fashioning a tale of social redemption, magical intercession and fateful resurrection from the dreariness of humdrum fate. The fairy tale is a remarkably democratic examination of the human condition. They are equal opportunity morality tales where everyone is worthy and at the same time potentially corrupt. The noble is just as flawed as the peasant, the butcher as seductive as the courtesan, and the duke can be as dumb as a bag full of dirt.

What is particularly ingenious about fairy tales is that, in as much as they strive to show how much we are alike, they are amazingly economical in the manner with which they convey our differences as well. For instance, it is a common tool to portray the hero as one of a set of three siblings, each of which exhibits very specific attributes. While the older sibling is the traditional object of great favor and affection, he or she is not always the most qualified for the exigencies of the fairy tale plot. We all love the Corleones' impetuous hot-head, Sonny, but his temper and tendency to take everything personally does not bode well for his tenure as acting heir-apparent.

It is the same with the middle sibling. The middle son or daughter is a mixed bag of qualities and attributes which might make them suitable champions in another fable, but right now they seem lost between the pig-headed confidence of the firstborn and the understated, as yet unrealized potential of the youngest. In the modern fairy tale of *The Godfather* (written by Francis Ford Coppola and Mario Puzo, based on the novel by Mario Puzo), Fredo is weak, unrealistic and sentimental. He aspires to be worthy, but is blinded by his own ambition. It would be one thing if he understood this about himself and accepted his lot, but tragically, he cannot see his own shortcomings, and so he is left to aspire for power, position and grandeur beyond his capabilities. These flaws make him prey to more cunning individuals outside the family, and thus bring him in to direct conflict with the true hero of the fairy tale, the youngest child. (Michael Corleone, being the youngest son of the youngest son, or, apocryphally, the seventh son of the seventh son, illustrates the propensity of fairy tales to vest legendary iconoclastic powers on the youngest protagonist.)

Like the fabled Goldilocks, who finds perfection in threes, the youngest fairy tale hero has all the "right stuff" to succeed. The perfect fairy tale hero is understated, innocent, humble and, as yet, a blank slate upon which the adventure ahead will demand the utmost. The youngest child has the most to prove. The others have made their mark, carved out their niche and have had their positions in the family hierarchy pre-defined, whereas the youngest has not. He or she is the baby, the spoiled one, the pampered. Whatever struggle has occurred in the family, it has occurred long before the youngest offspring arrived on the scene. If he or she is hampered in any way, other than by natural consequence in the family pecking order, it is at the hands of a curse.

### The Curse

The curse is a common device of the traditional fairy tale and its use in the modern screen story often supplants or accentuates the role of the inciting incident.

The curse can be a dramatic event from the outside that spurs the hero to adventure, or it may be the principle obstruction preventing him from doing so. Either way, it is this principle action levied against the hero, his community, or his beloved, that will prove itself to be the most persistent foe throughout the adventure. Whomever and however worthy the opponents to follow, be they mad dog or Morgan Le Fey, the curse shall remain the hero's primary objective and persistent adversarial force, right up to the tale's exciting conclusion.

The inner flaw of the mythic hero, or the much-beleaguered virtue of the outlaw, is replaced by the curse in the fairy tale structure. The hero or heroine must struggle to overcome this curse and either vigorously prevent it from spreading, or break it all together. If the kingdom is suffering from the curse in the beginning, the fairy tale hero must initially set himself free before relieving others from it.

### The Talisman

Fairy tales retain their link to the myth by creating special objects of intense power. Since these tales are about the low made high, the objects of power introduced are usually of common origin, i.e., the slipper, the magic bean, the spinning wheel, the rusty lamp, the spindle, the clock, the thimble, the watch, the tarnished bauble, or even the innocuous apple. The important detail here is to make the object, like the hero himself, of humble origins, so that its supernatural power is not immediately apparent, but grows with the increasing emancipation of the protagonist.

### The Climax

The constant in the fairy tale theme is one of human triumph over impossible odds (such as life achieved from vegetation, clay or dust), such as Adam and Eve, *Pinocchio* and *Pygmalion*. Mortality to immortality, as in *Cupid and Psyche*; poverty to wealth, *Cinderella, Aladdin and the Forty Thieves*; vanity to beast-liness, *Beauty and the Beast*; emotional release over ritual and superstition, as in *Moonstruck*; or inner worth validated over rigid elitism as seen in *My Fair Lady*.

The fairy tale evolved from the Greek myth, and later became Christendom's way of assimilating their inherent values into their own belief systems. For greater inspiration and insight into the origination of fairy tale structure, try finding their original roots in Greek myth. There you will find the basis for everything from *Snow White, Beauty and the Beast, My Fair Lady, Moonstruck, The Godfather* and *Pretty Woman*. For who is the model for the step-mother/Queen of Snow White, with her incessant querying, "Mirror, mirror on the wall," if not the vain and calculating Venus/Aphrodite? And who is the inspiration for noble Belle, in *Beauty and the Beast*, if not the valiant Psyche from Apulius' *Cupid and Psyche*? And who is the prototype of every sword-wielding hero if not the likes of Jason, Hercules, Perseus, Theseus and Ulysses?

### Thematic Content

Fairy tale stories often have strong thematic composition precisely because their purpose is to correct an imbalance in an artificial or unjust social taboo, be it the caste system or misplaced appreciation of material values. In *Beauty and the Beast*, the theme of inner worth is constantly juxtaposed between Belle's inherent beauty inside, and the Beast's grotesque exterior without.

In the modern Cinderella story, *Pretty Woman* (written by J.F. Lawton), these social values are further polarized, where you have the outwardly "successful" corporate raider played by Richard Gere matched against the socially "unacceptable" state of Julia Robert's prostitute character. These opposite traits are further examined when we find that the corporate raider, for all of his material success, is rotten to the core, whereas the hooker, despite her social failings, is the proverbial whore with a heart of gold.

In *The Godfather*, we are taught to empathize with Vito Coreleone and his sons, because of his open generosity and adherence to Old World values in spite of changing times. He patiently tolerates the undertaker, who treats him like a common thug. He keeps his distance from the terrifying figure of Luca Brasi, a feared dealer of death in the underworld. We watch as he chides, chastises and embraces his sons and daughters like any loving father would. And this allows us to align with him, and with his dream of taking the family legitimate. It is through this thematic texturing that our sympathies are bought for an otherwise murderous, ambitious and ruthless Mafia clan.

When the fairy tale kingdom is portrayed and perceived as idyllic, we are forced to draw on our pool of antagonists from powerful outcasts such as, the witch, the ogre, the dragon, the troll, the warlock, the enchantress, the wicked stepmother or the fortune hunting stepfather.

Today, with our skepticism about magic and divine intervention, we create characters who emulate the values of the fairy tale villain: So rather than the accursed beast/prince from *Beauty and the Beast*, we have the hardened, cynical, corporate raider in *Pretty Woman*. Rather than a beleaguered monarch and his three ambitious sons, we have the saga of the Corleone crime family; rather than the accursed sleep of a Sleeping Beauty, we show the less than romantic aspirations of a passionless widow in *Moonstruck*. By finding the original inspirations for these timeless archetypes, you can mine the riches of our storytelling past for endless updates and ever-meaningful variations on eternal themes.

## MODERN APPLICATIONS OF THE FAIRY TALE

In the movie *Moonstruck*, we open with a luminous full moon rising majestically over the fairy tale world of New York's Little Italy. Through the opening credits we are treated to scenes of the La Boheme Company coming to the Metropolitan Opera House, accompanied by "That's Amore," sung by Dean Martin. Immediately we are struck with two sub-stratas of a unique fairy tale kingdom: the sentimental, peasant musings of the kitschy love song, and the epic, romantic yearnings of Puccini's *La Boheme*. Two opposing sides of romantic love—the transcendent and the sentimental. As if to say, love can either be a drudgery or a blessing.

The next thing we see is an image of death, a man in a coffin in the funeral home where Cher's Loretta Castorini works as a bookkeeper. We learn that she is a nice lady, practical and caring, but a little cynical since the death of her first husband. She is cursed, believing that she was unlucky for not properly adhering to the formal rules of marriage and courtship. As a result she has long abandoned her heart in favor of efficiency, ritual and security. Under this curse she is condemned to marry the wrong man, Johnny Cammareri, played by Danny Aiello. Loretta is a princess. Her father is a wealthy plumber, a nobleman in the fairy tale kingdom of Little Italy. Loretta's mother is his long-suffering queen, obsessed with finding out why men are unfaithful. All of them, in their own way, are under the spell of the accursed moon and are paying the price for having settled for less than what they deserve (i.e., living life not for itself, but out of fear of death).

When her fiancé, Johnny Cammareri, is called away to his mother's deathbed in Italy, Loretta confronts a haggardly old witch waiting at the airport terminal. The old crone points to the plane and says her sister is on it and that she's put a curse on it that it should fall from the sky and crash into the ocean. Loretta abruptly dismisses the old woman's claim, compelled to hear her story about the bitterness of a life cheated from passionate love. The same mistake she is about make in her own life.

As promised, Loretta goes to invite Johnny's brother Ronny to their wedding (the inciting incident) and learns that there has been bad blood between them since an ill-fated accident that caused the loss of Ronny's hand. He too, is cursed, and his bitterness has transformed him into a type of fairy tale-type ogre. He is a tormented baker whose workplace surroundings of raging ovens and fiery kilns are akin to the under regions of a troll-like cavern. Ronny does what most ogres do and kidnaps the princess; he steals her away to his flat above the bakery where he takes her to bed. But, because he is a decent fellow, really, and because he awakens Loretta's suppressed emotions, the two are well-suited to break free of the stagnation that has ruined their lives. Through their personal choices, the transforming magic of the moon and the uplifting strains of "La Boheme," Loretta and Ronny are elevated beyond the bitterness of the past, the superstitions of the present, to embrace the future promise of romantic love. In the end, having learned to follow their hearts' desire over outmoded beliefs, life over death, love over superstition, the lovers break free of the curse and restore their respective families to a state of loving grace.

In *The Godfather,* Don Corleone is a benevolent patriarch of a stronghold shared by five powerful warlords. While relations are peaceful at the time of his daughter's wedding (the communal opening), we are forewarned that this peace will not last long. We are introduced to the good king's three sons: Sonny, the eldest, who is rash and impetuous; Fredo, the meek and envious; and Michael, the war hero who has aspirations outside of the family business. Immediately, because of the fairy tale structure, we sense a power struggle is imminent from within and without.

According to Sicilian custom, on the day of his daughter's wedding the Godfather must grant any boon requested of him. (This is a classic device of the Arthurian cycles.) So we begin by watching Don Corleone generously dispensing "favors" to noblemen and subjects alike. When he is approached by an undertaker, who insults the Don and treats him with disrespect, a curse-like unease settles over the Corleones. The curse comes to fruition when Sonny is mercilessly gunned down at a tollbooth and the undertaker, as prophesied, is pressed into service. It then falls upon Michael to avenge his brother's murder and restore his family's sovereignty. What follows is Michael Corleone's rise to power, proving himself the most worthy to take his father's place as Capo di Tutti Capi, "boss of all bosses." The film ends with Michael Corleone receiving the oath of loyalty from the most trusted knights of the realm.

Even though this saga takes place in modern-day New York, and among people we hardly associate with fairy tales—the strength of its structure compels us to identify and root for their plight. Watching *The Godfather* for the first time appeals to us from the time-honored archetypal realm, the realm of the eternal fairy tale. To determine whether your story fits the requirement of a fairy tale structure, ask yourself:

1.  Does my hero rise from within the provincial world?
2.  Is the hero afflicted with a type of curse?
3.  Can the inciting incident be a form of that curse being delivered?
4.  Must the hero free himself from the curse to obtain what he wants?
5.  Is the provincial world a self-contained community within a community, or should additional worlds be established?

If the fairy tale elements are strong, then use them to develop your story to perfection. Once again, your success will not come from *imitating* these structures, but by intelligently creating new stories through them. We choose the proper structure as a way of appealing to the audience's subconscious. Think of these structures not as formulas, but as prescriptions. Ultimately, all stories are constructed to remedy our most glaring social and personal ailments. The lay audience is usually unaware of a structure being myth or fairy tale, but when used properly, there is an unconscious recognition. Time and again, we watch how movies either fail in these traditions and collapse into cliché, or transcend them to become motion picture classics.

The next development in structure is the drama, and through it we see the further melding of myth and fairy tale elements into the most contained arena of all. While all structures grow out of one another, and contain many of the same qualities, they are unique unto themselves. Make it your business to understand the intrinsic qualities of every available structure, and pay homage to them, but do not enslave yourself.

It is unfortunate how we humans cleave to something wonderful, pure and original only to choke it to death with convention and cliché. The artist should never allow himself to fall into such a rut. We must continually grow, expand, depart and transcend. Storytelling and myth-making are living and organic arts. The artist/hero/writer knows and commits himself to this principle above all.

## DRAMA: A composition presenting in dialogue or pantomime a story involving conflict or contrast of characters.

In the drama, we generally move the center of conflict to a central arena to intensify the level of interaction. This is the New Orleans apartment house of *A Streetcar Named Desire*, the stark and efficient offices of *Glengarry Glen Ross*, the sleek, seductive bachelor pad of *Hurlyburly*, the one-room purgatory in *No Exit*, or the simple lifeboat in Hitchcock's *Lifeboat*.

Dramas look to pare down all superfluous outside influence to examine the psychological nature of human beings interacting on the most intimate of basis—i.e. real human beings with all their flaws, foibles, hopes and dreams in the same room, house, boat or elevator. The drama is the living proof that not only does proximity breed contempt, but also catharsis, conversion and conflict.

The dramatic structure is therefore a microscopic examination of how human beings relate to one another. The use of archetypes can be employed, but the flaws and virtues once outwardly evident are now concentrated and disbursed among an assembly of

MODERN FAIRY TALES
*All the Mornings in the World,*
*An American President, Beauty and the Beast,*
*Cinderella,*
*The Godfather,*
*A Heart in Winter (Un Coeur en Hiver),*
*Moonstruck,*
*My Fair Lady,*
*Pleasantville,*
*Pretty Woman,*
*Pygmalion, A Room with a View,*
*Sleeping Beauty,*
*Trading Places*

individuals in an extremely close environment. The intelligent use of dramatic structure warns us that we should not get too comfortable, the psychic crap is about to hit the fan.

### The Provincial World

In the drama, the provincial world becomes a waiting room, a house, an office, an apartment, a party, an airplane, a boat, a ship or any physical environment that will demand fierce scrutiny. When creating this part of your drama, pay attention to Aristotle's basic law of the Unity of Opposites. This determines why a group of contrasting individuals might come to together when under normal circumstances they would flee from one another.

### The Hero/Protagonist

The protagonist of the drama is the embodiment of the author's idea or theme. It is this belief or intense perception of man's nature that will emerge bloodied and defeated or wonderfully triumphant when the story is over. This medium is not for the meek of heart. Drama is the chosen form of masters. The weekend writer or struggling initiate is wise to put it off until his psychological maturity and mastery of craft has been aptly refined. If drama is your ultimate goal, be forewarned and respectful of the great giants before you.

In the drama, as in the fairy tale, we learn what all the main characters desire very early on in the story. It is the characters' individual desires and plans that will clash with others as the plot thickens. What the main character desires is usually very simple, but because of the antagonistic forces at work, it will be almost impossible to achieve.

### The Inhabitants

In the world of drama, the characters are drawn from real life situations. They are business people, salespersons, housewives, husbands, children, college graduates, high school students—sometimes even cockroaches. They might be deranged children, convicts, prisoners, concentration camp inmates or strangers on a train. They can be as disparate as college professors, truck drivers, longshoremen, or any other assortment of personalities drawn from everyday life. They represent the full spectrum of social standing and our deepest, darkest human foibles and frailties. Dramas are intensely cathartic tales with each character representing a particular flaw, a belief system or personal restriction awaiting exposure and final denunciation.

### The Inciting Incident

In dramatic structure the inciting incident is a powerful event that draws an unlikely group of people together, or pulls a closely-knit group apart. In James M. Barrie's play, the *Admirable Crichton*, liberal aristocrats and conservative house servants are thrown together on a deserted island to see who will survive. Although there is a mythic element to it, this wonderful comedy maintains its dramatic structure in two uniquely different worlds: the home of Lord Loam, in ultra-civilized London, and a primitive island where survival of the fittest is the only imperative.

In Tennessee Williams' *A Streetcar Named Desire*, a fragile and refined Louisiana belle comes to live with her sister and working-class husband in their run-down New Orleans apartment. The very set-up of such volatile individuals all under one roof is a sure promise that sparks will fly.

In Alan Ball's *American Beauty*, we watch ineffectual milquetoast, Lester Burnham, start peeling back the onion layers of his picture-perfect life, family and neighborhood, only to find everything and everyone—including himself—is rotten to the core. As he takes the necessary steps to extricate himself from this bourgeois hell, he finds gentleness, compassion, beauty and ultimately, death, where he least expects it.

### The Climax, Outcome and Revelation

The end of the drama is usually achieved through tragedy or personal victory, but whatever the outcome there is an ironic twist to it—the protagonist may get what he desires, but now it doesn't seem so desirable. The real hero of any drama is the writer's intention, and those in the audience who appreciate it. As these are usually highly personal revelations, they don't always present universal solutions. Blanche DuBois goes off to an asylum, Hamlet is killed in a sword fight, and even the Admirable Crichton becomes a butler again. In each case, while the hero comes out short of their goal, it is the writer's theme and the audience's revelation that are the true beneficiaries.

## MODERN MOVIE DRAMAS

In *Ordinary People* (written by Judith Guest, Alvin Sargent and Nancy Dowd), the first images are those of a peaceful Lake Michigan in autumnal splendor. Further along we are treated to pristine lawns, streets and stately homes in a Chicago suburb. It is a world immersed in perfect order. Pachabel's "Canon in D Minor" is heard sung by the high school chorus, comprised of nicely groomed boys and girls from good families. We are introduced to Conrad "Con" Jarrett, played by Timothy Hutton with dark circles under his eyes and an angry glare that sets him apart from the others. We later see that Conrad's father and most of his friends treat him deferentially. We soon learn that he is the sole survivor of some unspeakable tragedy of which there is more to learn.

While everyone else treads softly around Conrad, his mother, Beth (played by Mary Tyler Moore), and his swim coach (played by M. Emmett Walsh), appear particularly antagonistic, harsh and insensitive. While the Coach is simply a jerk, Conrad's mother strikes us as rigid and severe. She constantly nit-picks at her husband, Calvin, an unassuming tax attorney (Donald Sutherland). She tells him what tie to wear, when it is appropriate to laugh, and when he's had too much to drink. We also see that her house is impeccably ordered, as are her actions, mannerisms and rigid judgments. Yet for all of her outwardly flawless behavior she is emotionally dead inside, which explains her downright cruel treatment of Conrad. Conrad has just returned from a mental hospital after a suicide attempt, and is haunted by dreams of a storm at sea. Someone is drowning, but we do not know if this is a nightmare or an actual event.

According to the family plan, Conrad is to start seeing a psychiatrist, played by Judd Hirsch. At first the psychiatrist appears antagonistic, even callous. It is apparent Conrad will get little pampering here. But Conrad doesn't want to be coddled; he wants his self-control back. He wants to numb the emotional recklessness that led to his messy suicide attempt. We do not know it yet, but Conrad is just like his mother. His search for control is just a way to relieve the intense guilt for having survived a boating accident that killed his older brother. Under the guidance of the psychiatrist, Conrad starts to relax his need for self-control and forgive himself. The father, too, is compelled to delve deeper into the repressed feelings he's experienced since his son's death. We soon realize it is Beth who is the truly dysfunctional member of the household. Her desperate need to control comes from weakness, not strength. She fears her emotions and her need to control is just an excuse, a narcotic, a state of denial caused by her inability to accept life's unpredictable aspects. Because she refuses to deal with the "mess" of her emotions, she is ultimately expelled from the recovering family.

We are disturbed by this tragedy. It hurts us to see the mother's expulsion. No one wants it, but we know that she must leave in order for this family to heal. Obsessive control is not life, but a type of living death, and to live freely we must embrace all of life, with all of its terrifying mystery. This is undoubtedly a tragic drama, but we are left with an ironic feeling of hope expressed in the rekindled bond between father and son.

In *Kramer vs. Kramer* (written by Avery Corman and Robert Benton), the story begins immediately with the strains of a mandolin and guitar duet over the opening credits. Even the selection of a duet resonates on this movie's premise of a couple breaking up after eight years of marriage. The next image is of a disconsolate, brooding Joanna (played by Meryl Streep), stroking her little boy's forehead, sending him off to sleep, reciting a lullaby as part of their nightly ritual, "*Night, night. Sleep tight. Don't let the bedbugs bite. See you in the morning light.*"

But this time, Joanna Kramer won't be there in the morning light; she is packing to leave—her house, her marriage, her child—for good. The next scene is with Dustin Hoffman as Ted Kramer, a creative advertising executive shooting the breeze with his boss. The hour is late and we sense he should be at home, but like most modern males he is selfishly focused on his career. We learn that he is about to be promoted, and this excites him. Within the first five minutes of this excellent drama, we know what every character desires and what the problem is. Billy Kramer, played by Justin Henry, wants to see his mother in the morning. Ted Kramer wants a promotion and Joanna Kramer wants out of the marriage.

When Ted arrives home, Joanna tells him she is leaving, which barely fazes him (the inciting incident). Ted dismisses her, as he has repeatedly done throughout their unhappy marriage. When she finally walks out, he curses her, not for the loss, but for interfering with his ambition. As Joanna must leave her son Billy behind in order to pull herself together, Ted is forced to take parental responsibility for the first time in his life. The selfish Ted Kramer must learn to put someone else's needs before his own.

Billy is the perfect antagonist for the self-centered Ted, and represents the perfect opposition Ted requires in order to change and reprioritize his values. At first, Ted strives to keep his promotion and raise his son himself, rather than sending Billy away to boarding school. When this proves impossible and his career derails, he comes to understand that it is his son's welfare that matters most and Ted elects to take a new job—one far beneath his previous pay scale, but one that will allow him to spend time raising his son.

Having purged himself of the selfishness that destroyed his marriage, Ted Kramer gradually evolves into a loving and involved parent. It is here when Joanna enters the picture again, not to heal the marriage, but to get her son back. A custody battle ensues, with the lawyers casting aspersions on each parent's skill. Ted chooses selflessly to abstain from excoriating his ex-wife before the court. Having accepted the blame for their failed marriage, it would be selfish of him to use her abandonment against her, even when it is the only way he'll be able to keep Billy. This selfless act leads the court to decide in the mother's favor and return sole custody to her.

In the last scene, Joanna is also moved to act selflessly when she opts not to take Billy away from the only home he's ever known. Though the marriage is over, by acting selflessly, they are better individuals, better parents and more of a family than ever before. We are saddened, even shocked, by the seemingly unfair reversals and turns of this drama. It is tragic and unfair when Billy is given to his mother. The irony is that through this tragedy the individuals learn that life, marriage and parenting require true selflessness. When these qualities are present, outside of blame, shame and judgment, true relating can begin.

To determine whether your story will fit a dramatic structure you simply need to look at the nature of the world of story and determine whether it can be confined to a single arena. Do not be fooled if a certain character goes on a bus ride across town— look within the context of the tale. Where is the central arena of conflict?

## REVIEW

We've come to the end of our exploration of the nature external structure and how it can be applied to any story you wish to develop.

Returning to the *Richard Cory* premise, we can now intelligently decide what structure lends itself to the story we wish to tell. Is it myth, inverted myth, fairy tale or drama?

Let's revisit the premise once again, and consider which structure best suits its further telling.

*When* a young man's idol (Richard Cory) *commits suicide,* he becomes disillusioned and rebels. In defiance of his previous values he soon crashes and burns when he discovers a truth about himself and this spurs him on to re-examine his life and find personal fulfillment.

Question: Where is the central arena of conflict?
Answer: A small town.
Question: Who is our protagonist and what does he want?
Answer: He is a young man who idolizes the very wealthy Richard Cory. He wants to be like Richard Cory.

Question: What is the inciting incident?

Answer: A rich man's suicide.

Question: Is the inciting incident a journey? Or does the hero enter a provincial world from the outside? Does the tale involve any type of curse? Is there an event that brings a group of people together, or pulls them apart?

My choice: A curse. The whole town is afflicted by a kind of pervasive false perception.

Question: What external structure is best for the premise of *Richard Cory*?

Answer: The fairy tale.

By defining the structure as a fairy tale, we can now look at a contained world of a small town, a communal opening, a place where everyone and everything exists in its proper place. We start to conjure up images of a factory town where aristocrat and commoner are easily recognized for who they are.

The poem further tells us that everyone in the town looks up to Richard Cory. He is their idol. Once again our theme helps us shape the nature and personality of the protagonist, because our hero falsely perceives Richard Cory to be a happy man. So when he commits suicide, this causes all previous misconceptions to be called into question. As our hero reflects this disillusionment, he spirals downward, crashing and burning in self-destruction. We know that he must somehow escape the curse, and ultimately impact the township as well.

We are ready to move to the next stage of development—to explore and advance the plot of the main character.

# THE FIFTH STAGE
## Internal Structure

*PLOT: The plan, scheme or internal structure of a play, novel, poem or film*

Aristotle's *Poetics* questions what is the most important element of a play; character or plot? But we see time and time again that the two are inseparable. Without determining and planning the protagonist's *need to change in order to defeat his opponent*, we will merely construct a sequence of events with no integrity or spine. The spine of a story is achieved by following the protagonist as he goes about striving for what he wants and by changing his values in order to defeat the opposition and achieve his desire.

> *"Among plots and actions of the simple type, the episodic is the worst. I call episodic a plot in which the episodes follow one another in no probable or inevitable sequence. Plots of this kind are constructed by bad poets on their own account."*
> —Aristotle, *Poetics*

Actors are attracted to roles where the character expresses tremendous range. The range of a character's growth is the most compelling aspect of a myth, drama or fairy tale. It is the definitive thing of the story. So, which is more important, character or plot? The screenwriting masters prove time and time again: *plot is character and character is plot.*

We have examined the various worlds and external structures of how a character goes about changing his life; now we need to map the progression of these changes as they pertain to a story's internal spine. This vital stage will help you determine your main character's growth as he purges himself of his problems and goes about defeating his opponent and achieving his desire.

## TWELVE STAGES FOR PLOTTING THE MAIN CHARACTER'S GROWTH

1. The main character's shadow.
2. The inner flaw.
3. The moral consequence of the inner law.
4. The main character's immediate desire.
5. The inciting incident.
6. The main character's overarching desire as a result of the inciting incident.
7. The main character's objective to achieve the new desire.
8. Developing the Antagonist/Opponent.
9. The conflict between Protagonist and Antagonist.
10. The main character's realization as a result of the conflict.
11. The main character does or does not obtain his overarching desire.
12. The impact on the world of story.

## THE MAIN CHARACTER'S SHADOW (BACKSTORY): The shadow event in a character's past that looms over his everyday actions and sensibilities

Henry James wrote that no novel has a real beginning because the task of the storyteller is to create the illusion of time, circumstances and life before the onset of the story. In other words: we must give the audience a sense that our characters and their world have existed all along.

The purpose of developing your protagonist's shadow is to find out more about him and the cause of his problems and desires. It will give you important insights as to why he is acting the way he does and why he must change. While you should put a great deal of time and thought into developing your character's backstory, it is a mistake to feel compelled to include your audience in it or to always start your film there. It is far more effective to let these details unfold gradually throughout the script, rather than to dramatically spell them out for the audience.

Amateur writers often make the mistake of beginning their screenplays in the backstory. This creates a structural deficiency that throws the entire screenplay off-kilter. The professional screenwriter knows to begin the story, as with every scene in the script, as late as possible. The working maxim is, only provide as much information as the audience needs to know, when they need to know it. Irrelevant and unnecessary information, provided out-of-context, only serves to burden the story structure. Knowing when to impart pertinent details is an important part of the craft of screenwriting.

For instance: In *Chinatown* (written by Robert Towne), it would have been a mistake to begin the film with Jake Gittes' life as a beat cop in Chinatown. We don't need to know this up front. Later, as we see events leading him towards the same disastrous confrontation, the new information increases our doubts as to whether he will succeed or not.

In *The Verdict* (written by David Mamet), we do not need to know why Frank Galvin is an alcoholic ambulance chaser, only that he is deeply conflicted. Later, when we need to know that he once was a very honorable young attorney whose integrity was tarnished, we understand the circumstances of why and how he lost his honor and his intense desire to reclaim it.

In *In the Line of Fire* (written by Jeff Maguire), we do not need to begin with Frank Horgan's fateful day in Dallas at the assassination of Kennedy; we only need to know that he is impetuous, aging and flawed. Later, on as he attempts to stop the assassination of another president, it is much more powerful to learn that he did this once and failed. We intensify the audience's concern by making them wonder if he can purge himself of his self-doubt and succeed.

Following are some examples of compelling movie characters' "shadows" and how these can be used to create a sense of life and conflict prior to the beginning of a story.

In *The Sound of Music* (adapted for the screen by Ernest Lehman), Maria's *shadow* is that she is an orphaned free spirit whose daily communion with the glorious wonders of nature and the transcendent sound of music make her decidedly ill-suited for the monastic life she is living. The only experience we have of her is the opening musical sequence where she sings the title song. Later, in dialogue with the Mother Superior, we hear that Maria's spontaneous joy is not at all seen as a welcome attribute by the Sisters of Perpetual Suppression.

In *The Wizard of Oz* (based on the L. Frank Baum novel, *The Wonderful World of Oz*), it is Dorothy's *shadow* as an orphan that lends emphasis to her overarching desire to leave Oz and return home. We do not know who her parents are, or what happened to them. The fact that she lives with her Aunt Em and Uncle Henry is all we need to know of her past and of her intense desire to return to her parents.

In *The Godfather*, from the beginning oratory of the undertaker, we hear the experience of many Italian/American immigrants as they immigrated to America in search of paradise. This becomes an excellent exposition of Don Corleone's *shadow* as well (as we later see in the sequel). This simple narrative construction helps us understand the choices these men faced—either to subject themselves to this strange land and its uneven and biased implementation of justice, or to set up their own system, as Don Corleone so successfully did.

In *Kramer vs. Kramer*, we chance upon a family in the midst of dissolution and divorce. We are told through exposition that Joanna and Ted were married for eight unhappy years. It is the *shadow* of this unhappy union and Ted's selfishness that drives Joanna's departure. We do not need to literally dramatize the eight-year marriage, but only to refer to it within the course of the story.

In *Ordinary People*, the *shadow* of Conrad Jarrett's suicide attempt casts a pall over the entire Jarrett family, and sets up the mystery behind Conrad's continued alienated behavior. It is much more powerful to gradually reveal the boating accident and Buck's (Conrad's brother) accidental drowning, rather than dramatize it in the beginning.

In *Witness*, we know very little about John Book's personal life, except that he is alone and very arrogant. Though very few specifics are provided about his *shadowy past*, we see that he is overly confident and a bit jaded from living in a world where crime, murder and police corruption are commonplace. This might make anyone self-righteous, and it is precisely this moral drive that ultimately leads to his confrontation and flight from his more corrupt colleagues.

In *An Officer and a Gentleman* (written by Douglas Day Stewart), Zack Mayo's *shadow* is his relationship with his philandering and immoral Navy man father, whom we revisit in the opening credits. (Including the shadow in this instance is appropriate because it is this dysfunctional childhood that shadows Zack's inner flaw and obstructs his ambition to graduate from the Naval Academy and become a jet pilot.)

In *Moonstruck*, it is the death of her first husband and their unceremonious wedding that causes Loretta to obsess over her bad luck in love and marriage. Though we do not literally show her first husband, it is his *shadow* that drives her every motivation—and almost into the arms of the wrong man.

In the animated *Beauty and the Beast*, Belle's life with her eccentric inventor father *shadows* her separateness from the rest of the quaint provincial town. As a result, she is a bookworm and yearns for more than what the other girls would happily aspire to.

In *The Silence of the Lambs*, it is the death of Clarice's father and her experience as an orphan, growing up in poverty, raised by a relative, that *shadows* her interest in behavioral science and joining the FBI.

Through the deft articulation of a character's past and the intelligent placement of those details, we create a sense of history, tension and destiny before the actual events of the story begin to unfold.

Proficiency in creating multi-dimensional characters with compelling backgrounds is time-consuming, difficult and requires years of practice and experience. Because of the time and craft demanded, most aspiring writers either cut the process short or include the development process within the context of the script. This is like exhibiting a painting with the original pencil sketches still showing. It destroys the finished feel of the piece and makes for belabored viewing.

The screenplay is a blueprint of a complete motion picture from the writer's point of view. This will change as it goes into the collaborative process of filmmaking. For now your screenplay must come as close to the finished product as possible. Since most beginning writers do not take the necessary time in developing their characters before starting their scripts, they mistakenly leave the traces of development in, offering any experienced Hollywood executive an excuse to add your script to the dung heap. The clue to exploring the shadow of any character you develop is to go to the end point of your thematic equation and work your way backward. So let's look again at the template we've drawn for *Richard Cory*.

### Disillusionment/leads to/personal fulfillment

Following a logical sequence backwards, we see our main character has achieved fulfillment after being disillusioned. However, before he could be disillusioned, he must have been deluded in some capacity. How? If our main character idolizes a wealthy man because he perceives him to have everything, then what *shadow* from his past might have lead him to be so deceived?

What causes someone to idolize or envy a wealthy man?

Usually it is because they are in the opposite position. They are poor.

As dramatic values deal largely in opposites, we can consider detailing our young hero as impoverished. This is particularly apt since we have chosen a fairy tale structure. As fairy tales are about the lowly being made high, we can see how by detailing the main character with an impoverished past fits into the development of his *shadow*. By melding elements from the original poem with our working theme, premise and structure, we can start to see our story unfold.

The Beginning:
- A small town
- A rich man
- A *poor* young man who idolizes him, and who *desires* to be like him
- A suicide
- The young man becomes disillusioned

## THE MAIN CHARACTER'S INNER FLAW

We have previously isolated the two main types of stories: those where the main character undergoes change, and those where he is an agent for change (Batman, Ace Ventura, James Bond, John McClane of the *Die Hard* franchise). The best films and the best writers become proficient in the former, as it is the most difficult and rewarding. Since this book is chiefly concerned with the plot of those who change, this stage if internal development is the most vital.

You determine your main character's inner flaw through the theme of your story.

In *Blade Runner*, we have a sanctioned killer, a cop, whose distaste for killing leads him to leave the elite Blade Runner unit where he works. We first meet him on the street in a dark, over-populated, futuristic world where life is fast and cheap. We perceive him to be decent because right from the beginning he tell us of his disdain for the government-approved killers known as Blade Runners. Unfortunately for him, he is very soon compromised when he is coerced back on the force to combat a mutinous band of replicants headed for earth. The Division Chief tells Deckard bluntly that if he doesn't take the assignment he will be eliminated as well. It is this characteristic that illustrates Deckard's *inner flaw*, which can be stated thematically as: *It is better to kill than be killed.*

This sentiment is hardly heroic but helps us find the central core of Deckard's inner flaw. The mythic journey he goes on will lead him to a powerful transformation, that only completes itself when his life is spared by the very inhuman replicant he is assigned to destroy. In then end Deckard resolves his inner flaw by rescuing Rachel and escaping with her to an idyllic world outside the city.

In *Witness*, John Book's *inner flaw* is his self-righteousness. He believes that violence is a necessary evil for combating the forces of corruption. When he goes to live among an authentically righteous group of people, the Amish, he is slowly transformed, and learns to combat corruption with a well-earned and more intelligent moral authority.

In *The Wizard of Oz*, Dorothy's *inner flaw* is revealed as that of a spoiled young girl whose self-absorption is out of touch with the hard conditions of Kansas farm life. At first she is shown to be getting in the way of the farm hands, even falling into a pigsty and disrupting their work. The mythic journey she undergoes will teach her to act selflessly and make her capable of the heroic act of destroying the Wicked Witch of the West.

In *Moonstruck*, Loretta has become cynical about romantic love. Her *inner flaw* is that she has buried her private yearnings, and the curse of pragmatism has forced her into an engagement with an infantile Momma's boy.

In *Kramer vs. Kramer*, Ted and Joanna Kramer have the same *inner flaw* in that they both choose selfishness to remedy their problems. Ted is selfishly involved in his career. Joanna must leave her son behind out of a selfish need to heal herself. Both are justified, but it isn't until they eschew their selfish acting out that their problems will be solved.

In *The Verdict*, Frank Galvin is a pitiful wreck. His *inner flaw* is not that he is alcoholic; that is only a symptom. His real problem is that he has abandoned his integrity along with his faith in the justice system. The film ends aptly when he realizes that no system is inherently corrupt or just, it is the individual who makes the difference.

In *The Silence of the Lambs*, Clarice Starling is a woman in the masculine world of the FBI; she has hardened to her feminine self in a misguided attempt to succeed. As a result, she is constantly fending off the advances of men who sexualize her. Her *inner flaw* is that she has covered over the very nature that led her to become an FBI agent in the first place—her compassionate (feminine) desire to do good in the world.

In *Chinatown*, Jake Gittes has become a slick, somewhat cynical private detective succeeding in an unsavory line of work that exposes human beings in their least favorable light. It is a world of adultery, divorce, scandal and lurid headlines. His *inner flaw* is that he once tried to help someone and ultimately caused more pain. So now he is resigned to a line of work that helps some people and at the same time destroys others. His irreconcilable inner flaw manifests as a continuous self-fulfilling prophecy.

Determining a character's inner flaw is one of the most delicate and complex challenges a screenwriter faces. Your main character must be shown to have a problem without destroying his or her "likeability." This will require a great deal of finessing and rewriting. At first these problems may obscure your main character's better qualities but, through constant reworking, shaping and rewriting, you will find the delicate balance you need.

Novice writers tend to invest their main character solely with heroic qualities, and this makes the character appear shallow and one-dimensional—the equivalent of Tony Curtis in *The Great Race*, splendidly arrayed in white hat and a glistening Pepsodent smile—but without any real substance. Your heroes will be much more interesting by shading them with inner flaws and colorful idiosyncrasies without destroying their charm or interest. In the end their real natures will become apparent, not in isolation, but through the choices they make and the opponents they battle.

Hence:

Clarice Starling is only revealed as being truly good when she passes the stinging examinations, demented pronouncements and lurid projections of the contemptible Hannibal Lecter. *The Silence of the Lambs*

Jake Gittes' foibles and flaws pale to insignificance next to the incestuous lust and power-mongering of the malevolent Noah Cross. *Chinatown*

Frank Galvin's ambulance chasing and alcoholism are forgivable when compared to the polished, corrupt, silver-tongued manipulations of Ed Concannon. *The Verdict*

The best way to develop inner flaws in your main character is to mine dramatic situations and character traits from within your theme, and then weigh the characters' actions, desires and beliefs in relation to those of their allies and opponents. In *Richard Cory*, the main character's inner flaw is that he is ambitious and seeks to rise out of his impoverished condition by emulating a good man for the wrong reasons.

## THE MORAL CONSEQUENCE

*"Every disturbance, from the outbreak of world war to a child's temper tantrum, is caused by a restriction of consciousness."*
—Joseph Campbell

For every action there is a reaction. For every deep psychological problem within, there is a deep moral consequence extending without. This law of conflict and consequence determines the next stage in the development of internal structure. Your hero must not only be shown to be suffering from an inner flaw, but his or her actions must be shown to be impacting others as well. It is this "moral" connection within and without that must be confronted and ultimately corrected throughout the course of the story. This gradual confrontation and correction dynamic comprises the bare skeleton of your story's plot, character growth and story arc.

The dynamics are as follows:

1. The first scenes reveal the protagonist's inner flaw and the consequence it has on the world order. Hence John Book of *Witness* suffers from self-righteousness. He reveals this by erratic

behavior, bossing, sniping at everyone around him, and finally terrorizing a young Amish boy and his mother as he subjects them to a round-up of suspects through the harsh streets of Philadelphia.

2. The next step will be to reveal the protagonist in direct confrontation with the story's antagonist or villain. John Book learns that his fellow detectives are out to kill him and the boy.

3. The next phase of character plot is to show the protagonist struggling with his own allies. So as John Book recovers from his gunshot wound, he winds up compromising the Amish, who have protected him, with his violent, over-the-top defensiveness and continued arrogance. Eli Lapp chastises Book by warning him, "Book, it is not our way." John Book responds with his same arrogant manner, "No, but it's mine." And it is the return to his old ways that signal to the authorities where he is hiding out.

4. Finally, the protagonist must face their deeper, most inner flaw, and apply the right solution to defeat their opponent and obtain their desire. In the finale of *Witness*, the only way for John Book to disarm Paul Schaffer and save Rachel is to appeal to Schaeffer's humanity and reason.

This appeal is validated by the presence of the Amish patriarch "witnessing" the confrontation between Book and Schaeffer. It is classic confrontation between self-righteousness and true righteousness that Book is able to bring about with authority because we just watched him make the journey himself.

These important steps are a vital function of creative engineering as they will foreshadow the final impact on the world of story. (See Stage 12.)

In *The Verdict*, the moral consequence of Frank Galvin losing his integrity and faith in the justice system is that he is reduced to becoming an alcoholic ambulance chaser.

In *The Silence of the Lambs*, the moral consequence of Clarice Starling's suppression of her feminine instincts results in her being constantly objectified and sexualized by the men in her world.

In *Ordinary People*, the moral consequence of Conrad Jarrett's search for self-control is either emotional death or suicide, because it is impossible to control life's misfortunes.

In *Witness*, the moral consequence of John Book's self-righteousness is arrogance, alienation and the belief that violence is a necessary evil.

In *Chinatown*, the moral consequence of Jake Gittes' cynicism about helping people is a job mired in scandal, lurid headlines and sexual depravity. In other words, his profession as a private eye is the perfect expression of someone who helps people while inadvertently hurting others. (This scores a perfect ten in our ironic theme construction.)

In *Blade Runner*, the moral consequence of Rick Deckard's moral equivocation is that he is easily recruited back on the force once his own life is threatened. He is told, "You're either with us or you're little people," with the implication being that he will be killed if he refuses to cooperate.

In *Kramer v. Kramer*, the moral consequence of Ted and Joanna Kramer's selfishness is the dissolution of their family and the infliction of pain on their child.

In *The Wizard of Oz*, the moral consequence of Dorothy's lack of empathy for her hard-working aunt and uncle is that she is constantly disrupting their work schedules and getting in the way.

In *Moonstruck*, the moral consequence of Loretta's obsession with feeling cursed is her cynicism and subsequent engagement to the wrong man.

In each of these examples we see a direct and immediate impact on the hero's moral connection to the world and their relationships as a consequence of their inner flaw. In *Richard Cory*, the moral consequence of the main character's inner flaw is that he chooses goals and ambitions based on falsely perceived values of success. As a result he seeks friends, status and lovers based on social caste rather than inner worth, and eschews those who don't fit into his plan.

## THE MAIN CHARACTER'S IMMEDIATE DESIRE

The general operating theorem of motion picture stories as previously stated is: Someone wants something very, very badly, but must change somehow in order to defeat an opponent and obtain his desire.

This want or desire forms the central dynamic that fuels the character's growth and story plot. We stick around to see whether or not the hero achieves his desire—or not. There are often two or more types of desire lines within the course of one film: the immediate desire and the overarching desire.

While the immediate desire may (and often does) change, the overarching desire generally does not. While your protagonist may make various choices along the way that veer away from the overarching desire, in the end he or she must fail admirably in achieving it, obtain it against all odds, or find something much, much better to replace it. At this stage, we will focus on the main character's immediate desire as established in the first act.

In *The Silence of the Lambs*, Clarice Starling's *immediate desire* is to have Hannibal Lecter help the FBI track down a monstrous serial killer.

In *Chinatown*, Jake Gittes' *immediate desire* is to confirm the false Mrs. Mulwray's suspicions about her philandering husband.

In *Blade Runner*, Rick Deckard's *immediate desire* is to leave the Blade Runner unit.

In *In the Line of Fire*, Frank Horgan's *immediate desire* is to protect and train his rookie partner in the harsh and dangerous mission of the Secret Service.

In *Ordinary People*, Conrad Jarrett's *immediate desire* is to maintain control over his emotions and win his mother's affection.

In *Kramer vs. Kramer*, Ted Kramer's *immediate desire* is a promotion at the office. Joanna Kramer's *immediate desire* is her freedom. Billy Kramer's *immediate desire* is to see his mother in the morning light.

In *The Wizard of Oz*, Dorothy's *immediate desire* is to save Toto from the clutches of Mrs. Gulch and to find a world that is trouble free ("Somewhere over the Rainbow").

In *Beauty and the Beast,* Belle's *immediate desire* is for a life beyond the quaint provinciality of the small French village where she has grown up.

In *An Officer and a Gentleman,* Zack Mayo's *immediate desire* is to "fly jets," and to succeed at the U.S. Naval Academy.

In *Moonstruck,* Loretta's *immediate desire* is to get Johnny Cammareri to marry her in compliance with the proper "rules and rituals" (superstitions) of courtship.

The purpose of establishing an immediate desire line is to further define your main character in the beginning, so that after the inciting incident the audience is ready for your hero to undergo an immense change. This changed desire will forge the objective storyline and provide the spine for future acts. In *Richard Cory,* we can readily determine our main character's *immediate desire* as wanting to be like Richard Cory.


## THE INCITING INCIDENT

As described earlier, the inciting incident will force your protagonist out of the first act and into the second with great thrust and momentum. Obviously, this event will differ from one story to the next and vary according to what external structure you choose.

In *The Silence of the Lambs,* Clarice seeks to enlist the aid of Hannibal Lecter in stopping Buffalo Bill. She meets with Lecter and asks him to fill out a questionnaire. He is offended by her attempts to "dissect him with such a blunt instrument" and rebuffs her, telling her to, "fly away home, little birdie." When Multiple Miggs attacks her from the next cell, Lecter is shocked and disgusted by this act, and this is the *inciting incident* that compels Lecter to assist her. Lecter's appeal, despite being a cold-blooded psychopath, is that he is exceedingly well-mannered and charming.

In *Witness,* an undercover cop is brutally slain in a train station. The sole witness is a young Amish boy. When the murderer is revealed to be another detective on the force, and the crime revealed as a cover-up to departmental graft, John Book is determined to protect the boy. The *inciting incident* is when John Book is attacked and wounded in an underground garage, thereby forcing him to leave Philadelphia and hide himself and the boy in the Amish community.

In *Blade Runner*, the *inciting incident* comes when Deckard is re-enlisted to combat renegade replicants who have returned to earth. He is told that he will either submit or die. Deckard replies, "You mean I have no choice?" The tacit understanding that he must kill or be killed drives him out of the first act and into the second, while he tries to find a way out of his predicament. One might argue that it is the murder of the first blade runner that is the inciting incident of the story, and to a degree this is true. However, in so much that it is the threat of his own death that drives Deckard into action, it is this incident that proves most inciting to this story's theme and protagonist.

In *The Sound of Music*, the *inciting incident* comes when the Mother Superior senses a different destiny for the unpredictable Maria and assigns her to work outside of the convent, as a nanny for the Von Trapp family. At first Maria questions whether it is God's will or not. But the Mother Superior knows that God's will is very often mysterious and in time will make itself clear. Until then, she challenges Maria to, "climb every mountain," and "ford every stream,"—just as long as she does so sufficiently far away from the nunnery.

In *In the Line of Fire*, the *inciting incident* comes when Frank Horgan and his rookie partner are assigned to investigate an apartment where the landlord suspects an impending threat against the President of the United States.

In *Moonstruck*, Johnny Cammareri asks Loretta to invite his estranged brother to their wedding. After several attempts, she is forced to deliver the invitation in person. When in turn Ronny makes love to her, this *incident incites* her ardor and forces Loretta to confront her repressed desires and question her decision to marry Johnny.

In *An Officer and a Gentleman*, it is Zack's enlistment into the U.S. Naval Academy that forms the *inciting incident*, which will force him to purge himself of his selfishness and personal deficiencies and truly become and an officer and a gentleman.

In *Chinatown*, the *inciting incident* comes when Jake Gittes discovers he's been set up and the real Mrs. Mulwray threatens to sue him. He is then forced to investigate the ruse and the mystery behind the Water Commissioner's death.

In *Beauty and the Beast*, the *inciting incident* comes via Belle's father being imprisoned by an accursed beast and Belle's offer to take his place.

In *Ordinary People*, Conrad's first visit with the psychiatrist forces him to re-evaluate his need for self-control. He redirects his immediate desire to the overarching one of self-acceptance and forgiveness.

## THE MAIN CHARACTER'S OVERARCHING DESIRE

*"Always give the audience what they want,*
*but never what they expect."*
—Robert McKee

In *The Wizard of Oz*, Dorothy's immediate desire is to save Toto and to find a world that is trouble free. She runs away and meets a fortuneteller who shows her the error of her ways. She tries to return, but is waylaid by a tornado (inciting incident) and is whisked away to the Land of Oz. There she must purge herself of her spoiled, self-centered nature. Her mythic quest in the Land of Oz is driven by one *overarching desire*—to return home. Before she can do that she must learn the thematic lesson: *The search for a world that is free of trouble leads to the realization that there is no place like home.*

In *Witness*, John Book's immediate desire is to solve the murder of an undercover cop ruthlessly slain in a train station. His immediate action is to use the Amish boy as his chief witness. When the evidence points to departmental corruption, his *overarching desire* becomes that of protecting the boy and keeping him safe.

But Book can't leave. He must heal himself of the gunshot wound and his arrogant self-righteousness in order to prove the thematic lesson: *True righteousness and simplicity are more powerful forces against corruption than violence.*

In *The Verdict*, Frank Galvin's immediate desire is to get money anywhere he can find it. Because he has no integrity, he has been reduced to frequenting funeral parlors in search of wrongful death clients. When his old law professor surfaces to remind him of a case that goes before the court in ten days, his immediate desire focuses on winning the seventy thousand dollars he'll earn in contingency fees. Yet, as he uncovers the facts about the case, his immediate desire changes to an *overarching desire* of finding his integrity again, leading him to prove the thematic equation: *The search for integrity and justice, leads to the understanding that no system is inherently just; it is up to each individual to make the difference.*

In *Chinatown*, Jake Gittes immediate desire is to prove that the Water Commissioner is cheating on his wife. When Gittes discovers he has been set up, his immediate desire changes to an *overarching desire* of helping the real Mrs. Mulwray protect her daughter from the incestuous Noah Cross. This desire to help people leads to the rather fatalistic pronouncement in the end: *The search to help people often results in hurting them.*

In *The Sound of Music*, novitiate candidate Maria's immediate desire is to worship God and become a nun. But her free-spirited temperament clashes with the rigid order of the convent. Sensing she has a different destiny, the Mother Superior assigns her to work for the recently widowed Colonel Von Trapp, where she learns: *The search to serve God leads to understanding the transcendent quality of music and fulfilling our individual destiny.* (Or, more generally, the search for understanding leads to the fulfillment of our individual destiny.) Maria's immediate desire to become a nun changes to the *overarching desire* of serving God, family and humanity through music.

In *Kramer vs. Kramer*, Ted Kramer's immediate desire is to get the promotion and "bring home the bacon." When his wife walks out on him, his *overarching desire* becomes one of keeping his job and raising his son. To achieve this he must purge himself of the selfishness that lead to Joanna's desertion, thus proving the thematic equation: *Selfishness, however justified, leads to the disintegration of the family, whereas selflessness heals and transforms relationships.*

In *Ordinary People*, Conrad Jarrett's immediate desire is to control his emotions and conform to his mother's pathological demand for order. When he starts seeing a psychiatrist, his immediate desire gradually changes to an *overarching desire* of self-forgiveness and acceptance for all of life's mysteries, even his brother's tragic death, thus proving the film's maxim: *The search to control life leads to a kind of living death, whereas surrender and forgiveness set us free.*

In *In the Line of Fire*, Frank Horgan's immediate desire to train his rookie partner changes to an *overarching desire* of proving he has the courage to sacrifice his own life to protect the President of the United States, which proves the films theme: *Regardless of one's age or past failures, the search to prove one's mettle leads to success and personal fulfillment.*

In *Moonstruck*, Loretta's immediate desire of getting Johnny to propose to her changes to the overarching one of getting Johnny to marry her, in spite of her secret love for his brother Ronny. In this case, it is Loretta's foolhardy attempts to deny her heart in favor of reason and superstitious nonsense that indirectly proves the writer's theme, i.e. *the search for true love is not well-founded or even rational, but passionate and animalistic, and to succeed one must be willing to lose one's self.*

In each example we see the need to set-up an immediate desire for the protagonist and then change it to the overarching one after the inciting incident. This creates a more fully developed storyline and drives the character through the second act with increasing momentum. In *Richard Cory*, we can further detail the main character's immediate desire to emulate Richard Cory as it changes to the *overarching desire* of *not* emulating Richard Cory, after the inciting incident of Cory's suicide. This dynamic action will become even more powerful as we move towards proving the theme: *The search for success and self-fulfillment lies in neither wanting to be, or not wanting to be, like someone else, but by living life on our own terms.*

## THE MAIN CHARACTER'S OBJECTIVE: TO ACHIEVE HIS OVERARCHING DESIRE

Here we set up a "plan of action" or an objective of how the hero goes about obtaining his overarching desire. This objective is a way of layering in and foreshadowing certain expectations the audience will anticipate as the hero advances towards his goal. The operating maxim here is to give the audience what they want, but never what they expect. This frees the writer to employ the sleight of hand maneuvers of a magician in order to keep the audience in suspense. Alfred Hitchcock calls the technique of diverting an audience's attention the "McGuffin," and explains its use to Francois Truffault in this delightful anecdote:

An Englishman gets on a train and attempts to put his attaché case on a luggage rack when he notices a very large, oddly-shaped suitcase blocking his way. He inquires of the dour Scotsman sitting beneath it, "I say, is that your valise?" To which the Scot replies, "Yes, Sir, but that's no valise, that's a McGuffin!"

"A McGuffin?" the Englishman asks, taken back by the strangeness of the term. "What's a McGuffin?"

"My good man," The Scot replies indignantly, "a McGuffin is a type of gun used for hunting lions on the highlands of Scotland!"

"I see," the Englishman responds, not wishing to seem rude, but then is quickly overtaken by the preposterousness of it all. "But, there are no *lions* on the highlands of Scotland!"

To which the dour Scot shrugs, peering up over his *Edinburgh Times.* "Well then, that, Sir, is no McGuffin!"

However clever the tale, the point is to notice how the story focuses our attention on a specific object and holds it there for as long as we need it. Then, when we no longer require it, or are threatened with exposure, we dismiss it without further ado. We do the same when we establish the hero's objective. We set up a series of anticipated actions for the audience to expect and then constantly challenge them to keep the audience guessing.

For instance, in *Casablanca*, the hero's plan of action revolves around a set of stolen transit papers signed by Charles de Gaulle, leader of unoccupied France. We are lead to believe that whomever holds these documents has absolute free passage anywhere in the world, leaving the Nazis powerless to intervene. If we were to examine this McGuffin more closely, we would see it is a completely absurd construction. Charles de Gaulle was the leader of the French Resistance and a sworn enemy to both the Nazis and Vichy France. Historical fact would demand that possession of any such document by the hand of Charles de Gaulle would mean a one-way ticket to Dachau, but through skillful sleight of hand the audience's disbelief is suspended and the story artfully moved forward. Proving further the excellent point that: *Plot holes, objects of power and plans of action need not always be inscrutable. They can and must be dealt with via skilled and authoritative writing that uses creative problem solving.*

In *The Sound of Music*, Maria's *objective* is to serve God by teaching the Von Trapp children the transforming power of music, and in the process rekindle the stern Captain's affection for them. Her plan comes under attack by Captain Von Trapp when he sees his children growing more independent under her care. As Maria succeeds in awakening the Captain's affection for his children, and growing affection for herself, she comes under attack by the Baroness, who schemes to have her returned to the nunnery.

In *The Silence of the Lambs*, Clarice Starling's *objective* is to first win the assistance and trust of Hannibal Lecter so she can solve the Buffalo Bill murders. At first Lecter himself opposes the plan dismissing her as little more than a "rube." Then, mortified by Multiple Miggs' shameless behavior, he deigns to help her while also trying to better his own situation. The plans of both hero and opponent come under attack by Dr. Chilton, who seeks to usurp both of their objectives and win the glory of rescuing the Senator's daughter himself.

In *Chinatown*, Jake Gittes' *objective* is to solve the murder of the Water Commissioner and to help his widow and her daughter get out of town. His plan comes under attack by Noah Cross, who will use all of his power, wealth and influence to ensure Gittes' failure.

In *In the Line of Fire*, Frank Horgan's *objective* to prove his mettle requires him to stop the impending assassination of the President of the United States. His plan comes under attack by a cunning assassin who exploits Horgan's past and aging reflexes to wear him down and expose his deepest inner flaws.

In *Kramer vs. Kramer*, Ted Kramer's *objective* of raising his son forces him to juggle the demands of his high-pressure job while doing his best as a single parent. This plan comes under attack initially by Billy, who demands nothing less than total commitment and selflessness.

In *Ordinary People*, Conrad Jarrett's *objective* to obtain self-control has him seeing a psychiatrist and trying to numb the agonizing guilt that lead to his suicide attempt. His objective comes under attack by the psychiatrist, who knows that hyper-vigilant control of the emotions is a type of living death.

In *Blade Runner*, Rick Deckard's *objective* is to track down the renegade replicants and buy himself some time until he can find a way out of his 'kill or be killed' predicament. His plan comes under attack by the replicants, who seek to live. The story has a deep thematic flaw in that it creates antagonists who have come to earth to extend their lives, while the protagonist's objective is to stop them. This flawed thematic value has the effect of making the bad guys "good" and the good guy "bad" which ultimately took its toll at the opening box-office.

In *Witness*, John Book's *objective* to protect his star witness requires him to take shelter with the Amish and heal himself, while determining a way to implicate his corrupt colleagues. His objective comes under attack by the corrupt policemen who seek to find and eliminate him before he can expose them.

In *An Officer and a Gentleman*, Zack Mayo's *objective* is to become a pilot and graduate from the Naval Academy without being D.O.R (Dropped on Request), or by being ensnared by the working class girls of Puget Sound. His objective comes under attack by the Drill Instructor, who believes Zack is not officer material and also by Debra Winger's character, who loves him.

In *Moonstruck*, Loretta's *objective* is to break the curse of her bad luck by properly marrying Johnny Cammareri. Her objective comes under attack by Ronny, who seeks to awaken her passionate self.

In *Richard Cory*, the young man's *objective* after Richard Cory's suicide is to be as unlike him as possible, to rebel and break from the rigid ideals he held before Cory's suicide. This plan will come under attack by events that we will create through further development.

The main character's objective is directly related to the objective storyline and to the premise of your story. It is the way in which the protagonist proceeds along a certain path in order to achieve his desire. It is important to develop and communicate this to your audience, as it is how they track the success or failure of your hero's decisions. It is up to you to complicate this plan and effectively obstruct the hero's progress. The nature of this obstruction comes in the development of an ingenious antagonist with a carefully delineated objective of his own.

## DEVELOPING THE ANTAGONIST/OPPONENT:
## One who is opposed to or strives with another in any kind of contest; an opponent or adversary.

*"The more successful the villain, the more successful the picture."*
—Alfred Hitchcock

If a hero were to begin a journey and progress smoothly with nothing to oppose him the audience would quickly lose interest. Each of us faces adversarial forces in our lives and our fascination with movies comes from watching people overcome obstacles in order to obtain their heart's desire. So we measure a hero's mettle by how he succeeds in resolving his inner flaws, defeating his opponents, and getting what he wants.

Likewise we size up the adversary/antagonist by how effectively he obstructs, competes with or attacks the hero's progress. Very often the gauge of the opponent's effectiveness is based on his degree of familiarity with the hero. Sometimes the external structure we choose—myth, inverted myth, fairy tale or drama—will determine the level of familiarity between hero and opponent. For instance, in the myth, the ruler in the world of journey is the hero's opponent. Those who assist him in impeding the hero's quest are the opponent's allies.

The *Star Wars* franchise creates a pantheon of characters both allied with and opposed to the Rebel Alliance: Luke Skywalker's chief antagonist is Darth Vader, while Han Solo's principle adversary is Jabba the Hutt. While both Han and Luke share the combined goals of winning Princess Leia and destroying the Death Star, each must battle his personal opponent and inner flaw before he can achieve his desire. Luke is an orphan with incomplete information about the man who was his father and he struggles with his ignorance of his heritage. Meanwhile, Han is a cynical weapons smuggler, waffling between his maverick ways and a new-found commitment to the Alliance. Their opponents are effective because Darth Vader really is Luke's father, and Han still owes a sizable debt to Jabba the Hutt. Both opponents are intimately connected to the hero's inner flaws. The person best able to attack Luke's orphan status is Darth Vader, his own father; the best opponent for Han Solo's selfishness is Jabba the Hutt, the grotesque personification of greed.

In the outlaw myth, the outlaw's principle adversary is the Lord of the Underworld and/or anyone who obstructs the outlaw's timely escape from it. It doesn't matter if it's the police or any of the Underlord's countless minions; if they serve the function of obstructing the hero's escape, they are allies of the antagonist/opponent.

In the inverted myth, the orphan/magician's opponent is the distribution of power, with everyone in the provincial world striving for power of one form or the other. If they are against spiritual power, they are allies of the antagonist, if they are for it, they are allies of the protagonist.

The fairy tale hero's adversary is the curse levied by the opponent, and all those who fall under it. The hero struggles to be free of the curse and ultimately to free others.

In the drama, the hero faces the most powerful adversary of all: the spouse, boss, child, friend, parent or anyone who is intimately familiar with the hero by blood, circumstance or even coincidence.

In Shakespeare's *Hamlet,* the titular hero is a young prince obsessed with the murder of his father by his mother and uncle (now his stepfather), and this obsession creates problems for him and those around him. When the ghost of his slain father appears and asks him to avenge his murder (the inciting incident), Hamlet is attacked where he is most vulnerable. Can one who values life so passionately commit murder? "To be or not to be?" Though Hamlet is disgusted by his mother and stepfather's murderous intrigues, the burden of avenging his father's death quite literally drives him to the edge of sanity. It is this assault, both inwardly and outwardly, that leads to Hamlet's demise and the tragic outcome of the story.

The development of the antagonist in relationship to the hero forms the basis of the central conflict of every story. It is the opponent who plants the seed of doubt, prompting the question "Can the hero succeed?"

In the mythic-structured *The Silence of the Lambs,* Jodie Foster plays Clarice Starling, a candidate at the FBI Academy in Quantico, Virginia. We see that she is bright, brave, principled and physically fit, but we also see that she is an "orphaned" female in a society of men who sexualize and patronize her. Accordingly, she is compelled to mask her femininity in order to succeed in this "man's world." When she goes to interview the infamous mass murderer Hannibal "the Cannibal" Lecter, she is further objectified by the advances of Dr. Chilton, the crude ranting of Multiple Miggs, and even by Dr. Lecter himself who derides her for being one step above "cheap white trash" and ridicules her "good bag and cheap shoes." Throughout the course of her mythic quest to stop Buffalo Bill, Lecter heaps one degradation after another, convinced there is some "impure" motivation behind her becoming an FBI agent.

Hannibal Lecter is a classic "threshold guardian," as demanding and dangerous as any dragon, troll or sphinx and it is he, who

> "The dark shadow of intuition is the intuitive opportunism of the sociopath."
>
> *–James Hillman*

Clarice must outwit and even surpass if she is to obtain the necessary clues to proceed in her quest to stop the Buffalo Bill murders. With every lash of his dagger sharp "quid pro quo" interrogations, Clarice is stripped psychologically bare before him.

As a psychiatrist, Lecter has probed the mind of humanity and found it weak and self-serving. As a demented sociopath, he can do little more with this information than literally devour those who meet his cynical expectations (which covers pretty much everyone). There is no doubt that the archetype of Hannibal Lecter is the ancient riddle-posing, flesh-devouring dragon, whose infernal probing is designed to ferret out the hero's deepest flaws. Like the Sphinx in *Oedipus*, you either pass her test or face instantaneous destruction. Because Lecter is such a compelling interrogator, we immediately worry whether Clarice can withstand his searing inquisition—or will she too, be devoured?

In a compelling blow-for-blow battle of wits, Clarice defends Lecter's assault on her psyche with increasing mastery—finally delivering the ultimate revelation of the movie's theme when she solves the "riddle" of the silence of the lambs. "To stop the screaming!" she proclaims, at once proving her heroic stature and humanity. Take a second look and observe Lecter's reaction to this remarkable declaration, so surprised he is to find that Clarice holds no dark shadows of sexual abuse or child molestation in her past. That her motivation to become an FBI agent is pure and unadulterated—everything Lecter himself is not. He now deems her "worthy" to live, and so agrees to provide the missing clue of Buffalo Bill's identity.

Finally, in the lower dungeons of the Lord of the Underworld, (Buffalo Bill's basement chamber of horrors), Clarice slays the dragon and rescues the damsel in distress, symbolically reconciling her beleaguered feminine half.

When this film first came out, there was a loud public outcry against the film's perceived misogyny. Ironically, in my opinion, this is one of the best heroine myths of modern cinema. For who is Clarice Starling if not the modern feminine incarnation of St. George the Dragonslayer?

Moving on to the dynamic action of the fairy tale opponent:

In *Moonstruck,* it is the "curse" of her first husband's accidental death that causes Loretta Castorini to choose superstition over passion and results in her engagement to the fastidious, self-absorbed Johnny Cammareri; Ronny Cammareri, on the other hand, is the personification of raw animal passion. So, when he attacks Loretta where she is weakest, with wild and passionate abandonment, she sees her fears for the silly superstitions that they are, and casts off the shackles of the alleged curse.

In each case, the adversary is directly connected with the protagonist's inner flaw and outward desire. To develop the best adversarial relationship for your hero, determine what your main character wants, and what their innermost stumbling block is to getting it. When you have the answer, you can create the best adversarial opponent to impede their progress on both fronts: their inner flaw and their outward desire.

Returning to our development of the movie based on *Richard Cory.*

Question: What is our hero's inner flaw?

Answer: False perception; he idolizes a man for all the wrong reasons.

Question: What is the moral consequence?

Answer: His life is not his own, so he is hurting himself and others.

Question: What does our hero want?

Answer: He wants to be rich and respected like Richard Cory.

Question: Who is the best character to oppose the hero?

Answer: Richard Cory, because he commits suicide.

We know this because Richard Cory's suicide causes our idolatrous hero to become disillusioned. So, Richard Cory attacks the hero where he is weakest. Since our hero judges people on the basis of how they appear and not who they truly are, and because Richard Cory commits suicide, it is obvious that Cory is the best candidate for the role of antagonist/opponent. There is a potential problem with the death of the antagonist coming so early in the film. Without an antagonist, how do we maintain the tension of a conflict? We will have to create plot situations that will keep Cory at the center of conflict.

At this juncture it is important to point out that every problem that arises can be fixed with good writing. Do not shrink away from problems; fix them. Plot holes and illogical progressions are a part of the process of problem-solving and creative engineering. Sometimes they will appear to be insurmountable. They are not. But neither will they magically disappear, and they must be dealt with. If you reach a point where they overwhelm you, take a break, catch a nap, cook a good meal or sleep on it overnight. The answer will come.

We must strive to create a degree of familiarity between our protagonist and our opponent in what Lajos Egri (*The Art of Dramatic Writing*) and Aristotle call the Unity of Opposites. The working principle here is that under normal circumstances, antagonist and protagonist are such uniquely different individuals they would hardly associate in the same world. Hence, we need to create a situation where the two come together and confront one another. Since Richard Cory's suicide comes early on in the script, we know we must create this opposing unity through the use of backstory and the shadows of both protagonist and opponent.

Question: What is the most *ironic* connection between the protagonist and the antagonist?

Answer: The hero wants to be like someone who doesn't at all like being himself.

Question: Why?

Answer: For all his prestige and wealth, Richard Cory's life is not his own.

Question: Why?

Answer: Because Richard Cory chose to live a life based on how others perceived him, rather than one that might have made him happy.

Question: What is the opposing unity between protagonist and antagonist?

Answer: Both are living lives based on superficial values—how others perceive them, rather than what truly makes them happy.

Through the backstories of both protagonist and antagonist we start to see the ironic polarity of the forces involved. Two opposing themes that must come into conflict.

The protagonist's theme: A young man who has nothing aspires to be like someone who appears to have everything.

The antagonist's theme: Material wealth and prestige do not necessarily make one happy.

On the template, these opposing themes would look like this:

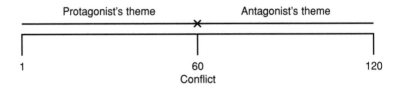

Let's examine the theme and the countertheme of previous films.

*Casablanca:*
Protagonist's (Rick's) theme: "I stick my neck out for no one."
Antagonist's (Ilsa's) theme: Duty is greater than love.

These ideals clash as our heroes wrestle between their passion for each other, and their duties to their respective countries.

*Unforgiven:*
Protagonist's (William Munney's) theme: Violence is always irrational.

Antagonist's (Little Bill's) theme: Violence is not only rational, but often necessary (and sometimes fun).

When these two themes clash, the sadistic Little Bill pleads, "I'm building a house. I don't deserve this!" (In other words, this is not rational!) William Munney responds, just before executing him, "Deserves got nothing to do with it." (Violence is not rational). With the triumph of William Munney over Little Bill, the theme of the film, rational violence leads to irrational violence is proven literally and figuratively.

*Witness :*

Antagonist's (Paul Schaeffer's) theme: Violence and corruption are necessary for one's betterment.

Eli Lapp's theme: " Violence is not our way."

Protagonist's (John Book's) theme: "No, but it's my way!"

In the end, with all the Amish elders gathered peaceably, with the intent of disarming Paul Schaeffer, the corrupt detective, John Book confirms his acceptance of Eli Lapp's theme when he asks, "What are you going to do Paul? Kill her, kill him, kill me? When does it all stop?" John Book changes from being a man of the gun, to a man of true moral authority.

*Moonstruck :*

Protagonist's (Loretta Castorini's) theme: Superstition and ritual is more important than passion.

Antagonist's (Ronny Cammareri's) theme: Passion may lead to tragedy, but it is better than living an empty life without love.

In the end, by choosing Ronny over Johnny, Loretta lifts the curse and chooses passion over superstition and fear.

*Chinatown:*

Protagonist's (Jake Gittes') theme: You can't help people without hurting them, so you might as well resign yourself to it.

Antagonist's (Noah Cross') theme: Man is inherently evil and wealth and power will always prevail.

As this is a tragedy, both the protagonist and antagonist's themes are proven in the end.

*Blade Runner:*

Protagonist's (Rick Deckard's) theme: It is better to kill (replicants) than to be killed.

Antagonist's (Batty's) theme: All living things must seek to live.

And after Batty saves his life, Deckard leaves Los Angeles with Rachel (a replicant)—and the writer's theme is proven: All life is sacred.

*Ordinary People:*
Protagonist's (Conrad Jarrett's) theme: To lose control of one's life leads to suicide.
Antagonist's (Beth Jarrett's) theme: Excessive control is necessary because life is cruel and unruly.
When Conrad learns that forgiveness and understanding are more important than control, the power of his revelation drives Beth from the family home.

*Kramer vs. Kramer :*
Protagonist's (Ted Kramer's) theme: Total commitment to one's career necessary for one's family and future.
Antagonist's (Joanna Kramer's) theme: Selfishness in redress to an oppressive marriage is necessary for one's mental well-being.
In the end, the writer's theme is proven—selflessness is the core of every successful relationship.

*The Silence of the Lambs:*
Protagonist's (Clarice Starling's) theme: To do good is to end suffering.
Antagonist's (Hannibal Lecter's) theme: No human being is inherently good, instead, humankind is weak, hypocritical and self-serving.
When Clarice proves to Hannibal Lecter that she is inherently good and well-intentioned, he helps her save the Senator's daughter and stop Buffalo Bill.

*The Sound of Music:*
Protagonist's (Maria's) theme: There is no greater service to God than music and celebration through song.
Antagonist's (Captain Von Trapp's) theme: Never mind singing, it takes discipline and a heavy hand to raise a family.
In the end, Maria proves that not only is music the salvation of the Von Trapp family, but it can be especially handy when escaping the Nazis, as well.

*An Officer and a Gentlemen:*
Protagonist's (Zack Mayo's) theme: Looking out for number one is all that matters.

Antagonist's (Paula Pokrifki's) theme: Looking out for number one does not make you a gentleman.

Second antagonist's (Gunnery Sargeant Emil Foley) theme: Looking out for number one will not make you an officer.

In the end, it is both antagonists' themes that are proven: To be an officer and gentleman, one must respect women (particularly one who loves you), and learn to put your classmates welfare above your own selfish desires and instincts.

*In the Line of Fire:*
Protagonist's (Frank Horgan's) theme: It's never too late to prove yourself when it comes to love, or duty.

Antagonist's (Leary's/Carney's) theme: The need to prove one's self is a sentiment that will not only get you killed, but could possibly help assassinate the President as well.

In the end, it is the protagonist's theme that wins the girl and saves the President.

*The Wizard of Oz:*
Protagonist's (Dorothy's) theme: "Life has to be better, safer, and more secure, somewhere, anywhere, than in Kansas."

Antagonist's (The Wicked Witch of the West's) theme: Even resplendent fantasy worlds have their problems with evil-doers.

In the end, it is the Glinda the Good Witch's theme that is proven, when she has Dorothy repeat, "There is no place like home."

*The Verdict:*
Protagonist's (Frank Galvin's) theme: As an attorney, having integrity means nothing when the system is corrupt.

Antagonist's theme: The legal system is not about justice, it is about winning at any cost.

Writer's theme: No system is either inherently corrupt, or just, it is the people that make it so.

In some of these examples we see the clash of two thematic notions resulting in a third concluding statement: The protagonist's point of view, the antagonist's point of view and finally, the writer's point of view. Sometimes the protagonist's view is triumphant. Sometimes the antagonist's theme prevails, but always it is the writer's belief that is proven in the end, which looks like this:

*Richard Cory :*
Protagonist's (the Young Man's) theme: A man who has everything will automatically be happy.

Antagonist's (Richard Cory's) theme: Material wealth and prestige cannot make you happy if your life is not your own.

Writer's theme: Being truly happy means *living life on your own terms.*

Now we will have to dramatize these character flaws and conflicts. As a screenwriter, it is not enough to have worked out a logical theme in your head. You will need to prove your point dramatically on paper through intense conflict and well-defined characterizations. You can't just have a bunch of talking heads moralizing and telling us who they are and what they want. You will have to reveal these psychological and dramatic developments through action. You must show these events unfolding rather than merely tell the audience about them. Create, don't narrate.

You will need to orchestrate these conflicts through a sequence of carefully chosen dramatic events over a common ground of conflict. If we have a young man who aspires to be like someone with great riches and respect, but is secretly very unhappy, then we have achieved the oppositional unity between protagonist and antagonist. Though they are entirely different in their values, neither of them is living a life based on their own terms.

How do we dramatize this? We must create a dramatic series of attacks and confrontations to prove this in a dynamic fashion. What then is the nature of the antagonist's attack upon the hero? Let's see where we are and what impetus there is to go on:

A. The main character's shadow: He is poor and socially ambitious.

B. His inner flaw: False perception.

C. His moral consequence: Not living life on his own terms, he judges others by their status and wealth.

D. His immediate desire: To be like Richard Cory.

E. The inciting incident: Richard Cory's suicide.

F. The main character's changed desire: He no longer wants to be like Richard Cory, in fact, he goes in the opposite direction and rebels.

G. The main character's objective to achieve his new desire: He contradicts all of his previous beliefs.

H. Develop the antagonist and subsequent attacks on the hero. Since we have already introduced the antagonist, we must design the nature of his attacks throughout the rest of the story. Which brings us to the remaining steps of internal structure:

I. The conflict between protagonist and antagonist.

J. The main character's realization as a result of the conflict.

K. The main character does or does not obtain his overarching desire.

L. The impact on the world of story.

## THE CONFLICT BETWEEN PROTAGONIST AND ANTAGONIST

The hero engages in battle on two fronts. First, he struggles with his inner flaw, while striving to achieve his overarching desire—which is in turn obstructed by the opponent, who also attacks our hero's inner flaw.

In Shakespeare's *Othello*, the hero is a valiant warrior and the honored commander of the armed troops of Venice. He has proven himself to be invincible in almost everything, except in his passionate love for Desdemona. Where then shall this noble fellow be undone? Through the hushed innuendoes and calumny of Iago, his duplicitous friend. Jealous and vengeful for having been passed over as Chief of Staff, Iago attacks Othello by implying that

Desdemona has been unfaithful with Roderigo, the rival who won the post Iago so covets. This illustrates the principle dynamic of how the opponent attacks the protagonist.

In *In the Line of Fire*, John Malkovich's portrayal as the ingenious assassin and master of disguise Leary/Carney goes about goading and attacking Frank Horgan through his self-doubt and aging reflexes. Will he once again flinch or does he have the personal courage to throw himself "in the line of fire" of an assassin's bullet?

In *Kramer vs. Kramer*, young Billy is the perfect antagonist for Ted Kramer's glaring ambition and selfishness: He goes about spilling juice on his father's advertising campaign, he makes Ted late for work and forces him to cut his time short at the office. Billy gradually moves into a central place in his father's life that once was reserved for his career. Through Billy Kramer's attacks on his father's ambition, Ted is transformed into a selfless, mindful and caring parent, even when he must take a job beneath his previous pay scale. When this self-correction is complete, a new opponent is introduced with Joanna, the returning mother, who attacks Ted where he is weakest—through his past patterns of selfishness and blind ambition.

In *An Officer and a Gentleman*, Louis Gossett Jr. plays a drill sergeant named Emil Foley, whose sole purpose is to weed out the weak from the strong in Officer Candidate School. He tells us of his intent to work them so hard they drop out at their own request, or D.O.R. (Dropped on Request). As the ensuing trials advance, Foley ferrets out Zack's lack of empathy for his fellow candidates and forces him to become true officer material by learning to help and care for his colleagues. But now Zack faces another challenge: his abuse of Paula's affections—because she is a working-class girl from Puget Sound, he treats her without respect. He behaves neither like an officer or a gentleman. Through the purging power of boot camp he is chastened and transformed and returns to marry the small-town factory girl, becoming, as the title suggests, a true officer and a gentleman.

In *Casablanca*, Rick is a self-absorbed, jaded, idealist, whose misfortune in love has turned him into a brooding, egocentric misanthrope. When reacquainted with the woman who spurned him, Ilsa attacks him where he is weakest and forces him to become a hero again, eschewing romance for idealism. It is very much as the film's popular theme song "As Time Goes By" suggests, "It's just the same old story, the fight for love and glory..."

In *Chinatown*, Private Detective Jake Gittes has made a career of being hired to help people, while invariably hurting others. He becomes the perfect dupe for Noah Cross, who hires Gittes to find his granddaughter in order to satisfy his own incestuous lust. Gittes' inner flaw of being a cynic with a soft touch winds up getting Evelyn Mulwray killed in Chinatown.

In *Ordinary People*, Beth Jarrett attacks Conrad where he is weakest—his wavering lack of self-control. By insistently demanding order and neatness, she drives Conrad again to the brink of suicide. The psychiatrist is also Conrad's opponent at first, because he obstructs Conrad's overarching desire for self-control. Ultimately he helps Conrad discover that self-forgiveness and acceptance are far more important than control. This important transition comes when Conrad, is spite of his antagonistic relationship with his mother, realizes how similar they are. In light of this understanding, he is able to forgive himself for surviving the boating accident that killed his brother and break free of his mother's soul-crushing hold over him.

In *The Wizard of Oz*, the Wicked Witch of the West is bound to intimacy with Dorothy through her need to possess the ruby slippers. Even though we don't know the shoes are Dorothy's means for returning home, the focus for both protagonist and antagonist to possess the ruby slippers keeps them involved with each other.

In *The Sound of Music*, the Baroness serves as Maria's foil while vying for the attentions of Captain Von Trapp. She attacks Maria where she is weakest, through her natural innocence and simple, unsophisticated ways. Von Trapp too, proves to be Maria's nemesis, by insisting on rigid discipline at the expense of joy, music and love in his children's life.

In *The Silence of the Lambs*, Hannibal Lecter attacks Clarice where she is weakest, by insinuating there is some unsavory motivation behind her becoming an FBI agent.

In *Witness*, the Amish community attacks John Book where he is weakest, in his self-righteous belief in his unflinching faith in the efficacy and need for blunt force. Through his trials amongst the Amish and his passionate yearning for Rachel, Book is transformed into a moral authority beyond the need for violence.

In *Blade Runner*, Batty, the replicant, attacks Deckard where he is weakest, in his belief that it is better to kill than be killed. The final transformation occurs when Batty shows greater humanity than Deckard, and saves his life.

In *Moonstruck*, Ronny attacks Loretta where she is weakest, by violating all known codes of ritual and courtship. He audaciously falls in love with his brother's fiancée at first sight and makes passionate love to her, provoking her response of, "Well, snap out of it!" In one last effort to break her down, he invites her to his favorite opera, where the swooning influence of "La Boheme," along with the luminous full moon, releases her repressed passions and allows her to find true romance.

In *Richard Cory*, by defining the relationship between hero and opponent, we can start to develop the particulars of exactly how the antagonist will attack. This is done by determining the most ironic and familiar connection between protagonist and antagonist, and by determining the main character's immediate desire as well as his objective in achieving it.

A. So, if the main character of *Richard Cory* has an immediate desire to be *unlike* Richard Cory, and his objective is to rebel, we can readily determine that their conflict will be a series of defiant acts waged against Cory, and everything associated with him.

B. Since Cory is not physically around we must create these dramatic attacks against Cory's property, image, holdings and ideals.

C. Since we have chosen a fairy tale structure, it is only natural that Cory's spirit will be felt in the small town where he lived. We keep Cory "alive" by detailing the town and various landmarks with his name and icon status.

D.   So, if the main character's desire is to be unlike Richard
     Cory and rebellion is the objective, we can dramatize this by
     showing the main character rejecting his old ways and will-
     fully drinking, smoking, quitting the football team, drop-
     ping his girlfriend/taking up with the wrong crowd and then
     escalating to vandalism, carousing and disturbing the peace,
     finally culminating in an outright act of destruction against
     Cory's property and namesake.

We keep Cory as the object of our hero's rebellion by detailing
his actions against Cory's holdings, estates and businesses. Now
we will need to establish a compelling detail of how Richard Cory
will strike back at our hero's objective. Since Cory commits suicide early on and is not physically around, we must turn to the
backstory.

What intimate detail from Richard Cory's past might further
obstruct our hero's desire to be unlike him? What if Richard Cory
is revealed to be the young man's father? This implies that no
matter how hard the main character rebels, since Cory is his
father, there is an inescapable hereditary link between our hero
and Richard Cory.

To serve the plot, we will need to keep this vital piece of information under wraps until the right moment, creating a terrific
twist to the story.

## THE MAIN CHARACTER'S REALIZATION AS A RESULT
## OF THE CONFLICT WITH THE ANTAGONIST

This is the final defining moment in the best motion pictures,
when the mystery is revealed and, as Arthur Miller says, "we finally understand what the story is about."

At this point the subjective storyline (theme) converges with
the objective storyline (premise) to become a wholly expanded
thematic revelation—delivered with all the impact of a lightening
bolt. It has this effect because it is exactly what happened to the
writer when he discovered what he really was writing about. It is
the deep subconscious gold he looked for when he first started the

piece, and the alchemical magic of transformation that all stories have the power to convey.

In the best of films, the audience shares the hero's final revelation. This is the real nectar of the screenwriting, myth-making, storytelling process. It is the entire reason we ultimately go to movies, and why we write them—to have a powerful, transcendent and transformational experience. Note too, how in the best of films, the film title unfolds to reveal a whole new and expanded meaning.

It is the moment in *Quiz Show* (written by Paul Attanasio), when we have expanded beyond the specifics of a famous game show scandal and are called to question our own integrity and lifetime ethics. In effect, the quiz show is no longer on the screen, but in the audience's mind.

It is that stunning revelation in *Witness*, when John Book drops his gun and disarms Paul Schaeffer with his moral authority and with the weight of the Amish community behind him. We are all asked to become "witnesses" to the power of truth over corruption and violence in our lives.

It is that gut-wrenching moment of horror in *Chinatown* when Jake Gittes finds himself right back where he started—having hurt someone he tried to help—and this lends incredible power to the last line of dialogue, "Forget it, Jake, it's Chinatown!" We are all left feeling equally helpless, hopeless and futile.

It is that payoff in *Moonstruck*, when Mrs. Castorini asks Loretta, despite all of her previous maternal admonishments, "Do you love [Ronny], Loretta?" And she answers, "Ma, I love him awful."

It is that defining moment in *The Sound of Music*, following the Von Trapp family's debut concert when they deceive the Nazis by slipping away under their noses, and thereby proving that music is not only transformational and uplifting, but a very practical diversion in dangerous situations.

It is the exhilarating moment in *An Officer and a Gentleman*, when Zack, having graduated against all odds, returns to sweep Paula off her feet and away from the drudgery of her working-class life.

It is the pivotal moment in *The Silence of the Lambs* when Clarice triumphs over Lecter's incessant badgering, finally answering his riddle when she shouts, "To stop the screaming!" Up until then we are unsure of what Lecter keeps driving at, what is this obsession with her past, what does he know that we don't? Note too, how Clarice's declaration, "To stop the screaming," immediately brings the movie's title to an active, heroic focus. Not only does this move redeem Clarice from victimization, it pronounces her as an honest-to-goodness hero. It is with this startling revelation that Lecter agrees to provide the help needed to stop Buffalo Bill.

In *Richard Cory*, it is the defining moment when the young man determines that it is not sufficient to be like Richard Cory, or even to be unlike him, but rather to live his life on his own terms.

## THE MAIN CHARACTER DOES, OR DOES NOT, OBTAIN HIS OVERARCHING DESIRE:
**Someone wants something very, very badly, but he must change in order to defeat his opponent and obtain his desire.**

We can use this general statement to determine the end of our story. For structural purposes it is not necessary that the hero obtain his desire; in fact, it works just as well if he doesn't. In each case the proper choice is determined by the author's theme. What is your point? What do you want to prove with your theme at the end of the film?

In *Moulin Rouge* (written by Baz Luhrmann and Craig Pearce), Christian (Ewan MacGregor) eventually gets what he wants, which is Satine, the courtesan (Nicole Kidman). Unfortunately, she dies soon thereafter and he is left to live in the shadow of that doomed love affair forever after.

In *Memento*, Leonard Shelly, the insurance adjuster played by Guy Pearce, gets much more than what he wants (revenge); but he also gets something he never bargained for, a reason to live. "Let's see now, where was I?"

"When I am called in to do a rewrite, the first thing I ask of the producers is, 'What do you want to say?'"

–Sterling Silliphant

In *Leaving Las Vegas* (written by John O'Brian and Mike Figgis), Nicolas Cage's character, Ben Sanderson, depressingly gets what he wants, which is to "drink himself to death." It is a sad, but telling sidebar, that the author of this gritty novella, John O'Brian, killed himself just after the release of the film.

In *The Wizard of Oz*, Dorothy learns she has the power to return home—wearing the ruby slippers, while reciting her mantra-like incantation, "There's no place like home." She gets what she wants when she awakens back in Kansas surrounded by loved ones.

In *In the Line of Fire*, Frank Horgan gets what he wants: to prove that he could put himself in front of a bullet to save the president. As a reward, and in conclusion, Frank redeems himself and wins the girl in spite of his advancing years.

In *Chinatown*, Jake does not get what he wants, which is to help someone without hurting them.

In *Ordinary People*, Conrad does not get what he thinks he wants, which is self-control, but does win self-forgiveness and acceptance, which are ultimately more satisfying.

In *Kramer vs. Kramer*, Ted gets what he wants—to keep his son with him—but only by his mature and selfless willingness to return Billy to Joanna.

In *An Officer and a Gentleman*, by becoming an officer Zack gets to fly jets, but he also becomes a gentleman, which earns him Paula.

In *Witness*, John Book gets what he wants, to protect the boy and nail his corrupt colleagues, but he also gets much more: true moral authority.

In *Blade Runner*, Deckard gets what he wants, personal survival and safety from the blade runner unit. In fact, it is one of the replicants he was hired to kill that saves his life, thus giving him a new-found reverence for all life, and the resolve to leave the city, and his thankless job, behind.

In *The Silence of the Lambs*, Clarice gets what she wants, to save the Senator's daughter and stop Buffalo Bill, with the added bonus of knowing her heart is pure. Lecter pronounces judgment on her in the last scene of the film, "You needn't worry about my finding you, Clarice, the world is more interesting with you in it."

In *Moonstruck*, Loretta does not get what she originally wanted, which was marriage to Johnny Cammareri; she gets much more: the curse is dispelled and she finds true romantic love again with Ronny, Johnny's younger and more vital brother.

The most important thing is to try to leave the fulfillment or non-fulfillment of desire to the last possible moment. The reasoning behind this is to allow the audience to track your hero's progress up to the moment of fulfillment. If you allow your main character to achieve, or fail to achieve, their desire early on, and then use the remainder of the film to tie up loose ends, you are only creating a series of false climaxes, which will wear on the audience's patience. We've all noticed that unnerving feeling when a picture is over and yet seems to go on (and on and on) indefinitely. This is usually because the pay-off comes too early, or because the director was too attached to his material (as was recently the case in *Training Day* [written by David Ayer], where rogue detective Alonzo Harris must suffer not one, but three separate endings, each with an increasingly violent demise).

In *Richard Cory*, the main character doesn't get what he wants, which is to be like and then not like his father, but he gets much more—the courage to live his own life on his own terms.


## THE IMPACT ON THE WORLD OF STORY

This is where the moral consequence expands to the world of story, after the hero fights his opponent. If the hero has a glaring deficiency at the story's inception, then it stands to reason it will be corrected after being purged by battle. This moral correction should be developed to further "impact" the community at large.

For instance, in the myth, the effect of the hero's purging himself will be to free the world of journey from the Evil Ruler, and head back to the return world with a remedy for the future.

The impact of Luke Skywalker's learning to master the Force under Obi-Wan Kenobi's direction leads to his destruction of the Death Star as a powerful new Jedi Knight for the Rebel Alliance.

The impact of Dorothy purging herself of her self-centeredness is the destruction the Wicked Witch of the West and the end of her tyrannical hold on the Land of Oz. Dorothy awakens back in Kansas with a new-found sense of commitment and appreciation of her life there.

The impact of Frank Galvin's realization that no system is inherently just, but instead comprised of individuals who try to make the difference, leads a "galvanized" jury to decide in his favor. On a personal level, Frank now has the strength to quit drinking and reclaim his integrity. We can assume that Frank will go on to become a much more honorable force in the justice system.

In *Witness*, the impact of John Book's newly found moral authority allows him to overcome the forces of corruption and the wisdom to know that he must return to his life in Philadelphia.

In the outlaw structure, there is little or no impact on the world of story, because these are harrowing tales of rugged individualism. Thus the outlaw does not impact the world, but concentrates only on saving his own neck.

In the inverted myth, the orphan/magician has an overwhelming impact on the provincial world, with the level of impact varying with each sub-structure. For instance, In the messiah structure, the messiah's death has little impact on the provincial world except through the message he imparts to his disciples. There is a dichotomous sense that while the status quo is maintained, the messiah's life takes on an ethereal, Holy Ghost-like resonance that will in time rectify itself. (Hence, the resurrection.)

In the vengeful messiah structure, he destroys the world of story, and the world is forced to start over again.

In the blithe angel structure, the provincial world becomes a better place of laughter, merriment and joy.

In the fairy tale, the hero frees himself of the curse, and in turn frees the kingdom.

In the drama, the hero solves a personal problem with little or no impact on the world at large.

In *Richard Cory*, we have yet to determine the impact of the hero's actions on the world of story. We know the town is suffering from the same false perception he was, but the particulars of how our main character will dispel this are still undetermined. This is perfectly acceptable, for now. To better flesh this problem out, we will need to advance to the next stage and return when we have worked things through a bit further.

# THE SIXTH STAGE
## The Five Character Relationships

- The Protagonist (Hero)
- The Antagonist/Opponent
- Allies of the Protagonist
- Allies of the Antagonist/Opponent
- The Romantic Interest

With the central and opposing themes of our story fully embodied in the relationship between protagonist and antagonist, we can begin to see where all others characters will fall into place. They will assist either the protagonist or the antagonist—sometimes they will assist both.

We develop ancillary relationships for the hero because it is through them that his changes are dramatized. We see what his friends and foes are like through the prism of his relationship with them and this reveals the various stages of his progress.

When adapting a novel, short story, poem, magazine article or even a parable, begin by making a list of characters who fall into place as either allies of the antagonist, or allies of the hero. This can be determined by which theme they align themselves with: the protagonist's or the antagonist's. If you are dealing with scant material to begin with, you will need to create additional characters. If you are dealing with an epic, you will need to reduce, condense and sometimes even combine characters who fulfill these functions.

We have seen many instances where an antagonist's position changes from one of opposition to that of assistance. Generally this switch comes after the immediate desire changes to the overarching one. The next transition point comes when the hero hovers on the brink of fulfilling, or not fulfilling, his desire—which should occur toward the end of the third act. When and how this happens is entirely up to you. Screenwriters have solved this problem in various ways.

In *The Silence of the Lambs*, Hannibal Lecter is both opponent and ally to Clarice. While helping her to accomplish her overarching desire, he attacks her inner flaw. Her true opponent is Buffalo Bill, who obstructs her overarching desire of saving the Senator's daughter. Dr. Chilton then, is an effective ally to Buffalo Bill, because he thwarts Clarice's efforts to win Lecter's trust.

In *The Wizard of Oz*, Dorothy's allies are the Scarecrow, the Tinman, the Cowardly Lion, the Wizard of Oz and Glinda the Good Witch. Her opponents are the Wicked Witch of the West, the flying monkeys, the castle guards and ultimately Oz itself.

In *Moonstruck*, Loretta's allies are her father, mother and Johnny Cammareri, who line up on her side to support the curse. The old man pulled around the city by an enthusiastic herd of dogs is an unknowing ally to Ronny, because he is a representation of unbridled animal passion and lunatic exuberance, as represented in the mystic power of the "Bella Luna." The love interest, Ronny, as is true in most love stories, proves to be Loretta's most effective opponent, because he attacks her overarching desire to go against her nature and marry Johnny.

In *An Officer and a Gentleman*, Zack's most effective opponent is the drill instructor in that he directly attacks Zack's overarching objective to become an officer. Likewise, Paula proves an effective opponent when she exposes Zack's ineptitude as a gentleman and a lover. At first, Zack's fellow candidates are the opponent's allies because they align themselves with the D.I. to expose Zack's glaring flaw of looking out only for himself.

In *The Sound of Music*, the Mother Superior is Maria's most effective opponent in that she thwarts her efforts to join the nunnery; when Maria's overarching desire becomes one of serving the

Captain's children and awakening them to the sound of music, the Mother Superior becomes her ally, while Von Trapp and the Baroness become her opponents.

As films are often more like short stories than they are long-form novels, they can really only support relatively few sets of relationships. You can go back later and color these relationships as richly as you might like, but in the development phase you should relegate them to a specific relationship through one of the five selections.

In *Richard Cory*, we have not developed these specific relationships as yet, but we do have a general idea of which side of the conflict they will fall.

Which leads us to consider the next relationship: The Romantic Interest.


## THE ROMANTIC INTEREST

Yesterday's movie romance: Boy meets girl. Boy loses girl. Boy gets girl back.

Today' movie romance: Boy meets girl. Girl has girlfriend. Girlfriend tells boy to shove off or she'll kick his ass. Boy looks for another girl. Girl has boyfriend. Boyfriend suggests a threesome. Boy gives up searching, seeks a pet iguana. Girl with iguana finds Boy. They have great sex, but argue over who gets to feed the iguana.

Obviously, with today's jaded audiences, we demand much more from our romantic heroes than in our romantically simplistic past. These days, the convoluted machinations of romance, dating and relationships are far more realistic in films like *Being John Malkovich* than they are in *Moulin Rouge* or *Titanic*. The latter films seem better suited to supreme adolescent yearning than actual adult male/female relating.

With today's sophisticated audiences, we mistrust a movie hero whose sole obsession is for romantic alliance. Whether male or female we ask that our heroes be somewhat successfully individuated first, before we care to see them couple. Hence, it is far more satisfying to watch an intelligent—if somewhat beleaguered—

William Shakespeare as he pursues and is met, challenged and mutually adored by the equally magnificent Viola De Lesseps in *Shakespeare in Love.*

In the modern remake of *Little Shop Around The Corner, You've Got Mail* (written by Nora and Delia Ephron), it is interesting to see Meg Ryan's intelligent and defiant shopkeeper fall in love with her arch-business rival and equal, Joe Fox, played by Tom Hanks. The film offers up one of the great lines in modern storytelling when it declares, "if you want to get a glimpse of someone's neuroses, just see who they're in relationship with."

So many of Nora Ephron's romantic comedies are refreshing precisely because they reflect the intelligence of male and female relating, as opposed to the neurotic and depressingly co-dependent aspects of it. In contemporary times, the age-old lover's anthem, "I cannot live without you" is more likely to inspire fear and paranoia than rapturous joy.

In a much deeper perspective, the love story is a parable of integration and individuation. Carl Jung suggests each of us holds male and female archetypes within our psyches, which he labels as animus (male) and anima (female). Thus, the outward search for a partner is actually a metaphor for the internal quest to unify the archetypes within us. The screenwriter knows that the love story is actually an allegory for his own unification and balancing of anima and animus.

The ability to create compelling male and female characters will be in direct proportion to the writer's psychological health. If you are a male, you will have a hard time creating female characters with any dimension if you are not in touch with your own feminine nature. In contrast, female writers may have a much easier time creating male characters because they have already had to adjust to a patriarchal mind-set that is thousands of years old and permeates every aspect of our society. The concomitant result of five thousand years of male-worshipping culture is that we not only idealize men who are men, but also women who act like men. To break free of this archaic and lopsided mentality, the writer needs to revolutionize his own thinking and re-consider what, in fact, is male and what is female. An intelligent examination of both necessitates going beyond the obvious gender and body part distinctions.

According to author Angeles Arien, in her archetype-inspired, *The Tarot Handbook*, "The male animus is the doer, the builder, the action-taker, the visionary, the knower, the leader, the explorer and adventurer. The animus is the world-traveler, pioneer and initiator of new realms of human experience. He makes his world safe for the advancement of culture, civilization and evolution. (It is important to reiterate and emphasize that all men and all women possess these qualities.)"

If a woman acts in accordance with these aspects of herself, she is drawing deeply from her own animus. It is as much a part of her natural consciousness and birthright as any male's. We are all capable of so much more than traditional societal roles impose on our specific genders. The writer must learn that to create compelling new heroes and heroines he or she must delve further into understanding of all facets of the human psyche. Again, according to Arien, "the anima is the principle of love, wisdom, intuition, nourishment, agriculture, the birth-giver, the mystic, the portal and holder of the unknown. She creates ritual, order, alignment, grounding and peace."

Or this, my favorite passage from Joseph Campbell's *The Mythic Image*, on the ineffable female energy, known as shakti: "The important Sanskrit term 'shakti,' meaning 'power, energy, capacity, faculty, or capability,' is used typically to convey a thought basic to all Oriental religious thinking; namely, to denote the active power of a male divinity as embodied in his spouse. Carried further, every wife is her husband's shakti and every beloved woman her lover's. Carried further still: the word connotes female spiritual power in general, as manifest, for instance, in the radiance of beauty, or on the elemental level in the sheer power of the female sex to work effects on the male. It is operative in the power of the womb to transform seed into fruit, to enclose, protect, and give birth. Analogously, on the psychological plane, it is the power of a woman to bring a man to his senses, to let him see himself as in a mirror, to lure him to realization-or destruction: for it is the power, also, to bewilder and destroy.

Goethe epitomized the idea in his frequently quoted concluding lines of Faust, 'Das ewig-weibliche zeit uns hinan,' 'The eternal feminine draws on onward.'"

When a male acts in accordance to these more subtle qualities he is doing so in natural correspondence to his innate feminine aspect. We are all born of men and women, and as a result possess the qualities of each. When either male or female act with a predominance of one aspect over the other there is an imbalance. Traditionally, we seek to correct this imbalance through a physical coupling. Unfortunately, it is too great a burden for one partner to carry all the qualities of one over the other, there must be a proper and equal integration of both aspects from both parties for there to be a true alliance. In many ways the entire history of human kind has been a search to harmonize these polarized aspects of self. Every religion, myth, poem, parable, story, fairy tale courtship or marriage has as its underlying purpose an integration of the individual psyche.

Likewise, the creation and culmination of any romantic liaison should be portrayed as a type of allegory for the hero or heroine's completion and self-fulfillment. Today, the boy can only get the girl if he undergoes a type of integration of both anima and animus. This is the fundamental element of a character's change. When a character changes, it means that they have undergone a re-balancing of their animus and anima as a result of their ordeal.

In the movie *The Mask* (written by Mike Werb), Stanley (Jim Carrey) is a nebbish bank clerk completely out of touch with his masculine animus. He is taken advantage of and abused constantly by his more aggressive male and female counterparts. When he finds a Nordic mask with supernatural powers, he transforms himself to an overly confident, rumba-dancing Lothario with vastly masculine, super heroic powers. In the end, he wins the girl (Cameron Diaz) not through his larger-than-life super ego, but through his more balanced, benign and sweetly transformed persona.

In *The Truth About Cats and Dogs* (written by Audrey Wells), a female radio show host with traditionally masculine qualities (Janeane Garofalo), seeks to woo the man she loves by having her ultra-feminine girlfriend (Uma Thurman) represent her physical self. In the end, with the ruse exposed, she wins his heart through the more feminine mien of truth, self-acceptance and intuitive wisdom.

In *Witness*, the overtly masculine John Book is softened through his alliance with Rachel and his experience among the wise and peaceful Amish. This softening and rebalancing results in Book becoming a greater moral force than before.

In *Dead Poets Society* (written by Tom Schulman), a group of young men are transformed by the transcendent, feminine, "geni" of poetry and romance literature. The tragic confrontation of these ideals with the patriarchal school authorities leads to a suicide and the expulsion of the teacher who dared to introduce and encourage them.

In *Thelma & Louise* (written by Callie Khouri), the transcendent journey of two women as they shed their traditional subservient roles becomes a tragic parable and symbolic quest for gender emancipation.

Virtually every story and character arc can be attributed to a sense of correction between masculine and feminine imbalance. The more the writer understands the archetypal traits of each, the better drawn and more realistic his characters will become. Turning back to the development of *Richard Cory*, we may assume that the romantic interest in this story will provide important insights into to the choices our hero will make throughout the story.

Generally, we choose partners who best mirror our deepest aspirations and innermost flaws; because our hero will also make several choices in this regard, we can immediately see the potential need for two romantic interests—one to emulate our character's desires before the inciting incident, and another one who reflects his changed desire afterwards. To further dramatize our hero's plight prior to Richard Cory's suicide, we create a romantic interest who aligns herself with our hero's lifestyle and desires while he still idolizes Richard Cory. When this changes, we create another romantic interest to further reflect the hero's altered and overarching desire.

Which leads us to ponder another point in the unity of protagonist and antagonist. If our main character progresses through a series of choices from one romantic interest to another, what if Richard Cory faced a similar dilemma? Because we know Richard Cory's choices led to death by his own hand, will our hero make the same bad choices, or does he have the power to change before it's too late? The creative step of considering the romantic interest character has led us to an exciting plot point and a potential twist to our story.

What if Richard Cory is the young man's biological father? What if Richard Cory had to choose between the young man's mother and a more "socially acceptable" girl? What if the weight of that choice caused a lifetime of grief for Richard Cory, eventually leading to his suicide? This development in the backstory would link protagonist and opponent together on an intimate basis, potentially creating a very exciting plot twist in the story.

Now let's see if all the steps of internal structure are met, after which we will write a working treatment to organize and create a seamless flow to the story. We do this knowing full well that everything may change at any time. We want to ensure the story works on its own and not just because we want it to.

A. Main character's shadow: He is poor and socially ambitious.
B. His inner flaw: False perception.
C. His moral consequence: Not living life on his own terms, he judges others by their status and wealth.
D. His immediate desire: He wants to be like Richard Cory.
E. The inciting incident: Richard Cory commits suicide.
F. The main character's overarching desire: He no longer wants to be like Richard Cory.
G. The main character's objective to achieve his overarching desire: He contradicts all of his previous beliefs and values, goes in the opposite direction and rebels.
H. The antagonist: Richard Cory.
I. The conflict between protagonist and antagonist: The hero rebels through personal acts of abuse, which escalates into acts of destruction against Cory's estate.

J.  The main character's realization as a result of the conflict:
    The hero discovers that Richard Cory is his biological father,
    so no matter how hard he tries to rebel, they are more alike
    than he ever imagined. In order to achieve his desire and
    escape Cory's fate of crushing despair, our hero must start
    living life on his own terms.

K.  The main character does or does not obtain his overarching
    desire: In this scenario, the hero does not obtain his imme-
    diate desire because he finds out that he is Cory's biological
    son; this makes him even more determined to break free
    from the ties that bind.

L.  The impact on the world of story: The hero leaves town the
    day of his own wedding (to find the romantic interest), and
    the shock of this dispels the curse.

# THE SEVENTH STAGE
## Writing a Working Treatment

It is helpful and necessary to write a working treatment in order
to organize your development strategy and flesh out your characters and plot. This is for *your purposes only* and should not be
shown around, commented on or critiqued by others—yet. It is
an essential phase of development and a very fragile one. If you
reveal your story too early, any negative comment may discourage
you from completing it.

Experienced writers have been known to let a story "cook"
inside their heads for six months (Lewis John Carlino, for example). Others have been known to work their stories out at cocktail
parties and on writer friends before committing them to paper
(William Bowers). My advice to aspiring screenwriters is to not
talk about your stories at this level of development. You may trick
yourself into believing your story is finished, or even worse, hopeless—and this can turn your enthusiasm for the project to dust.

While filmmaking *is* a highly collaborative process, most inex-
perienced writers look to their friends, family and others for
indiscriminate support and approval. The fact is that you cannot
allow yourself to depend on these non-professionals because you
cannot rely on their objectivity. They will want to please and
encourage you as much as they can (even as they roll their eyes
back in their sockets wishing you'd just give up this nonsense and
get a "real" job).

If they are in the film business, that is one thing, but even still,
stories and story ideas are extremely subjective material. As
William Goldman says most succinctly, "*Nobody* knows."

> "They recently held
> a co-dependency
> seminar, and I
> really wanted to
> attend, but I
> couldn't find
> anyone to go with."
>
> *—Anonymous*

Bear in mind that the treatment to *Star Wars* was turned down by Universal Studios *and* United Artists before it finally received a "green light" from Alan Ladd Jr. at Twentieth Century Fox. Even still, he told George Lucas, "I don't really understand this, so I'll have to trust your instincts." Lucas had previously made two films that warranted such trust: *THX 1138* and *American Graffiti*.

Another mistake that beginners make is to take on a writing partner out of a sense of deficiency. They believe that by sharing the load with another their own inadequacies will be reduced. Unfortunately, this can create even more problems as you both jostle time schedules and personality quirks. The process of writing is one of constant improvement and self-reliance. If you hastily take on a writing partner, you may cut yourself off from the tremendous independence this art form offers. There is little room for co-dependency. You must learn to develop a keen sense of your own abilities and shortcomings, then practice mastering them. Do not look for partners to buffer the painstaking process of your own mastery. In many ways the "talent" is in your own determination and will to improve.

The treatment stage is where you will personally solve the questions and answers you've come up with and organize their inherent logic, drama, conflict and dynamic actions into a beginning, middle and final resolution. Here is where you will start to name your players and flesh out their relationships and conflicts. Of course, this is also where a chorus of inner critics will chime in from inside your head, talking you out of your story, running it down, diminishing your efforts, telling you that you do not have the talent to succeed.

The only way to tame these voices is by proving them wrong, and the only way to prove them wrong is to show them—by doing all that it takes to write a terrific motion picture. What happens after this depends on your personal commitment. When you are committed to the art of writing and story craft, it is no longer a matter of merely selling one screenplay, but creating an entire body of work that defines your genius. This ideal will compel you through copious rewrites and other works as you move towards becoming a great storyteller.

### RICHARD CORY
A working treatment for a
two-hour motion picture.

RICHARD CORY was born into a very wealthy family. As in many such dynasties, the course of his life was predetermined for him: he would attend the right schools, marry the right girl, join the family business, and settle down to a life of quiet nobility. Except, Richard Cory met and fell in love with the wrong girl and was stubbornly determined to marry her in defiance of his family's objections. A fierce ultimatum was handed down: submit or be disinherited. Unable to stand up to the demands of his family, he relented and condemned himself to a life that was not his own. He broke off his relationship with the girl from the "wrong" side of town, and married a girl his family approved of. He settled into a life of bitterness that would later define his act of suicide.

Now consider the girl he jilted, PATRICIA MADDINGLY. Pregnant by Richard Cory, but too frightened to tell him, she turns to the only other suitor in her life and deceives him into believing he is the biological father. The two raise their son in relative calm, but owing to her deceit and broken heart, she withers away and dies prematurely, leaving her son to be raised by the man she deceived. JIM FOSTER, as it turns out is a decent man—a security guard at one of Richard Cory's businesses—and does his best to raise young WILLIAM with a strong sense of small town values.

William grows up in Coryville, idolizing the town's patriarch and assigning to him (as does everyone else in the community), an almost god-like stature. The boy works hard at various odd jobs, excels in school and athletics and wins honors and accolades in his pursuit to make something of himself. Naturally, he wins the socially correct girl, MARISA FRICK, along the way. He has become the living embodiment of the delusional curse that permeates this middle class factory town—one that draws its very name and identity from a false god and desperately manipulates everyone within it to fit the vision.

One day Richard Cory goes home and puts a bullet through his head. The scandal and shock of this act sends our hero into an emotional and ontological tail-spin. He becomes listless and demoralized, and finally rebellious, taking up with the underside of small town life. He quits the football team, gets high, rejects the prom queen and meets up with the "wrong" girl who better suits his defiance and disillusionment. LILLITH CANTRELL is wild, reckless, willful, and free—a poet, free thinker and all-around hellion—who affects Will in a way he has never known before. The fiery nature of their relationship leads them to plan a collective act of defiance—to burglarize the CORYVILLE factory.

One night, after drinking and carousing, Will breaks into the factory and rifles through Richard Cory's office and private papers while Lillith combs the building and sets it on fire. The fire rages precariously out of control as Will discovers an alarming piece of evidence: Richard Cory is his biological father.

As police and fire engines converge on the scene and Lillith escapes, Will hears the desperate pleas of the SECURITY GUARD trapped inside. Clutching the new-found evidence in his hand, Will turns back for him and the two, overwhelmed by smoke, collapse outside.

Will is now hospitalized and unconscious, leaving the security guard, a friend and colleague of his adoptive father, to talk to the police and divert suspicion away from the boy, proclaiming him a hero.

(Now remember, this is a town that willfully assigns values and ideals to people even when they aren't true. So, while Will may be poised to break free of the fulmination of false perception, the town still suffers from it and the fairy tale structure determines that the hero must free himself and impact the kingdom before the story ends.)

As the news of Will's heroic act spreads, along with the evidence that Richard Cory is his natural father, he is readily accepted back into the same social circles as before: The Cory Trust awards him a sizable cash inheritance, his old girlfriend takes him back and he turns his back on Lillith. He now finds himself as he was in the beginning—his life is not his own.

As circumstances lead Will to fall back into his old patterns, we understand that he will marry MARISA and enjoy a life of wealth and prestige. As the town convenes at the church in anticipation of the much-celebrated union, we have a sense that the curse has prevailed. Will he too, one day, be driven to suicide, as Richard Cory was before him—or does he now have the strength to change?

We end the story with Will riding his newly acquired motorcycle to the nuptial ceremony. The entire community has turned out to honor its new idol. But Will passes the church and keeps on going, straight into the arms of Lillith.

We pull back to show Lillith and Will racing out of town to a life and destiny that is theirs alone—the townspeople are left to wallow in their own disillusionment. The removal of the curse comes in Will's rejection of their values and opting to live a life of his own making.

> A good screenplay is not written, but rewritten."
>
> *—Ernest Lehman*

Of course, this is only one of many endings available to us, but ultimately we determine the proper ending by choosing one that best proves the story's final theme: *The search for success and self-fulfillment lies in neither wanting to be, or not wanting to be like someone else, but by living life on our own terms.*

We have now developed a story with a beginning, middle and end, with some of the necessary twists and turns to proceed to the next stage. Of course, there are some apparent and even not-so-apparent flaws to the story, but we can elect to work through them as we proceed. If at this point your story seems contrived or hokey, do not be discouraged; this is still very early on in the development stage.

You will need to calm your critical and editorial voice by neither giving it undue credence, nor dismissing it altogether. Rather than discarding your story in disgust, you will want solve the problems through writing and rewriting. If one element seems too obvious or cliché, you may need to complicate and construct some sleight-of-hand maneuvers. Not all the answers will come at once. Most problems require hours, weeks and months of problem solving to come up with the correct solution.

*Work* the problem, *write* the solution.

The primary difference between the amateur and the professional is that the amateur usually confronts a problem and then gives up during or after their first screenplay is completed. The professional keeps on going, script after script, through failure and success, until he's learned the art of creative problem solving.

As screenwriting is the art of translating the unseen into the seen, we now direct our efforts to the geographical setting of *Richard Cory,* known as the world of story. Where will this modern day fairy tale take place? How can we use our location to communicate the subtle thematic messages of conformity, individuality and false perception? As the original poem dictates, as does our choice to use a fairy tale structure, we start to conjure up images of a small factory town in the Midwest.

The nature of a fairy tale structure will indicate a communal opening, as well as establishing shots of the town, in order to convey the world at a glance. Using our visual sense and drawing upon our theme and external structure, we can start to fill in the details of the world. We can now envision an opening and a detailed first act.

A billboard says, "Welcome to Coryville"—depicting a small, idyllic community in vibrant colors, while the other side is nothing more than support beams and props, representing a type of facade (false perception).

We immediately pull back to reveal the billboard hovering over an imposing, brick-walled factory that bears the Cory family name.

We introduce our protagonist riding his bicycle. He stops in at the local sporting goods store, where he works after school, and deals with some business there before cycling on to the high school. We are careful to detail this moment with Will's impoverished status. We will also show his desire to improve himself his desire to emulate his idol, Richard Cory. The shop owner wishes him good luck, before Will continues on through the town. At Coryville High, students arrive in various cars and trucks that suitably inform us of their status in the community.

An assembly is in progress (communal opening). The special guest is none other than RICHARD CORY, who has come to award this year's Junior Achievement Award honoree.

Will is selected and gives a touching acceptance speech thanking his teachers, his father, his girlfriend and especially Richard Cory.

After the assembly we meet MARISA FRICK, Will's girl. We see that she and her friends are spoiled and a class above him, but because of his achievements in athletics and his desire to improve himself, they have grudgingly accepted him. We will next want to show Will's relationship with some of the underachievers. He strives to be "better" than they are, and this proves hurtful and demeaning. We also see that though he is accepted by the in-crowd, it does not mean he can freely enjoy the same advantages: They have their own cars; he rides a bike. They have lavish allowances; he must work hard at the sporting goods store after school.

By detailing the world of story with the situations, characters and conflicts, everything in the town of Coryville will be set up to resonate metaphorically on the story's themes.

The factory will be shown in contrast to the idyllic village with the church and downtown square and merchant shops.

Richard Cory's Victorian mansion will sit high on a hilltop.

Will's home will be in the poor section of town, dotted with company houses and trailer parks.

Coryville High School will be a melting pot for all the town's kids, rich and poor alike.

Marisa and her friends will hang out at a local ice cream parlor.

The underachievers will frequent the pool hall, parks and back alleyways.

We will be sure to divide the town between the haves and the have-nots. Everything from their automobiles to their clothing and manner of speech should fall into two categories: either to support the protagonist or the antagonist.

By drawing your visual world from the story's theme, there will be a reason for your descriptions. You won't just describe things for the purpose of filling up the page (and boring the pants off your readers). The arrangement of details will provide your story with subtext—a way of saying more and writing less.

Remember:

*The amateur screenwriter begins by asking,*
*"How can I fill up one hundred and twenty pages?"*

*The professional screenwriter asks,*
*"How can I fit it all into one hundred and twenty pages?"*

Of course, not all your stories will take place in small towns. So, the next chapter is designed to stimulate your interpretation of various locales and how they communicate thematic values on a purely visual level.

There is nothing more stultifying than reading a screenplay that enters every scene or introduces each character by describing what they are wearing or how the furniture is arranged. There must be an underlying thematic reason behind the details you include in your script, otherwise—lose them. As Henry James himself once said, "You must be willing to kill all your precious darlings."

# THE EIGHTH STAGE
## The World of Story

1. Where does the final conflict of *The Fugitive* take place?
2. Where does The Terminator meet his demise?
3. Why does *The Godfather* open on a wedding ceremony?
4. What telling landmark does Hitchcock use to open his excellent *Shadow of a Doubt*?
5. What do the opening shots of Casablanca convey?
6. Why does *Witness* open on the Amish community and not Philadelphia, where the hero lives?
7. Where does the last scene of *Chinatown* take place?
8. Why does the movie *Moonstruck* take place in New York's Little Italy?
9. What is the first shot of *Unforgiven*, after the opening credits?
10. In *The Wizard of Oz*, why is Dorothy's Kansas farm shot in black and white?

Answers:

1. The real murderer in *The Fugitive* is hunted down in the *laundry room of a hotel*. The laundry is a place where things come clean. Hence, this is the perfect setting to resolve the tale about a man falsely accused of murdering his wife ("soiled").

2. The first Terminator is put to rest in a metal *foundry*, a place where machines are made. Is there a better location to conclude this epic tale of machines at war with humankind?

3. *The Godfather* is a fairy tale about a powerful Don and his three sons as they struggle to settle in the socially "legitimate" world of Nevada gambling. The communal opening (as in all the *Godfather* movies) provides us with an overview of their unique society and their social standing in it.

4. *Shadow of a Doubt* (written by Thornton Wilder, Gordon McDonell, Sally Benson and Alma Reville) shows what happens when a sophisticated mass murderer escapes the city and takes refuge with his unsuspecting relatives in an idyllic small town. What better image to roll credits over, than the cityscape of a solitary bridge wending its way out of the cold, impersonal city? Upon first examination, the somewhat static shot of the bridge seems peculiar, if not empty and meaningless, but appreciating Director Alfred Hitchcock's flair for landmark symbolism, it is impossible to ignore its deeper implications. The bridge, innocuous and unthreatening as it appears, is a focal point of social transition and symbolism directly related to the theme of the story. The bridge itself is an impassive conduit where the depravity and corruption of the inner city can depart to find refuge in the sanctity of small town, USA. In this light, something as commonplace as a bridge can take on ominous overtones. It is especially interesting to note that *Shadow of a Doubt* was filmed only two years after the attack on Pearl Harbor—a time when Americans were deeply worried about the encroachment of other foreign evils upon their way of life.

5. The underlying theme of *Casablanca* revolves around the prisons we build for ourselves. Prisons built of commitment, honor, love, bitterness, disappointment and politics. Rick is a prisoner of his own cynicism: "I stick my neck out for no one." He drinks alone and reveals himself to no one. In other words, he is just as caged as every other person who comes to Casablanca. So we are barraged with images of incarceration—both subtle and gross—from the opening shot right through to the end.

6. *Witness* is an example of mythic structure, with the added innovation of opening in the world of journey—with its golden pastures, simple farmhouses and community at prayer—when convention might have dictated opening the story in crime-rid-

dled Philadelphia. This choice for the opening is perfect when we stop to consider the movie's theme. The power of true righteousness, as exemplified by the Amish, being a stronger force than the self-righteousness of Detective John Book, or the corrupt machinations of rogue detectives.

7. *Chinatown* is a disturbing murder mystery about a slick, cynical—but well-intentioned—detective, Jake Gittes, whose search for the truth inadvertently winds up hurting the people he tries to help. Chinatown is a world where decency, purpose and humanity are supposed to mean something, but do not. It is a place where justice, truth and morality should count, but don't. We are left with a world, a society, where might rules over right and wealth and depravity triumph over basic human respect. In the end, the audience is forced to admit, "It's all Greek to me!" Or, in the writer's own words, "Forget it, Jake, it's Chinatown!" The whole world makes no sense.

8. *Moonstruck* is a wonderful story of transformation where virtually every word, song, or locale is drawn from the writer's theme. What more colorful canvas to place this tale than in the eclectic, vibrantly alive world of New York's Little Italy?

9. *Unforgiven* is a masterpiece of conflicting themes based around man's need to rationalize his violence. The town of Big Whiskey is introduced at the foot of a vast mountain range to further demonstrate man's feeble efforts to raise himself out of the muck in the face of the more elemental, majestic grandeur of nature itself.

10. Kansas in *The Wizard of Oz* is shot in black and white, not as a marketing ploy to further exploit recent advances in Technicolor, but to further resonate on the story's theme. Auntie Em and Uncle Henry's farm is not paradise, in fact, it is rather bleak, desolate and run down. It is a place where you have to work very, very hard to eke out a living. Kansas, the writers tell us through exposition, is a state where the rich have power over the working class and justice only exists to serve their every whim. It is going to take Dorothy's journey to Oz, with all of its resplendent wonder and tribulation to realize, "Be it ever so humble, there is no place like home."

It is the writer's task to detail his story with subtle thematic values and compose a veritable symphony of characters, conflicts, dialogue, music and visual settings. These myriad worlds are born of theme and creating them is one of the truly great joys of cinematic storytelling. If you are not building thematic images, then you are window dressing. You are describing, rather than detailing. We should not describe characters by what clothes they wear, but by their actions, flaws and desires. Similarly, the setting of a script is a visual metaphor for the challenges facing your characters.

## GEOGRAPHICAL ARCHETYPES:
## Topographical symbolism in THE WORLD OF STORY

### THE CITY

According to Pericles, "all things good" flow from the city. As storytellers, we know that the inverse is often just as true. The city is simultaneously man's most calamitous act and greatest achievement. Everything wondrous about civilization is to be found here, but so is everything vile, horrific and evil. In the city there are museums, theater, opulence, commerce, transportation on a mass scale, cinema, literature, cuisine, music, opera, fashion, art, poetry, dance, education, universities, and all varieties of intellectual, creative, cultural and economic pursuits. In the city there are parks, shops, amphitheaters and architectural wonders by the score. But there is also abject loneliness, despair, poverty, crime, addiction, depravity, murder, conspiracy, violence and degradation. It is the very best of who we are and the very worst. The city is the perfect modern fairy tale kingdom, because in one shot you can show the highest of the high socially and economically (the skyscraper) and the lowest of the low in the subways, sewers and street life.

These days, we have the option of choosing cities with different social significance. For example, San Francisco is the perfect locale for extraordinary love stories, sex crimes and murder mysteries since it has been long been identified in the public's mind as being tolerant of decadence and gender-bending lifestyles. (*Point Blank, Dirty Harry, Basic Instinct, Jade, Nine Months, Jagged Edge, 48 Hrs., What's Up Doc?, Bullit, The Big Fix, The Killer Elite, Time After Time, Chan Is Missing, D.O.A., San Francisco, Pacific Heights, Gentleman Jim, '68*)

Los Angeles is synonymous with glamour, glitter, greed and gangs. (*Angel City, Blow, Lethal Weapon, Chinatown, Blue Thunder, Pulp Fiction, To Live and Die in L.A., The Player, Against All Odds, American Gigolo, Beverly Hills Cop, The Big Picture, Boulevard Nights, Colors, Boyz N the Hood, Bugsy, Barfly, The Big Sleep, True Confessions, Who Framed Roger Rabbit, The Graduate, American Gigolo, Down and Out in Beverly Hills, L.A. Story, Night on Earth, The Terminator, The Truth About Cats and Dogs, Nick of Time*)

Philadelphia is old money, high society and social climbing of one type or another: *The Philadelphia Story, High Society, Philadelphia, Rocky, The Philadelphians, Trading Places*. Philly can be easily replaced with Boston, which has similar traits, except that Boston has the added distinction of a rich Irish heritage, and Ivy League affiliations. (*The Brinks Job, The Verdict, The Bostonians, Blown Away, Altered States, The Paper Chase*)

Chicago used to be known exclusively as mob territory or the hotbed of political cronyism, thanks to such colorful characters as Al Capone, The Untouchables and Mayor Richard Daley. Recently, John Hughes and Robert Redford have shown it to be an ideal setting for middle class angst, teenage chicanery and sometimes all three as in the example of Paul Brickman's masterpiece, *Risky Business*. Other Chicago backdrops include *Backdraft, The Blues Brothers, Bound, Ferris Bueller's Day Off, Robin and the Seven Hoods, Home Alone, Some Like It Hot, The Untouchables, Pretty in Pink, Sixteen Candles, The Breakfast Club* and *High Fidelity*.

New Orleans is as "Olde Worlde" as you can get (in the United States, at least), so it can accommodate more exotic, erotic tales of sensuality, sex crimes, racial tension, political corruption and even a little bit of gothic horror (*Easy Rider, Palmetto, This Property Is Condemned, A Streetcar Named Desire, The Big Easy,*

*Cat Woman, Pretty Baby, Blaze, Interview with A Vampire, Storyville).*

Las Vegas, Reno and Atlantic City are all flash and little substance—perfect locales for stories about man's lower impulses and addictions: *Ocean's 11, Leaving Las Vegas, Casino, Atlantic City, The Gambler; Bob, Carol, Ted and Alice; Honeymoon in Vegas, California Split, Lost in America, Bugsy, Forty Pounds of Trouble.*

London is about Cinderella stories, sex crimes born of rigid oppression, political scandals, rebellious youth, and the escapades of the rich and Royal, as well as the misadventures of the bourgeoisie (*Tom Jones, 39 Steps, Blow up, Frenzy, Four Weddings and a Funeral, The List of Adrian Messenger, Murder by Decree, Agatha, Scandal, The Crying Game, Time after Time, The Elephant Man, The Day the Earth Caught Fire, 84 Charing Cross Road, A Fish Called Wanda, Darling, Repulsion, To Sir With Love, Mona Lisa, The Krays, Hope and Glory, Remains of the Day, Howard's End, Notting Hill, From Hell*).

Paris is rich with tales of the artist's struggle, along with sophistication, fashion, passion, sexual perversity, romance and international intrigue. In Hemingway's words, it is "a moveable feast." (*Alphaville, Dangerous Liaisons, Camille, A Man and a Woman, Moulin Rouge, Lust for Life, Charade, Funny Face, Round Midnight, Pret-a-Porter, The Moderns, Frantic, French Twist, Last Tango in Paris, Henry and June, An American in Paris, Under the Rooftops of Paris, Belle de Jour, Irma La Douce, Gigi, Metropole, American Dreamer, Bob Le Flambeur, Bitter Moon, The Four Hundred Blows, Small Change, Camille Claudel, Stavisky, Can-Can, The Red Balloon,* the *Pink Panther* series, *The Tenant, Is Paris Burning?, Night on Earth, Jefferson in Paris, A Tale of Two Cities, The Scarlet Pimpernel, Les Miserables, The Nine Gates*)

Washington D.C., Baltimore, Virginia and vicinity are the citadels of power—perfect for stories of high-placed corruption, political conspiracies or intense investigations by the FBI or Secret Service (*Absolute Power, Broadcast News, No Way Out, In The Line of Fire, The Hunt for Red October, Clear and Present Danger, All the President's Men, The American President, Advise and Consent, The Silence of the Lambs, Seven Days in May, First*

*Monday in October, The Star Chamber, Dr. Strangelove, The Next Man, Wrong is Right, Bedroom Window, Avalon, Diner).*

New York is the Big Apple and is fit for almost anything. For references of New York at its breathtaking best, watch these films: *Breakfast at Tiffanys; Bright Lights, Big City; How to Murder Your Wife, Ragtime, The Thrill of It All,* every Woody Allen movie ever made, *Taxi Driver, Married to the Mob, Mean Streets, The Godfather, Goodfellas, The City, Dog Day Afternoon; New York, New York; Little Odessa, Miracle on 34th Street, New York Stories, French Connection; Fort Apache, The Bronx; An Affair to Remember, Kramer vs. Kramer; Author, Author; After Hours, Times Square, Network, When Harry Met Sally, My Favorite Year, Moscow on the Hudson, Next Stop Greenwich Village, Rear Window, Please Don't Eat the Daisies, Moonstruck; The Taking of Pelham One, Two, Three; Wall Street, Kids, If Lucy Fell, Eyes Wide Shut, Sleepless in Seattle, You've Got Mail, Vanilla Sky* and probably a billion more to come.

Miami is to the Colombian Drug Cartel what Chicago was to the Irish/Italian/Jewish mobsters of the prohibition era, with the swaggering gold-chained set of cocaine cowboys, drug runners, renegade airplane pilot and linen-clad sleuths. *Michael, Miami Blues, Scarface, The Birdcage, Black Sunday, Ace Ventura, Goldfinger, To Die For, The Perez Family.*

Atlanta, St. Louis, Kansas City, Houston and Omaha are often viewed as marginal places and are therefore almost interchangeable. If you can spin a compelling yarn about any of these lesser-known cities, you might be forever linked as the screenwriter who made so-and-so exciting again.

Seattle and Denver are interesting locales as depicted in *Singles, Sleepless in Seattle, An Officer and A Gentleman* and *Things To Do in Denver When You're Dead*, but as of this writing they have yet to impress themselves upon the national psyche as distinct urban archetypes. Of the two, Seattle is most likely to break through due to its spectacular islands, ferry boats, distinctive space needle, grunge rock and other alternative music developments, as well as its eye-opening riots against the World Trade Organization. Seattle could well be the perfect location for future thrillers featuring home-grown terrorists.

At one point (during the *Urban Cowboy* craze), Dallas had the chance to emerge as something other than its flashy, somewhat tasteless namesake. It has all the amenities of any big city with a natural association with oil: big cars, big hair, big business, technology and shit-kicking cowboys (*Love Field, Nixon, Kennedy, Giant*). For this author's money, Austin is the next up and coming Texas town to host your film-intended imagination.

Nashville is the Country Western scene's answer to Hollywood. They didn't like the values of their Western counterparts so they created one that is as equally garish and over-the-top (*Nashville, The Thing Called Love*).

Detroit is the 'Motor City' and heavily identified with major industrialization, the Motown Sound, blue collar workers, labor unions and urban blight: *Blue Collar, Robocop, Compulsion, The Betsy, Beverly Hills Cop, Swoon* and *Detroit Motor City.*

San Diego is most notable for The Hotel Del Coronado, used in *Some Like It Hot, Grand Hotel* and *The Stunt Man.*

The least filmed urban location in the United States is Minneapolis/St. Paul, which offers not only some incredible landmarks, but a burgeoning music scene, opera house, children's theater, The Mall of America and one of the hippest museums in the world. The people are robust, the girls svelte, and those frigid winters are rife for tales of simple stalwart values matched against growing urban decay, brutality and decadence. Don't believe me? Check out the Coen brothers' *Fargo.*

Italy, Greece, Spain and other Mediterranean locales pique our more adventurous sides and conjure up notions of light-hearted comedy, romance, exotic fun, marital affairs, sexual experimentation and exhilarating romps through sensual locales, such as the beach, the countryside, or quaint farming villages and opulent estates (*Barcelona, Three Coins in a Fountain, Roman Holiday, Shirley Valentine, Luna, Daisy Miller, Stealing Beauty, Topkapi, Who's Killing the Great Chefs of Europe?, Amarcorde, La Dolce Vita, A Little Romance, Blume in Love, The Bobo, A Room with a View, Enchanted April*). But they can just easily host our darkest fears of, kidnapping intrigue, terrorism and brutal murder. Just ask *The Talented Mr. Ripley.*

The glamour and intrigue of the Orient; places like Tokyo, Kyoto (Japan) Hong Kong, Peking, Shanghai, Formosa, China and Seoul, Korea, are almost too exotic from most filmgoers' interests. Thankfully, this is changing with the impressive quality of films, directors and actors capturing the world's stage: *Crouching Tiger, Hidden Dragon; Rising Sun, The Yakuza, Karate Kid II, You Only Live Twice; Walk, Don't Run; Hiroshima, Mon Amour; Sayonara, Tokyo Moon, Eat Drink Man Woman, Shanghai Triad, Raise the Red Lantern, M. Butterfly, Empire of the Sun, The Last Emperor.*

Munich, Frankfurt, Stuttgart, Hamburg, Berlin, Budapest, Vienna, Moscow, and the former Eastern bloc countries are ideal cities for political pot-boilers and international intrigues. They are among the cleanest and most sophisticated cities in the world—featuring an eclectic mix of historic and post-war architecture along with modern technology and residual design elements from the Baroque and Rococo periods: *The Magic Bullet, Wings of Desire; Far Away, So Close; Iron Curtain, The Prize, One Two Three, The Third Man, Torn Curtain, Amadeus; Mission: Impossible; The Sound of Music, Cabaret, Russia House, The Victors, The American Success Company; Europa, Europa; The Blue Angel, Three Penny Opera, The Young Lions, Schindler's List.*

Israel, Egypt, Lebanon, Morocco, the Middle East and Northern Africa. One suspects because these troubled regions are still playing themselves out in real life dramas and contemporary headlines, there is less enthusiasm for audiences to rush out to see movies based there. With Osama Bin Ladin and his band of Taliban thugs dominating the news, they have ceased offering any production values to your movie script. In fact, they are more of a liability than at any time before the stomach churning events of September 11th. Who in their right mind would want to see a political thriller set in the Middle East right now? What filmmaker could think their fiction could possibly compete with what's unfolding around the world on a daily basis? Nevertheless, these locales do provide some excellent backgrounds, mostly drawn from the rich mythological/archeological traditions inherent of the region: *The Peacemaker, Three Kings, Raiders of the Lost Ark,*

**DESERT MOTIFS**
*Beau Geste,
The Desert Fox: The Story of Rommel,
Dune, The English Patient,
The Greatest Story Ever Told,
Heat and Dust,
Ishtar, King of Kings, The Last Temptation of Christ, Lawrence of Arabia, Lost Horizon, Passion in the Desert,
The Searchers,
The Sheltering Sky,
The Ten Commandments,
Woman of the Dunes, Dr. Zhivago*

**ICE MOTIFS**
*Alaska, Alive,
The Eiger Sanction,
The Empire Strikes Back, Galahad of Everest, The Golden Seal, Ice Palace,
K2, Kundun, The Road to Utopia,
Salmonberries, The Savage Innocents,
Seven Years in Tibet, Superman,
The Thing, Top of the World, When the North Wind Blows, White Fang*

*Stargate, The Omen, The Exorcist, Courage Under Fire, The Ambassador, Cast A Giant Shadow, Exodus, The Awakening, The Wind and the Lion, The English Patient, Lawrence of Arabia, The Sheltering Sky.*

## THE DESERT/ICE MOTIF

The desert/ice region is where the hero exhibits the attributes of individualism, faith, sacrifice, resolution and determination, as if to declare, "I am who I am until the last breath of life—and I will not be dissuaded, dissipated or diluted while that life breathes within me!"

In religious traditions, the desert is where the hero seeks his vision and is tempted from his resolve with delusions (promises?) of wealth, power and abundance. Somehow the mere sight of these mouth-watering delights in the middle of so much deficiency intensifies the hero's choice, so we are impressed when he ultimately declines them. Once his inner resolve is proven, all that glistens is promptly returned to dry, empty particles of sand and illusion.

### A List of Contrasting Values Expressed by the Desert/Ice Region

• Spiritual strength versus material strength
• Spiritual weakness versus material strength
• Spiritual strength versus material weakness
• The rarity of life (Oasis)/ versus the inevitability of Death (Desert)
• Scarcity versus abundance
• Surrender versus endurance

## UNDERWATER/ OUTER SPACE

These are entirely foreign and openly hostile habitats whose very nature requires extraordinary and artificial measures for survival: Breathing apparatus, space suits, wet suits, gravity boots, flippers, spaceships and submarines are just some of the extreme requirements necessary to function on a day to day basis. Because of the dependency on technology, these realms are rich arenas for exploring the psycho/spiritual dimensions of excessive reliance on artifice.

The Sea/Space realms are rich situations for introducing new and unique life forms, which challenge our present notions of being human. Since we marvel at the wide variety of species spawned in habitats here on earth, we can readily accept the existence of extra-terrestrial life, even without scientific proof. In this archetypal way, everything we write about draws validity from our collective consciousness. It is the screenwriter's job to know what these playgrounds are and how best to utilize them.

### A List of Contrasting Values Expressed by the Underwater/Outer Space Motif

- Evolution versus creationism
- Social dependency versus rugged individualism
- Tribal consciousness versus "I am" consciousness
- Known versus unknown
- Prejudice versus tolerance
- Ignorance versus science
- Monogamy versus polygamy or polyandry (the space colonies of the future are excellent locales to explore creative alternatives to male/female relations outside of the normal traditions we maintain here on earth)
- Space and time versus eternity
- Past versus future
- Limitations of time and space versus the continuum
- Cosmic truth versus religious dogma
- Reaction versus pro-action
- Isolation and alienation versus individualism and community

**JUNGLE MOTIFS**
*The African Queen, Aguirre: The Wrath of God, Apocalypse Now, At Play in the Fields of the Lord, Bataan, Bird of Paradise, The Emerald Forest, Farewell to the King, Fizcarraldo/Burden of Dreams, Gorillas in the Mist, Greystoke: The Legend of Tarzan, Heart of Darkness, The Jungle Book, King Kong, The Mission, The Mosquito Coast, Mutiny on the Bounty, The Piano, Platoon, Predator, Sorcerer, South Pacific, Tarzan, The Wages of Fear; White Hunter, Black Heart*

## THE JUNGLE AS METAPHOR

The supreme law of the jungle is that life feeds on life. There is evidence everywhere of life springing from decay and death giving birth to new life. There is no real death in the jungle in the physical sense. Everything that dies creates a new life. So there is a feeling of timelessness, a recognition that however mighty and grand the cities we build, we are still only renting space from nature. Eventually everything will be reclaimed. There is an ironic sense of impermanence within the timeless region of nature—as if to say that unless we become as predatory as nature itself, we will never survive.

The jungle is the ideal place to compare notions of civility and social affectation with man's unfettered animal nature. It is no wonder that the rigid, highly civilized Victorian age spawned so many tales in this milieu: Joseph Conrad, E.M. Forster, Rudyard Kipling, Edgar Rice Burroughs and Robert Louis Stevenson. Even James M. Barrie, author of the beloved *Peter Pan*, wrote of "civilized" man's fate in the savage wilderness in his work, *The Admirable Crichton*.

### A List of Contrasting Values Expressed in the Jungle Region

- Permanence versus impermanence
- Civilization versus primitive
- Pretense versus innocence
- Education versus animal instinct
- Ancient taboos versus contemporary mores
- Breeding versus survival of the fittest
- Education versus evolution
- Passion versus repression
- Grand artificial schemes versus unbridled nature
- The hunter versus the hunted

## THE FOREST

The forest separates the known and inhabited world from that which is yet to be discovered. It is the very realm that challenged the knights of King Arthur and kept the Puritans of Salem in check with fears of witchcraft. The forest is a metaphor for finding one's way through the quagmire and carving out one's unique destiny in life. Whatever you can imagine, however terrible or wonderful, it lives somewhere out there in the forest: The Castle of the Grail, the Gingerbread House, the Green Chapel, or the lair

---

"They thought that it would be a disgrace to go forth as a group. Each entered the forest at a point that he himself had chosen where it was darkest and there was no path. If there is a path, it is someone else's path and you are not on the adventure."

—Joseph Campbell

FOREST MOTIFS

*Alice in Wonderland, Bambi, Beauty and the Beast, The Blair Witch Project, The Company of Wolves, Darby O'Gill and the Little People, Dracula, Excalibur, Andy Warhol's Frankenstein, The Last Unicorn, The Legend of Sleepy Hollow, A Midsummer Night's Dream, Sleeping Beauty, Snow White, Werewolf, The Wizard of Oz*

of the Blair Witch. The deeper you penetrate it, the more you must redefine yourself, or risk your own sense of self. Ultimately the forest is unending, impenetrable and as unknowable as the mind itself. Any attempt to pass through without a map or a qualified guide is to risk losing your way, your sanity, your life—or perhaps all three.

*A List of Contrasting Values Expressed by the Forest Motif*
- Sanity versus insanity
- Seen versus unseen
- Magic versus science
- Fantasy versus the mundane
- Sacred versus profane
- Simplicity versus sophistication
- Technical proficiency versus the supernatural
- Hunter versus hunted (nature versus man)
- Feminine wiles versus masculine aggression

## THE MOUNTAIN SYMBOL

In the sixties, two significant "mountain" pieces emerged in the counter culture: One was a novel, and the other a film unofficially inspired by it. The unfinished novel was the 1944 publication by Rene Daumal entitled *Mount Analog* and the film that borrowed extensively from it was *Holy Mountain*, by the surrealist filmmaker Alexandro Jodorowsky. Both deal with a ragtag group of believers who come together to climb the highest mountain in the universe. (While the movie sets the story in outer space, the book gathers its expedition from around the world). The book is the definitive piece on mountain symbolism and is a must-read for anyone planning on doing anything with mountains.

The mountain region is the visible road to the invisible, the stairway to Heaven: the ziggurat, pyramid, the tower of Babel, and throne of the most high sky gods of our ancestral past. The mountain zenith is the bridge between earth and sky, heaven and earth, consciousness and super consciousness. It is where God communes with man and offers gifts and knowledge: The Ten

MOUNTAIN MOTIFS
*Alive, The Blue Light, Close Encounters of the Third Kind, Dracula, The Eiger Sanction, The Fearless Vampire Killers, Frankenstein, Holy Mountain, Kundun, The Last Unicorn, The Lost Horizon, A Passage to India, Seven Years in Tibet, The Ten Commandments, Young Frankenstein*

Commandments to Moses, fire to Prometheus, Soma (heavenly nectar) via King Indra. It is also the source of the sacred Ganges (from Mount Kailash) and the most high seating place of the Dalai Lama, Jehovah, Thor, Zeus and the great Olympians, as well as Shiva and Parvati (Daughter of the Mountain) and a thousand other saints, mystics, gods and goddesses of the ancient world.

The mountain realm is one of cruel treachery and tyranny as well. It is where Vlad the Impaler built his chamber of horrors and had a thousand Turks impaled on stakes along the road. It is also where another bloodthirsty Count traditionally retires after restocking his personal blood bank from unwitting donors in the village below.

### A List of Contrasting Values Expressed by the Mountain

- Aristocracy over democracy
- Superior over inferior
- Monarchy over peasantry
- Tyranny over simplicity
- Spiritual law over human matters
- Transcendence over the mundane
- Supreme benevolence and wisdom over ignorant squabbling and materialism
- Immortality over mortality
- Spiritual law over material law
- Adventure over complacency
- The road to enlightenment through physical challenge
- Purity over decadence
- Wisdom over ignorance

## THE TOWNSHIP

If fairy tales are about leveling the playing field between rich and poor, then the perfect setting for this remains small town, USA. Here, we have all the elements for a complete society at a glance. Without spending a lot of time establishing the dynamics of such a place, we can readily get down to the nitty-gritty of our story. Since screenwriting is about economy, the choice of a small town for your world of story will set up all the characters and situations with as little exposition as necessary.

You can intensify the values of a small town and compress it to even more specialized arenas like a monastery, a private upscale boarding school, or even a summer camp.

### A List of Contrasting Values Expressed by the Township
* Upper class rigidity versus home-spun values
* Personal worth versus social status
* Middle class values versus individual ideals
* Conformity versus iconoclasm
* Racial, social or class bias versus independent thinking
* Small town virtues versus urban threat
* Ambition versus inherited wealth

## THE HOME

Due to economical or structural requirements, it is not always necessary to create sweeping world epics in order to develop intensely dramatic situations. All one needs is a single dwelling place. This is the mainstay of dramas, taut thrillers and horror stories, where the house itself often proves to be a type of "monster." These stories draw their suspense from their claustrophobic intensity.

When choosing a home setting, take care to detail the rooms as you would separate environments—create distinct qualities from one room to the next. Extremely self-contained situations like *My Dinner with Andre*, *Reservoir Dogs* and *Twelve Angry Men* use waiters, doorways, stairwells, bathrooms, water fountains and windows as well as chairs, desk tops, and even window curtains to break up scenes and underscore emotional intensity.

### A List of Contrasting Values Expressed in the Home
* Familiarity breeds contempt
* Insecurity within intensely secure conditions
* Terror from within the commonplace
* Unknown from within the known

*HOME MOIFS*
*The Amityville Horror, Beetlejuice, The Big Chill, The Black Cat, Blind Witness, Castle Keep, Down and Out In Beverly Hills, The Exorcist, The Fifth of July, Frankenstein, Halloween, The Hand That Rocks the Cradle, The Haunting of Hill House, Home Alone, House on Haunted Hill, Home for the Holidays,; Hush, Hush Sweet Charlotte; La Grande Bouffe, The Last House on the Left, The Lodger, Lost Highway, Mr. Blandings Builds His Dream House, The Nanny, Neighbors, Nightmare on Elm Street, Poltergeist, Rules of the Game, Scenes From the Class Struggle; Sorry, Wrong Number; Whatever Happened to Baby Jane?, You Can't Take It With You*

- Psychological or supernatural adversity versus familial and normal conditions

## THE APARTMENT

To take the qualities of the familiar and amplify them in extremely intensified situations for: drama, romance, horror or comedy, the apartment setting can be especially suitable, economic, and ruthless in its examination of human foibles and relationships.

## THE ISLAND

The exhilarating rush from moving rapidly over turbulent blue waters to white sandy beaches and lush tropics transports us to a world that is uniquely self-contained. The island world is the world that stands apart—a civilization where the rules are much different than our own. There are a wide variety of peoples, cultures, customs, and traditions that have evolved wholly out of context with the rest of humankind.

These separate kingdoms are either futuristically ideal, primitively unspoiled, or inherently corrupt. As we land, either by being marooned or through invasion, we are eager to learn the ways of this awesome and peculiar terrain as fast as possible. Unfortunately, it is not that easy. The island is a vast laboratory to explore the rich diversity of evolution, culture, sexual mores and other moral issues, while speculating on what future developments might offer.

The island is a place of natural aggression against idyllic peace, where danger lurks all around from warring tribes, head-hunters, beasts of prey, and perhaps most alarmingly, through the outside agency of modern predators: man himself.

### A List of Contrasting Values Expressed through the Island Locale

- Modern avarice versus simple virtues
- Technology versus simplicity
- Imperialism versus self-contentment

- Political ideology versus survival-of-the-fittest
- Utopia versus modern civilization
- Material wealth versus spiritual wealth
- Individual greed versus communal well-being
- Animal nature versus modern schemes

## THE RIVER

In Hermann Hesse's *Siddhartha*, the young mendicant is asked by his teacher to find one place in the entire universe where he could see the past, present and future in one sitting. The answer is in the incessant flow found along the riverbank. Looking downstream, Siddhartha could see the past feeding into the present and then wending its way up stream, into the future and out of sight. Hence, the river world is one of constant transition; past present and future joined confluently to bring us to full transformation.

The river journey is the supreme realm of the myth. We start out in the jungle of our provincial realties and gradually make our way to larger waters of vision and understanding. As in the myth, we are not the same people when we finish the journey. Each of the outposts and adventures along the way drive us further to completion—to either madness or emancipation—depending on which direction we are heading. In *The African Queen* it is to love and political commitment. In *Apocalypse Now* it is a backward regression from civilization to depravity and horror.

RIVER MOTIFS
*Apocalypse Now, The African Queen, Banjo on My Knee, Fizcarraldo/Burden of Dreams, Heart of Darkness, The Mission, Night of the Hunter, A Passage to India, Phoolan Devi: The Bandit Queen, The River, River of No Return, A River Runs Through It, The River Wild, River's Edge, Siddhartha*

### *A List of Contrasting Values Expressed by the River Motif*
- Constancy versus change
- Transience over permanence
- Adventure over complacency
- Growth versus stagnation
- Dogma versus truth
- Experience versus the commonplace

## MINI-CITIES

The prison, the hospital, the psychiatric ward—each of these is a self-contained metropolis. Each can be drawn to reflect either a timeless quality or a dark, foreboding, impersonal nature. They are all provincial worlds that embody an extreme conflict the hero must endure. These are tales of intense individuality against rigid conformity or teeming, faceless humanity.

## CITIES OF THE FUTURE

The movie *Blade Runner* begins with a burst of fire exploding on top of a mile-high skyscraper, as air mobiles soar over the City of Los Angeles, circa 2025. This is a futuristic city, overpopulated with characters and foreign sights far different from anything we've ever previously experienced. Immediately we perceive that the future is an unpleasant place, where individuality means nothing and life is cheap and expendable. As Bryant (M. Emmett Walsh), the chief of the Blade Runner unit, tells Deckard, "You're either cop or you're little people," implying that if he doesn't take the assignment, Deckard will be killed. This theme is given further intensity when we see our hero begin his quest at street level and finish by dangling precariously from a mile-high rooftop at the mercy of his opponent.

An additional tool for creating new and exciting variations of film locales is to take the archetypal values of one and transpose them on another. This has been done to great effect in films like *The Asphalt Jungle, Escape from New York, Escape from Los Angeles, Up the Down Staircase, Crocodile Dundee, Streets of Fire, The Warriors* and *Do The Right Thing*.

## ETERNAL CITIES

They appear out of nowhere every hundred years or so, when the people frolic and make merry before quietly disappearing back into time. The eternal city is the provincial world embodied with messiah-like, magical propensities, so it usually appears for the sole purpose of absorbing a single anachronistic traveler whose life is disastrously out of synch with contemporary times.

## BORDERLANDS AND FRONTIERS

The frontier separates civilization from the unknown and the uncivilized. Beyond the border lies adventure, magic, savagery, enlightenment, paradise, hell or anything else the imagination can conjure. These are tales that challenge or complacency and false notions of security and civility.

In *Dances with Wolves*, Lieutenant Dunbar, being cheated of suicide in an attempt to die a whole person, chooses the next best thing to it—to be exiled to the westernmost post of Civil War-torn United States. From the rumors of savagery that exist there, we are lead to believe it is just a more prolonged way of dying. But Dunbar has nothing to lose, and from this place of emptiness, he begins his life anew. Far from the dire warnings, Dunbar finds love, harmony and wisdom among the Native Americans. All previous misconceptions are dispelled when Dunbar realizes it is not these gentle people who truly threaten, but the war-mongering, deceitful and militaristic "civilized" government he left behind.

*A List of Contrasting Values Expressed by the Borderland*
- Civilization versus tribal values
- Known versus unknown
- Imperialism versus indigenous peoples
- Preconceptions and bias versus the truth

## THE VILLAGE

From the barren wasteland of the frontier outpost springs the first offshoot of civilization. Through the progression of technology, people, culture and natural law, we see society in its process of maturation. These are sub-worlds in constant change. Will the values and barbarism of the frontier past prevail, or will this burgeoning experiment progress into a full-fledged city?

---

ETERNAL CITIES
*Brigadoon, Gulliver's Travels, Holy Mountain, The Little Mermaid, The Lost City of Atlantis, The Lost Continent, Lost Horizons, The Man Who Would Be King, Somewhere in Time, Splash, The Time Machine*

BORDERLANDS AND FRONTIERS
*Apocalypse Now, Assault on Precinct 13, The Crucible, Barbarosa Black Robe, The Border, Borderland, The Buccaneer, El Norte, Enemy Mine, Fort Apache: The Bronx, The Frontiersman, Heart of Darkness, Indochine, Lone Star, The Last of the Mohicans, M.A.S.H., The Mission, Northwest Passage, Outlands, Platoon, The Scarlet Letter*

There is a timeless fascination with the best Westerns because the idea of one person having a direct impact on the community at large is important to us. Rarely do we see this anymore. The more sophisticated we get, the more cynical we are about the corporate bureaucracy that rules our lives. We're told, "You can't fight City Hall!" The Western world is not like that: one Sheriff, drifter, gambler, schoolmarm/madam/barkeep, is all it takes to make a difference.

## AUXILIARY LOCALES

*He stands in the threshold, never quite managing to make it inside, and so we are left with a sense that he will never be at home.* This classic pose of John Wayne in *The Searchers* supremely expresses the use of the commonplace architecture to underscore a powerful theme. Since we are in the business of translating the unseen to the seen, we are left to devise physical metaphors from the world around us for the following purposes:

A   To underscore an emotional or thematic value

B.   To establish a concise plan of action

C.   To geographically identify the exact whereabouts of the hero or opponent

D.   To punctuate the nature of the hero's predicament, goal or destination

E.   To intensify an objective, conflict, request, revelation or outcome

F.   To reveal a particular character trait, problem or idiosyncrasy

To achieve these results, screenwriters, directors, producers and film crews have created a metaphorical film language that employs doorways, passages, windows, thresholds, maps, miniatures, paintings, hallways, scale models and objects such as table settings, curtains, cameos, jewelry, books, illustrations, flashbacks, hallucinations and dreamscapes. Each of these auxiliary locations can be treated as a separate world in your overall world of story.

**VILLAGE MOTIFS**
*The Big Country, Big Hand For A Little Lady, Cat Ballou, The Cheyenne Social Club, Gunfight at the O.K. Corral, The Gunfighter, High Noon, High Plains Drifter, The Legend of the Lone Ranger, A Man Called Horse, The Man Who Loved Cat Dancing, The Man Who Shot Liberty Valance, My Darling Clementine, Pale Rider, Rio Bravo, Shane, She Wore a Yellow Ribbon, The Shootist, Silverado, The Skin Game, The Sheepman, Support Your Local Sheriff, Three Amigos, Tombstone, Unforgiven, Wyatt Earp*

The following are examples of how such artifacts have been used and how you can use them to further enhance your storytelling.

## WORMHOLES AND THRESHOLDS

*The looking glass, the wardrobe, the rabbit hole, the cupboard, the mousehole, the arch, the storybook, the airlock, the fireplace, the doorway, the attic, the basement, the window...*

When Dorothy wakes up after the tornado has knocked her unconscious, she leaves the black and white world of Kansas and enters the Technicolor world of Oz through a hallway. Look how the corridor is shot to form a threshold between two worlds: the world of origin and the world of journey. The placement of such a threshold literally takes us from Act One into Act Two, approximately thirty minutes into the film. As discussed in earlier chapters, usually there is a threshold guardian waiting on the other side, whom the hero must defeat before continuing the journey.

Use of these thresholds can convey wanderlust, ambivalence, surprise, reluctance, hesitancy, cowardice, curiosity, revelation, breakthrough or a host of other emotions. The careful use and placement of such metaphors will go a long way toward building a relational value between your world of story and the hero's plight.

In *The Sound of Music*, when Maria leaves the nunnery to embark on her life with the Von Trapps, she exits through a series of gates, arches, and corridors. When she finally arrives, she faces wrought iron gates, a doorway and even an implacable butler who impedes her entry.

Look how a simple pawnshop exit becomes an insurmountable threshold for Butch in *Pulp Fiction*. It would be so easy for him to escape and leave Marsellus Wallace to the hillbilly rapists, but he can't leave without sacrificing his own honor. (He comes from a long line of war heroes.) This way, he is forced to return to the underworld, but only after selecting a weapon suitable to his more valorous aspirations.

In *The Exorcist* (written by William Peter Blatty), the door to Linda Blair's bedroom grows and glows more eerily with each visitation, making us all the more leery and reluctant to go beyond it.

In *Ghostbusters* (written by Dan Ackroyd and Harold Ramis), a refrigerator door becomes a threshold between reality and the supernatural realm.

## LEGENDS, MAPS and COMPASSES

The on-screen inclusion of a map can go a long way toward graphically showing where the hero is and where he must go. Don't waste these excellent devices by being too brief. They are a vital and visual way of involving the audience and informing us of the topographical locales pertinent to your hero's quest.

*Casablanca* opens with a long introduction, replete with a map to show the isolation of the story's locale. This will later take on new poignancy when we end the story at an airport—the only way out.

*Raiders of the Lost Ark* uses maps, models, miniatures, jewelry, book illustrations and talismans to inform us of the mystical nature of the Ark of the Covenant and the globetrotting involved in finding it. Though we hop from South America to an American university, to Tibet and the Middle East, the audience can see and understand just where the story is taking place from scene to scene.

## SCALE MINIATURES AND MODELS

*Gladiator*, which won the Best Picture Academy Award® in 2000, provides an excellent example of miniature in the world of story. Commodius has a scale model of the Coliseum in his quarters, which he uses to plot the humiliation and ultimate destruction of Maximus. As his obsession with the Festival of Games grows, we see him brooding over the model as he plots his nefarious plans.

In *The Bridge on the River Kwai*, we see David Lean's excellent use of a miniature bridge to heighten the stakes in our hero's quest to blow it up. Likewise, in Stanley Kubrick's *The Shining*, a scale model of the sinister labyrinth foreshadows the ending when the young boy uses it to ensnare his ax-wielding father. In George Pal's *The Time Machine,* a tiny scale model of Well's invention increases our anticipation of seeing the real thing. In *Star Wars,* the use of miniature holographic projections informs us of Princess Leia's desperate need of assistance from Obi-Wan Kenobi. In *Citizen Kane,* the metaphorical placement of the miniature snow crystal evokes a time of nostalgia and innocence and lends great emotional power to the hero's primal incantation of "Rosebud."

The use of scale modeling and miniature effects is so profound they have become entire motion picture subjects, for example: *Tom Thumb; Honey, I Shrunk the Kids; The Incredible Shrinking Man, The Golden Voyage of Sinbad, The Borrowers, Jurassic Park, Gulliver's Travels, King Kong, Godzilla* and *Stuart Little.*

Arthur Rankin, of Rankin Bass Productions, the producer of those classic stop-motion family perennials such *as Frosty the Snowman* and *Rudolph,* the *Red Nose Reindeer,* once said (in a story meeting to a team of animation writers I'd assembled), "Oh yeah, Give me lots of big, little, little, big. Kids love that kind of shit!"

## PASSAGEWAYS, ENTRYWAYS AND GATES TO THE BEYOND
*Tunnels, tornadoes, vortexes, whirlpools, eddies, chimneys, launch pads, time tunnels...*

In situations that call for intensified action or dramatic emphasis, the screenwriter employs a physical narrowing of space. Sometimes these condensed arenas are used at various act breaks to further emphasize the segueing from one act to the next.

In *Moonstruck,* Johnny Cammareri asks Loretta to invite his brother to their wedding just as she is driving him to the airport. The scene takes place in the Midtown Tunnel and serves to intensify Johnny's request (the inciting incident) for Loretta to be the go-between and peacemaker between the two estranged brothers.

In *The Magnificent Seven* (written by William Roberts, Walter Bernstein and Walter Newman, based on *The Seven Samurai* by Akira Kurosawa), Yul Brynner and Steve McQueen come together in the beginning at a funeral procession in order to deliver an Hispanic man to a cemetery. A gauntlet is formed and the heroes must fight their way through it, emphasizing their willingness to fight to the death for extremely unpopular causes.

In *On the Waterfront* (written by Malcolm Johnson and Budd Schulberg), Marlon Brando has to leave the docks through an angry crowd of longshoremen, cursing and berating him for turning state's evidence against the mob boss who controls them. The entire thematic thrust of the motion picture is summed up in the one powerful *mise en scene*.

*The Fugitive* uses a wide variety of condensed locales and labyrinthine tunnels to intensify the hero's constant flight to freedom.

The finale of *The Terminator* (written by James Cameron, Gale Ann Hurd, William Wisher and Harlan Ellison), as well as the opening of *Terminator II* (written by James Cameron and William Wisher), uses a wide selection of tunnels, roadways, river basins and gauntlets to increase the intensity of action.

In *Mary Poppins* (written by Bill Walsh and Don DaGradi, based on the books by P.L. Travers), chimneys, sidewalk paintings, staircases and fireplaces play an important role in drawing fantastic and magical situations from commonplace urban settings and household artifacts.

In *The Silence of the Lambs*, Clarice gains entry to Hannibal Lecter through a maze of corridors, staircases and cell blocks inhabited by prison guards and the criminally insane. When she finally confronts Buffalo Bill, she battles him in pitch darkness and narrow basement passageways.

## TALISMANS, JEWELRY, ARTICLES OF CLOTHING, ANIMAL FAMILIARS

*The magic sword, the shield, a common bean, the cigar box, a spinning wheel, the apple, a music box, the glass slipper, the magic ring,*

*the magic crayon, a musical instrument, the parrot, raven, ferret,
dog or cat...*

A common device of the myth and fairy tale is to bring in various baubles, totems, gewgaws or animal companions that help humanize the hero, or sometimes his opponent. These numerous and sundry objects are very often nondescript and commonplace. At first, we do not attach a lot of importance to them, though our hero generally does. As the story unfolds, we see there is a lot more to it than we originally thought and this gives us insight as to the hero's good qualities of loyalty, vision and foresight. Similarly, when we endow particularly nasty villains with objects of power or animal familiars, it serves to humanize them and counteract their maniacal obsession with conquering the world.

When designing any of these devices, try to define an ironic, complimentary or contrasting theme to the character possessing it and then go to the opposite value. This will go a long way toward making your characters come alive on-screen. The following is a list of films where these objects of power are put to original and highly effective use:

In *Pulp Fiction*, Butch cleaves to his father's watch as a token of his connection to his ancestral war heroes. A family legacy of four generations of heroism in battle, makes Butch's return for the watch all the more crucial, and ultimately defines his choice to return to the basement where Marsellus Wallace is being viciously abused, and rescue him from the pit of pawnshop hell.

The bandit in Sergio Leone's *For a Few Dollars More* clings to a musical pocket cameo that belonged to a young woman he raped and killed. The object becomes an important device for bringing in elements of the backstory as he reminisces through a foggy haze of marijuana induced memories.

In *Witness*, John Book's gun takes on a talisman-like quality as it serves to define his crippling moral deficiency and heavy reliance upon blunt force. This becomes especially significant later, when, in the absence of the gun, he defeats his enemies by drowning them in grain, or disarming them with his newfound moral awareness.

In *Experiment in Terror, Fatal Attraction, Kramer vs. Kramer, Sorry, Wrong Number, Dial M for Murder, I Saw What You Did, Twin Peaks* and *Rear Window,* a simple telephone becomes a pivotal device for intensifying the suspense and outcome of the story. With each piercing ring, our sense of well-being grows increasingly on-edge and unnerved.

## FLASHBACKS, DREAM SEQUENCES, MONTAGES, AND HALLUCINATIONS

Contrary to popular use, these devices should be used as a part of the forward movement of the story. Most new writers make the mistake of hitting a wall in their natural story development and then resort to flashbacks or dream sequences to keep their personal momentum going. Unfortunately, this breaks up the flow and can create aggravating lulls in the pacing. If your story requires the use of flashbacks, make sure they serve the forward progression of a tale, and are not just employed out of laziness, cliché, or to fill (valuable) page space.

For example, in *Casablanca* the writers interrupt the storyline midway through the film to show Ilsa and Rick's relationship in Paris. While arguably, this was an effective convention for that time period, it hopelessly dates the material and wears on our interest. The use of this flashback only serves to dramatize what we already know. The real information is not that they were in love, but why Ilsa abandoned Rick at the train station.

In *Memento,* the Polaroid snapshot is used ingeniously as an ongoing plot device to trigger new details, flashbacks, flash forwards and other important expository information that continually update, refresh or introduce new plot detail and information.

In the absence of such brilliant plot devices, do not use flashbacks, montages or dream sequences to rehash old material, or to exposit superfluous details. This information can best be imparted through clever foreshadowing, personality traits or inventive dialogue. If your script relies too heavily on flashbacks, try restructuring the story. Overuse of flashbacks is a sure signal to studio readers that they are reading the work of a novice.

In *In the Line of Fire*, a simple photo pinned to an assassin's wall links Secret Service Agent Frank Horgan to the Kennedy assassination. Since that fateful day in Dallas, Horgan has been consumed by self-doubt, unsure he has the fortitude to throw himself in the line of an assassin's bullet. This inner flaw makes us wonder if he can succeed or not. By placing the exposition of this fact in the hands of his opponent, the writer has expertly turned the backstory into a series of attacks by the opponent, and thus moves the story forward, rather than backward.

Imagine *Chinatown* if we stopped Jake Gittes relentless pursuit of the truth to flashback to his days as a beat cop in Chinatown. To do so would be totally unnecessary as this information comes out gradually through the forward progression of the story. All that we need to know is that he tried to help someone then and wound up with an innocent getting hurt. This memory resonates more as events conspire to return Gittes once again to his old nemesis, Chinatown.

## FILM LANGUAGING AND ACTION SEQUENCING

Forget about trying to impress the reader with the use of film school lingo such as montage, parallel edit, smash cut and the like. You will succeed in boring them rather than interesting them. Technical language and redundant technical descriptions only serve to put barriers between your story and the reader.

Montage is just another name for action sequencing and is used to convey rapid plot progression. It should not be imposed upon your story just because you've grown tired of solving problems. The movie *Blow* is one of the most amateurish examples of montage sequencing in modern cinema. The story spine is so wildly all over the place, all the director can do is move his characters around like stick figures in search of a story. I'm not saying that this is the writer's fault, for the entire project evokes a head-scratching, "What were they thinking?"

Action sequences are a series of shortly linked scenes that build a story's momentum and emotional core in rapid progression. They are a function of structure and plot and should move quickly along to determine a plot point or strike an emotional chord. You will need to write these scenes with powerful hard-hitting words, and suspense-filled details. Do not label these sequences. Done correctly, your reader should have no problem understanding your process.

Dream sequencing and hallucinations should not be arbitrary contrivances, but should be drawn from the story's theme, the main character's shadow and inner flaw. To write these effectively you must know a great deal about your character's psychological makeup, problems and aspirations.

Hence, Alex, the psychopathic killer in *A Clockwork Orange* (written by Anthony Burgess and Stanley Kubrick), is obsessively driven by the music of Beethoven, hallucinogens, wild acts of cruelty, robbery and "ultraviolence," all out of an intense desire to elevate himself from his dreary working-class roots. He delights in torturing his upper class victims in order to feel equal, if not superior, to them. So, when he unwittingly becomes the "cause celebre" for two vying political parties, he fancies himself as having joined their ranks, and being free to resume his obsessions with their approval. The dream sequence at the end features Alex in a sexual romp with a beautiful society girl, while elegantly dressed noblemen and women look on and applaud. The use of dream sequencing, hallucination and surrealistic fantasy is an excellent medium to express this scathing look at modern society and its corrupt culture of politics.

## TIMELINES, TIME BOMBS AND TICKING CLOCKS

The screenwriting adept uses a wide variety of tools to intensify the action, emotion and visual outcome of a story, while also creating an overall time frame that focuses the audience's attention on events that must transpire before the story concludes.

Alfred Hitchcock illustrates the timeline principle to François Truffaut by relating the story of a couple seated in a dining car holding a pleasant conversation. "Now put a bomb under the table and watch the whole dynamic change." With the introduction of bomb on a plane, a bus, a train, or a roller coaster, a story's timeline shrinks dramatically. By condensing the timeline, your main character will have to defeat his opponent and obtain his desire within a finite amount of time. This simple plot device can help increase the suspense and action of any story.

In *D.O.A.* (written by Russell Rouse and Clarence Greene), a man stumbles into a police station to report a murder: his own. Through the agency of a slow-acting poison, he has only twenty-four hours to solve his own murder.

In *Murder on the Orient Express* (written by Agatha Christie, Paul Dehn and Anthony Schaffer), famed Belgian detective Hercule Poirot must investigate a gruesome murder that has been committed on a luxury train trapped in a snowstorm. As a plot device, the murder must be solved before the train is rescued, or risk the outside incursion of authorities, who might be less sympathetic to the high class conspirators onboard.

In *Nick of Time* (written by Patrick Sheane Duncan), Johnny Depp's character has until 1:30 PM to assassinate the Governor of California or his daughter will be killed. The gimmick of this action film is that the story is told in real time. Decide for yourself if it works or not.


## SEASONAL, SOCIAL AND MAGICAL TRANSITIONS

By placing a story around a particular holiday, the audience anticipates the final resolution coming in time for the big celebration. The holiday event you choose should have a significant social theme that contradicts, compliments or transcends your story's theme. This allows feuding family members who clash and conflict to adjust and accommodate before the final Thanksgiving or Christmas Day feast (*Hannah and Her Sisters, Home for the Holidays, Parenthood, Home Alone, A Christmas Carol, All I Want for Christmas, Holiday Inn, Jingle All the Way; Planes, Trains and Automobiles*).

*The Big Chill* hosts an impressive ensemble of characters who gather together for a friend's funeral. The characters reflect, renew acquaintances and reminisce over a three-day period, with the film's beginning and ending staged appropriately around their arrivals and departures.

*Independence Day* stages its alien invasion around the Fourth of July, a day of great cultural significance for most Americans. What better social event exists for this tale of imperialistic aggression and the need to fight back?

*Groundhog Day* uses this comically bizarre and arcane ritual to tell the hilarious and provocative story of a misanthropic weatherman trapped in time.

*Halloween, Friday the 13th, The Wicker Man, Sleepy Hollow* and *E.T.* also use their holiday settings as plot devices to evoke the traditions, costumes and superstitions of past belief systems.

*Close Encounters of the Third Kind* creates its own spectacular social event and concludes its omnibus telling of alien contact by converging on Devil's Tower for the grand finale.

*Sense and Sensibility, Much Ado About Nothing, Four Weddings and a Funeral, Sleepless in Seattle, My Best Friend's Wedding* and about a thousand other love stories, use the occasion of a wedding or coupling to resolve their lovelorn characters' plight.

### Magical Transitions

In the myth, the fairy tale, or even some of the inverted myths, the world of story will undergo a "magical" change as a result of the hero's actions. While action films will find a way to blow something sky high at the film's finale, fantasy films will require an entire "magical" make-over.

In both Disney and Cocteau's *Beauty and the Beast*, the enchanted castle of the beast is transformed to its fairy tale grandeur after the beast performs his final heroic act of self-sacrifice.

In *The Wizard of Oz*, when Dorothy breaks the spell holding the flying monkeys and guards when she unwittingly melts the Wicked Witch of the West.

In *The Music Man*, Professor Harold Hill vindicates himself and transforms the stern countenance of Iowa City into a musical, magical place of wonderment and joy.

In Dickens' *A Christmas Carol*, Ebeneezer Scrooge's transformation ends on Christmas Day, and all of his hard-earned soul-searching makes Christmas morning an even more joyful occasion than usual.

In *Field of Dreams*, one man's obstinate belief in his own inner voice transforms a simple cornfield into a magical baseball diamond.

In *High Plains Drifter* and *Unforgiven*, the avenging angel brings down murder and mayhem, and this cathartic action on the town initiates a cleansing and need to start over again.

## PERIOD PIECES AND COSTUME DRAMAS

It is my ardent belief that there is no reason on earth to do a costume drama or period piece unless you can shed some light on our contemporary human and social dilemmas. The films of James Ivory and Ishmael Merchant teeter back and forth precariously in this regard. While *A Room with a View* and *Howards End* are excellent examples of telling a story in period while commenting on the soul-crushing effects of an overly mannered society, *Jefferson in Paris* leaves us wondering what exactly they had in mind. As handsome as these productions are, without relevant thematic resonance to our present mores, we are left with little more than pleasant diversions (and for my hard-earned ticket dollars, I want provocation and not just evocation).

In adapting *Sleepy Hollow* for live-action, I was faced with a troublesome flaw at the very core of the tale. Washington Irving's story is little more than a social parody about a Jewish schoolteacher aspiring to marry the daughter of a wealthy Dutch landowner (Ichabod, in Hebrew means "no glory"). It remains a slightly racist, if not, dated, social commentary for its time (circa 1810). The problem I faced was how to shape real flesh and blood characters from what were essentially caricatures.

While researching and visiting East Hampton, New York and other colonial British and Dutch enclaves, I chanced upon a local cable station where the Reverend William Sloane Coffin was giving a televised speech. He was talking about the difficult leaps in consciousness we must make as we stand on the brink of a new global awareness. With the prospect of instant worldwide communication, multi-national corporations and glaring ecological and environmental issues, we can no longer afford to consider ourselves exclusive nationals of one body-politic, but as ever-expanding members of a vast global community.

He went on to point out how, in many ways, our modern situation mirrors that of our colonial ancestors who faced becoming citizens of a newly forming "United States," The idea of the provincial folks of one colony "uniting" with their distant neighbors in another, was as inconceivable then, as it is for us to now envision the prospect of paying world income tax.

Unwittingly, the good Reverend gave me the "hook" for my adaptation. What were the people of Sleepy Hollow afraid of? What might drive a simple country bumpkin like Bram Van Brunt to adopt the drastic measures of dressing up as a headless phantom, just to chase off a hapless suitor? To lift this out of its cartoon origins into a true to life, flesh and bone horror story there had to be something modern audiences could relate to, root for and ultimately, fear.

So, what do we share in common with the simple folks of Sleepy Hollow? Fear: of the future, of change, of cultural integration and expansion. Fear, of a foreign family settling in next to us and despoiling our in-bred notion of Americana. It is the same today as we witness the current proliferation of militant race groups. The "hook" then for my story was that of a small community crippled by fear and how their ignorant, petty and misguided machinations lead to an even greater evil. Thus providing the theme, *fear of change leads to ghostliness.*

Sleepy Hollow became a metaphor for all of us whose fear of change condemns us to live in the past—to become as living ghosts forever doomed to repeat the same haunts and unconscious patterns. This insight became even more startlingly real when I visited the modern day Sleepy Hollow: North Tarrytown, NY. It is a historical preserve, where they still farm, cook, dress and live exactly as they did in Washington Irving's time. In other words, they got what they wanted!

## NARRATION

Beginning writers often resort to employing a narrator or explanatory crawl as a means of finding their own voice or setting up the world of story in the opening act. Unfortunately, this device is overused and usually abused. Remember, screenwriting for film where you have to give the audience what they want, but not what they expect. In other words, you have to always play against the obvious. So, like the flashback, the use of a narrator can be either an unnecessary contrivance or a compelling tool—in the right hands. The fundamental disadvantage is that it serves to set up an unnecessary buffer between the audience and the characters of your story.

If narration is still your first choice, I would have to advise against it. Try to find more challenging ways to reel your audience in. If nothing else works, try to draw the power of your narrative from the theme rather than just describing what you're seeing. It is a disaster to simply have your narrator point out what is already visually presented on the screen.

*Don't tell—Show!*
*Don't narrate—Create!*

The diagonal crawl that appears in the opening sequence of *Star Wars* serves a dual function of introducing us to a completely foreign environment, while simultaneously evoking the cliffhanger film serials of the past. "A long time ago, in a galaxy, far away. . ." This technically innovative introduction establishes an immediate sense of wonder, awe and suspense.

The pedestrian and rather perfunctory "dedication" that introduces the film *Rob Roy* only serves to anchor the story in the past without contemporary relevance. Why go out of your way to tell us we are about to see a historical reenactment? It's kind of obvious, isn't it? When I go to the cinema, I want to be a part of the characters and feel their challenges and conflicts. I want to draw my own conclusions about their lives and struggles—I don't want to be told how heroic they were.

In *Unforgiven*, the lyrical fairy tale-like music and silhouette of William Munney burying Claudia Feathers sets up a haunting, yet sympathetic, tone to an otherwise extremely violent story. Note how the crawl brilliantly bookends the film with this simple, poetic legend.

In *True Romance* (written by Roger Avary and Quentin Tarantino), Patricia Arquette's unassuming and sweetly accented Southern drawl speaks to us over shots of Detroit. This sets up a contrast of values: the zeal of romantic love juxtaposed with the hard, impersonal blight of the city—the last imaginable place for true romance to occur.

In *Barry Lyndon* (written by Stanley Kubrick, based on the novel by William Makepeace Thackeray), Michael Hordern's eloquent narration evokes the literary richness of Thackeray's original story. Unfortunately, its overuse weighs the material down and reduces the characters to robotic stick figures. It is a stunning visual masterpiece, but in the end a sadly deficient drama. In contrast, the use of narration in Tony Richardson's *The Adventures of Tom Jones* serves not only to evoke Fielding's literary masterpiece, but also plays perfectly along with the hero's unspoken psyche and pantomime.

In *Romeo and Juliet* (1968) (written by Franco Brusati, Maestro D'Amico and Franco Zeffirelli, based on the play by William Shakespeare), the opening and ending narrative evokes a moral authority to the film and book-ends the tale with a succinct emotional imperative: "For never was there a tale of woe more than that of Juliet and her Romeo." Simply exquisite.

In *To Kill a Mockingbird* (written by Horton Foote, based on the novel by Harper Lee), Kim Stanley's narration at the beginning and end of the film serves to punctuate this bittersweet coming of age drama in the American South. I saw the film when I was eleven years old and have never forgotten it. So much so that— twenty years later—as I sat watching *Sophie's Choice*, the same lyrical narration sent me swooning back to that moment. It was no small coincidence that Alan Pakula directed *Sophie's Choice* and produced *To Kill a Mockingbird*.

In *Blade Runner* (the original theatrical release), both an explanatory crawl and narrative voice are employed to set up the world of story and to evoke a "film noir" resonance to the piece. The crawl is pure exposition and not particularly poetic or involving, while Ford's Chandleresque voice-over proves more of a gimmick. In the final sequence, Ford's terse wrap-up seems almost comical. (Note that the cult success of the film led to the release of the Director's Cut, which is blessedly free of this pedantic narration.)

In *Sunset Boulevard* (written by Charles Brackett, D.M. Marshan Jr. and Billy Wilder), William Holden's narrative gives a blistering account of Tinseltown mores and ambitions in the Golden Age of Hollywood. His relentless acidity accentuates the humor and tragedy of this inverted Cinderella story. The whole effect of seeing his body floating in a pool while his voice-over tells us the story of how he got there becomes a scathing social commentary of the period, as well as a timeless satire.

In *A Clockwork Orange*, Malcolm McDowell's narration as Alex evokes sympathy in both a self-serving and contradictory fashion. On the screen, he feigns compliance and conversion to the prison chaplain, while the narrative and dream sequencing on-screen conveys hilarious visions of a psychopath's affinity for the Bible.

The need to find a narrative voice is both good and proper, but your energy is better spent applying it to the written style of your screenplay, rather then creating a separate and specific voice-over. A separate narrator can be redundant and should be used sparingly, if at all.

# THE NINTH STAGE

## Working in Genre

*GENRE(s): A kind, sort, type or category in which films are classified*

Determining the type of genre you want to specialize in is a quest. It is similar to finding the theme you most believe in. Most writers begin their careers by experimenting with a wide variety of genres. This is healthy because it expands your vocabulary and knowledge of story structure and character development in all areas. The goal is to create a body of work and proficiency in craft that is uniquely your own.

The selection of a genre not only determines the subtle characteristics of your film's dialogue, world, theme and characters but is also an essential tool for determining its intended audience. Whatever you decide, be it horror, drama, romance, action, comedy or adventure, it helps to ask yourself, "Who is going to want to see this film?

If the predominant qualities favor romance, comedy and fantasy, this will indicate a more general audience. If it is slanted towards action, adventure and violence, an entirely different audience should be considered. It is important to know the advantages and disadvantages of whatever genre you choose, so you can make intelligent decisions accordingly.

When I am working in a specific genre, I like to immerse myself in the attitudes, worlds, action, characters and dialogue of my story. That is to say, if I'm writing a love scene, I watch only love stories; an action sequence, action films; period piece, period films. In this way I not only build on my film references, I take in only what I'm putting out.

The greatest way to earn respect from directors, actors, studio executives and other industry craft persons is to have a profound and well-versed expertise in motion pictures. Be very careful about naming these references within the text and dialogue of your script. Most film or television references tend to be highly personal or obscure, and this connotes a kind of laziness on the writer's part. For instance, Quentin Tarantino and Roger Avery use various tag lines from television shows, movies and radio of the '70s to humanize their outlaws. It is funny to hear a hitman talking about Arnold the pig from *Green Acres*. It is shocking to watch a sadistic murderer torture a policeman to the lyrics of "Stuck in the Middle with You." In lesser hands (as in the movie *Fled*), the arbitrary use of film references becomes tiresome and hokey. One has the cloying sense of the writer's ego overtaking his on-screen characters.

Don't be discouraged if you don't possess an elaborate reference system as yet. Knowledge, as with everything else in life, is an accumulative process that begins at birth and shouldn't end until you do.

## TIMING IS EVERYTHING

*"Observe due measure, for right timing is in all things the most important factor."*
—Hesiod

Certain types of genres wax and wane in popularity with the vicissitudes of contemporary culture: Westerns, science fiction, musicals and horror films all seem particularly susceptible to this ebb and flow. Most "down times" are corrected with the introduction of a hit movie in one specific genre, after which an onslaught of terrible follow-ups will send the genre back into oblivion. You will need to anticipate these trends as a part of your job as a screenwriter. Do not be disheartened if your love of a particular genre seems outdated and unpopular with current trends, it will return, and perhaps it will be your innovative work that brings it back.

With the recent release of Baz Luhrmann's *Moulin Rouge*, a rash of articles appeared in the nation's newspapers trumpeting either the demise, or the Lazarus-like "return," of the movie musical as a genre. Of course, this is a lot of hyperbolic claptrap (the musical has been quite successfully revived since the mid-eighties with Ashman and Mencken's brilliant collaboration with Disney animators on *Beauty and the Beast, The Little Mermaid* and *Aladdin*).

While a film release can renew or even awaken mass interest in a particular genre, each film must be evaluated on its own. No matter how good or bad the movie experience is, the next genre-related film down the pike must be able to stand on its own merit. Just look at the number of films being touted as "the next *Pulp Fiction*" years after the debut of the original. *Pulp Fiction* was not just the re-emergence of a genre; it was the birth of a new one. Sure, its anti-structural theme has deep cinematic and archetypal roots, but the pace, originality and authorship raised the bar on how outlaw stories should be told.

I remember the dismay of some of my colleagues at the College of Santa Fe film school as the student body (and certain subversive faculty members) uniformly embraced *Pulp Fiction* with wild, unbridled, enthusiasm. You would have thought old Elvis was shaking his hips again. "Pornography!" one erudite professor moaned, "Sheer pornography!" Yet, its box-office and critical acclaim at both Cannes and the Academy Awards confirmed the authentic birth of a cultural and artistic phenomenon.

On the other hand, James Cameron's *Titanic* was one of the most successful pictures of all time, and yet it certainly did not spawn a herd of costumed romantic tragedies in its wake. Maybe the studio pitch for *A Perfect Storm* was for a "poor man's *Titanic*," but I can't imagine any self-respecting film executive actually believing this would translate to success at the box office.

The makers of *Moulin Rouge* publicly compared their effort to the precedent-setting *Titanic*, because it happened to be a romantic tragedy costume drama. While they may have been initially encouraged by the latter's success, so many years between releases should have sobered any chance of a generic tie-in.

I think it was Alan Ladd Jr. who once opined that "in Hollywood, 'forever' means about three years." I think this is a good rule of thumb for all comebacks, professional careers and genre-related offspring.

Obviously, you should try to avoid releasing that big-budget space opera script you just completed after the last four bombed at the box-office. After I sold my screenplay, *Cupid*, to Amblin Entertainment, I began looking around for another animated musical to write. I focused on biblical stories, not for their theology, but for their rich blending of magic, romance and myth. My eight-year-old son often remarked how *The Ten Commandments* was his favorite film, and indeed, I recalled the very same sentiment when I was his age. I eventually settled on King Solomon as my hero, for no other figure in history is more associated with wisdom, mysticism and romance. Halfway through the script I convinced myself that Hollywood was not ready to produce an animated musical in a biblical setting and abandoned the project. Six months later, my lawyer/agent inquired about the script and urged me to finish it. I spent the next three months completing, polishing and preparing to pitch it. The very day I finished it, DreamWorks announced their first animated release would be *The Prince of Egypt*, based on the story of Moses. I can only speculate that if I had not given up when I did, DreamWorks might have been persuaded to produce *The Song of Solomon* instead. The lesson here is that while market savvy is good, following your instincts is always preferred.

The following is a list of movie genres with historical and analytical guidelines. It is not a complete list of all films in all genres, but merely ones that I feel have been influential.

## THE MUSICAL AND THE ANIMATED MUSICAL

When *The Sound of Music* debuted in 1965, it remained the reigning box-office champ for many, many years. Then, in the early seventies, interest in both musicals and animated films seemed to have died out altogether. In the late eighties, with the debut of Disney's animated musicals like *The Little Mermaid, Beauty and the Beast* and *Aladdin,* new life, wonder and merriment resuscitated both art forms. An examination of how this happened gives invaluable insights into the nature of both genres.

After the death of Walt Disney, with the lackluster performance of films like *Robin Hood, The Fox and the Hound* and *The Black Cauldron,* the Disney studio strongly reevaluated its commitment to the art that Uncle Walt pioneered. Then, through the hard fought enterprise of Roy Disney, Walt's nephew, and a young protégé, Peter Snyder, a ray of hope appeared on the horizon. Disney and Snyder were touting the work of a relatively unknown composer/lyricist team of Alan Mencken and Howard Ashman. While the two had enjoyed some mild successes off-Broadway with *Little Shop of Horrors* and *God Bless You, Mister Rosewater,* the true showcase of their genius would come with their first animated feature for Disney, *The Little Mermaid.*

In the seventies, when the Walt Disney company was trying to emulate Walt's unique gift for storytelling, Ashman and Mencken were developing their craft for the musical stage. Matching them up with the floundering animation department at Disney proved to be pure inspiration. All that was missing was the new shift in management to Michael Eisner and Jeffrey Katzenberg, and the rest, as they say, is history. What made the difference?

Ashman and Mencken understood that for musicals to work, the songs had to originate from within the characters, rather than appear just as entertaining interludes. This simple innovation helped define what worked and what did not work in the animated story. With the need to create characters that complimented the sophistication, wit and emotional depth of Ashman and Mencken's songs, the Disney animators were forced to develop more complicated characters and storylines that did not merely rely on animation for animation sake. In other words, having a bull and a frog sing and dance together may be a perfect use of music and animation, but is it emotionally involving or even desirable?

One thing Walt Disney understood, as did Ashman and Mencken, is that animation is not just for children. To succeed in the marketplace, the characters and story must appeal to adults as well. When this simple principle is ignored you have stories such as *The Secret of N.I.M.H, An American Tale, All Dogs Go to Heaven, Thumbelina, The Swan Princess* and *Ferngully*. When the characters, story and music achieve a sophistication of fantasy and emotion, you have films like *The Lion King, The Little Mermaid, Beauty and the Beast* and *Aladdin*.

With the advent of Ashman and Mencken's theatrical sensibilities, all of a sudden we were watching scenes like Ariel, the little mermaid, in her secret grotto singing about her most heartfelt desires and yearnings. Or the intelligent and bookish Belle longing for a life beyond the commonplace in *Beauty and the Beast*. What child—or adult, for that matter—could resist such soulful musings? Well, they couldn't, and the result has led to some smashing blockbuster successes and the subsequent revival of two classic art forms.

## MUSICALS

Musicals seem to work best when tied to either the myth (*The Lion King, Cabaret, The Sound of Music*), the fairy tale (*The Producers, Beauty and the Beast, My Fair Lady*), the blithe angel (*The Music Man*), or tragic/dramatic structures (*Moulin Rouge, Evita* and *Les Miserables*). Recent attempts to develop musicals from horror genres have met with decidedly mixed results. In the case of Andrew Lloyd Weber's *Phantom of the Opera*, the achievement was massive. Less so with the unfortunate *Jekyll and Hyde*, by the confounding Frank Wildhorn, where the love story is but an obvious and awkward contrivance. *The most important consideration in writing any musical is to determine whether or not the underlying material is inherently musical.*

The star-crossed assignation between a writer and a courtesan working at the famed Moulin Rouge in fin de siecle Paris should be the perfect setting for an old time musical extravaganza. And indeed, it might have been a great success were it not for the unfortunate choice of music that mires it down in fifties and seventies Americana. For my taste, the unfortunate choice of "Diamonds Are A Girl's Best Friend," "Your Song" or "Silly Love Songs" gives this otherwise exhilarating extravaganza the sense of riding a roller coaster in a cart with square wheels. I suspect the misfortune to be more of cultural faux pas than a creative one. How was Baz Luhrmann, an Australian director, to gauge the deadening impact his musical repertoire would make on an otherwise delightfully original effort?

I must admit a bias against the operetta style, where the players constantly sing to one another. As a writer I yearned for the more old-fashioned musical that mixes story and dialogue with music. I found John Leguizamo's Toulouse-Lautrec absolutely wonderful, but disappointingly underutilized. My writer's mind wanted to see the relationship between Christian and his bohemian mentor better defined.

*The Wizard of Oz* is a perfect musical myth, as the songs spring from the hopes, fears, and desires of the main characters.

*The Sound of Music* is an excellent example of an underlying story that is inherently musical, as it tells of a talented novitiate enlivening an oppressed household through her gift of music.

*Cabaret* gives us an ingenious insight to the social attitudes of pre-Nazi Germany as the country spirals from moral decadence into fascism. The deft interweaving of musical numbers between Liza Minelli's Sally Bowles and Joel Grey's Master of Ceremonies portrays an especially poignant and haunting view of a society in total moral collapse.

*Mary Poppins* is an excellent blithe angel musical where the fantastical adventures of Mary, Burt, Jane and Michael counter-balance the stern, overly mannered, child-quashing remonstrations of George Banks.

*Meet Me in St. Louis* is a sublime look at turn-of-the-century values as the future comes to a traditional, small town household in the form of the St. Louis World's Fair of 1903. The soulful romantic yearnings and disappointment of this family of young women coming of age generated more than its share of popular songs and remains one of the best musicals ever filmed.

MUSICALS
*Absolute Beginners, An American in Paris, Bells Are Ringing, Blue Hawaii, The Blues Brothers, Bye-Bye Birdie, The Commitments, The Cotton Club, Cry-Baby, Dirty Dancing, Fame, Footloose, Funny Face, Funny Girl, Gigi, Grease, High Society, Holiday Inn, Inside Daisy Clover, Jailhouse Rock, The Mambo Kings, Mo' Better Blues, Nashville, Popeye, The Rocky Horror Picture Show, Sarafina, Sgt. Pepper's Lonely Hearts Club Band, The Slipper and the Rose, A Star is Born, Tommy, Top Hat, West Side Story, The Wiz*

The singing and dancing antics of a group of street-hustling Dead End Kids in Disney's *Newsies* is anything but musical fare. Critics described this lackluster attempt as *Matewan* with music, or *Oliver* without it.

Studying musicals is a great way to learn about narrative structure and the required art of segues and sequencing. Musical plots are generally lucid and uncomplicated, because of the time allotted for the actual songs. This same principle applies to action as well as comedies, where one must sacrifice plot complexities in a compressed need for time. The extent of how successfully you balance these elements will contribute to the effectiveness of your musical.

Here is a general template for successful musicals:

1. Introduce the main character's world(s), its problems and virtues in a communal opening (song).
2. Focus attention on the main character and show his or her unique placement in the world (plot).
3. State the main character's desire (song) and reveal the relationships with close allies and the romantic interest (plot and possible song).
4. The inciting incident (plot).
5. Introduce the opponent and reveal his overall scheme (song and plot).
6  Link the main character with the opponent and emphasize their thematic differences (song).
7. Follow the main character as they act to fulfill their desire (plot).
8. Reveal the main character at the mercy of the opponent (plot and song).
9. Show the main character's personal triumph (plot).
10. Reveal the impact on the world of story (song).

When including lyrics in the body of your script, either original or published, make sure there is either a thematic, character-driven or structural purpose for doing so. Otherwise, it is best to simply indicate the song parenthetically within the narrative text (i.e. "suggested song here") and leave the rest to the composer.


## ANIMATION

Never has there been a more schizophrenic film legacy than that of the animated film. What started off as a stop-motion novelty (Georges Meliere), developed into a windfall for comic strip merchandisers, tabloid cartoonists, and political satirists (Windsor McKay, Max and Dave Fleischer, Tex Avery, Chuck Jones and Bob Clampett). Eventually it became the mainstay for children and family fare through Walt Disney's animated dream machine. In the wake of Walt's demise, animation became forever targeted towards children and families, and for a while this made it indistinguishable from other mindless pabulum. Even today, novice studio executives don't quite know what to do with animation and the result is that they second-guess, water down and eviscerate the stories into oblivion.

If you intend to write for animation make sure that the material is reasonably sophisticated and inherently animate in the first place. Unless there is a natural fantasy element to the story, you might ask yourself why not do it in live action? The rule of thumb for animation used to be based on the number of animal or fantasy characters within the text of the story. However, with recent advancements in computer animation, the line between live-action and animation is practically nonexistent.

For animation to work best it must support two areas of engagement: fantasy and emotion. Obviously it is much harder to suspend an audience's disbelief when your characters are—by their very construction—two-dimensional. To breathe life into them, the audience must care about their hopes, dreams and problems, and really fear the forces that oppose them. (Because of the wrongheaded notion that animation is for kids, and that kids are supremely stupid rather than simply immature, most studios shy away from compelling arch-villains; this serves only to dilute the conflict.) The overarching problem of a family of field mice trying to move their home out of the way of a housing development (*The Secret of N.I.M.H.*) is hardly blockbuster fare. Fantasy and emotional involvement must be inherent in the underlying elements of the original premise.

Thankfully, animated films like *Ferngully: The Last Rain Forest, The Swan Princess, The Pagemaster* and *The Trumpet of the Swan* are a dying breed, as they aspire to add fantasy elements to "reality" (read: human) based stories forcing every effort to fantasize them to come off as being contrived and artificial. Talking books, frogs and feisty fairies—while certainly unusual enough—do not a fantasy make. The story itself must be inherently fantastic, such as *Beauty and the Beast, The Little Mermaid, Shrek, Toy Story, Aladdin* and *A Bug's Life*. These stories work because they deal in worlds and characters that are magical to begin with. Meanwhile Disney's *Pocahantas, Hunchback of Notre Dame* and *Hercules*, and Dreamwork's *El Dorado* and *The Prince of Egypt* fall disappointingly short of the mark because the fantasy elements are added on rather than being indigenous to the world and characters of the original story.

Ralph Bakshi, who had some initial success with his X-rated feature of *Fritz the Cat*, failed miserably when animating reality or human based subjects such as *American Pop*. Failing to understand the subtle texturing of fantasy, his attempt to cross over with efforts like *Wizards* and 1978's *The Lord of the Rings* proved equally disastrous. Animation requires a natural talent and imagination for the fantastical and emotional. It has proved merciless to all pretenders regardless of their credentials. For example, the computer-animated fairy tale *Shrek* required nine producers, seven writers and two directors to make it to the screen successfully. While in comparison, author/illustrator William Steig (of *New Yorker* fame) needed less than three pages of copy to tell the original story.

The result is a stunning visual treatment of an eighty-nine minute tale so insecure about itself, it has no choice but to overcompensate with an Eddie Murphy tour de force, that makes Gilbert Gottfried seem mellow. All of this while managing to reduce the comic genius of Mike Meyers to little more than a walk-on cameo. In the absence of true story craftsmanship, pro-

**ANIMATED FILMS**
*Allegro Non Troppo, An American Tale, Animal Farm, The Land Before Time, Snow White and the Seven Dwarfs, Pinocchio, Fantasia, Bambi, The Lion King, The Sword and the Stone, Sleeping Beauty, The Little Mermaid, Beauty and the Beast, Aladdin, Pocahontas, The Hunchback of Notre Dame, Hercules, Where the Wind Blows, Who Framed Roger Rabbit? The Prince of Egypt, Shrek, Toy Story, Antz, A Bugs Life, The Last Unicorn.*

ducers and studio executives are cowed into one contrivance after another, while missing the fundamental point of their story. Arguably, if there was more meat to it, Eddie could have taken a breather and some of us might have enjoyed the ride a little bit more. Don't get me wrong, I think Eddie Murphy is a brilliant voice-over artist, as evidenced in his *The PJs* television series, but the editorial decision to let him go, sadly limits this otherwise promising effort. It may be an historic achievement in technology, but the lackluster storytelling only leaves us wistful for what could have been.

When writing for animation you will need to consider the overall design of your characters. In this regard, Disney has set the standard for decades. However, with the ongoing breakthrough in computer animation, we are seeing a whole new wave of innovative character designs that may break the Disney franchise for good.

Over the years, movie-going audiences have embraced Disney as the King of Animated Film. Today's animation studios must meet or surpass the Disney standard, or risk losing their audience altogether. Sadly, this was my experience with *The Last Unicorn*. A stellar cast, a great screenplay, a bestselling novel, great music and an enchanted subject like the unicorn all could not overcome the poorly executed character designs, stilted animation and mediocre marketing campaign.

## COMEDY:
Any film, play, character, musical or literary composition dealing with a theme suitable for laughter, merriment or satire.

> *"The difference between a comedy and a tragedy is that in a comedy the characters figure out reality in time to do something about it."*
> —Bennett W. Goodspeed

The fundamental component of comedy sets itself up to attack specific people, institutions and beliefs that have become entrenched in superstition, dogma and convention. The great drama critic Horace Walpole observed, "The world is a comedy to those who think and a tragedy to those who feel."

While satire is the most direct and acerbic approach, it can quickly veer off into black comedy. Natural comedy seeks to expose our most commonplace human and social foibles with the abject purpose of making us laugh. It works on the same principle as the fairy tale, only in a more condensed fashion, as it deflates the mighty and uplifts the lowly. This set-up and pay-off cadence forms the dynamic in which the best comedies work. You slowly build it up and then very quickly pay it off. Just like when telling a joke, there is a long preamble and then the punch line. Slow inflation, quick deflation. Set-up, pay off. It is as natural as breathing.

The key in determining any genre you are working with, be it musical, animation, action or comedy, is to first evaluate the underlying comedic quotient if it is a comedy; the underlying fantasy quotient if it's a fantasy; the underlying musical component if it's a musical, and so on.

*Any comedy, whether character or plot driven, depends on the actors drawing on the strength of the primary theme in order to convey its underlying humor.*

The simple plot of five characters learning of the whereabouts of a vast sum of money becomes a comedy of epic proportion because of the aspirations and lengths we would all got to, to win that pot of gold. *It's a Mad, Mad, Mad, Mad World.*

The wild turns of a Black street hustler trading places with a Brahmin commodities trader at the mere whim of his eccentric employers is not only inherently funny, it becomes hysterical when we see them team up to bring their masters down. *Trading Places*

The comedic antics of a put-upon seven-year-old left alone to fend for himself works surprisingly well, especially when he is forced to match wits against two hapless burglars. *Home Alone*

The efforts of an unemployed, self-absorbed actor dressing up as a woman and becoming a major soap opera star are not only intrinsically funny, they become hysterical when we see him become the victim of male chauvinism. *Tootsie*

The idea of four eccentric eggheads forming a private enterprise that combats paranormal phenomena is very funny indeed, especially when their efforts lead them into battle against the primary forces of evil. *Ghostbusters*

The basic premise of sex-obsessed males in modern-day Los Angeles, trying to affect the "cool" lingo and fashions of the fifties, becomes a very funny and touching commentary on a new generation of "twenty-somethings." *Swingers*

If you are mixing genres—a desirable feature in this day and age—you will need to evaluate the underlying value of each generic component. The task is to mix and match them as an artist would a palette of primary colors. The result can provide a wide variety of desirable cinematic combinations. In each case, be sure to determine whether each specific genre is inherently funny, horrific, musical, suspenseful, fantastic or romantic.

Some examples of mixed comedy genres are:

Horror/Comedy/Romance
Romantic/Comedy/Thriller
Comedy/Action/Mystery
Musical/Comedy/Fantasy

When you decide to mix genres, it is good to stay true to the principles of each, lest you send crossed signals to the audience and confuse them. You want to surprise them, yes, but confusing them is an absolute no-no.

Confusing the audience is often the result of adding genres that destroy or alter the overall tone of the piece. For instance, in Jonathan Demme's *Something Wild* (a comedy/romance/thriller), the story starts out as an quirky and delightful comedy, quickly develops into a romance, then becomes darkly serious. Personally,

COMEDIES
*Abbott and Costello, Ace Ventura, Airplane, The Awful Truth, Big, Bill and Ted's Excellent Adventure, Blazing Saddles, City Slickers, The Curse of the Pink Panther, Fast Times at Ridgemont High, Father of the Bride, Ferris Bueller's Day Off, A Fish Called Wanda, Ghostbusters, The Graduate, Harold and Maude, Harvey, Heathers, The Jerk, Little Shop of Horrors, Manhattan, The Man Who Came to Dinner, Mermaids, Modern Times, Monty Python and the Holy Grail, The Player, Police Academy, Porky's, Repo Man, Risky Business, Ruthless People, The Seven Year Itch, Sleeper, Splash, Stir Crazy, This is Spinal Tap, Tootsie, Trading Places, Victor/Victoria, What About Bob?, Zelig*

I liked the film, but this confusion seems to have limited its broad-based appeal at the box-office (though it did go on to become a bit of a cult hit).

Another example of confusing genres is *Boys on the Side* (a comedy/road picture/chick flick*)*. It starts out as your basic road picture, becomes a girl power movie, then collapses into a maudlin AIDS story. The mix and match creates an unsettling feeling in the viewer's mind and leaves audiences wondering, "What happened to the movie I was watching?"

In the hysterically funny, *Some Like It Hot* (an action/comedy/romance), the natural components of three genres blend easily to become one integrated whole, while keeping the underlying pace and tone light and upbeat. In this case, the basic premise is hilarious: Two struggling male musicians join an all-girl band in order to evade the Mob.

It is possible for a film to be too funny at the expense of the plot. The trick is to pace your comedic moments as you would any action film or musical. In each case, the plot stops while the action unfolds on-screen. The plot in the musical stops while the character's sing. In action genres, the plot stops while the action plays itself out and we wait for the outcome. In the limited environment of film stories, you can easily wear your audience down if you don't pace your comedic moments properly. This was exactly my experience when watching *Ace Ventura: When Nature Calls*. Because Jim Carrey is such a remarkable comedian, I laughed myself sick for about two thirds of the movie—and then promptly fell fast asleep. The comedy overwhelmed the plotline until I just didn't care anymore.


## LOVE STORIES

*"Love is a story we tell ourselves about someone else."*
—Virginia Woolfe

Oddly enough, love stories rarely have anything to do with love. The original romantic ballads of the eleventh century more often sought to correct a heavily patriarchal Judeo-Christian cosmology than they reflected on true masculine/feminine relationships. The birth of chivalrous love sought to restore a beleaguered feminine deity (The Virgin Mary) who had been suppressed by the church for thousands of years. Later, in the eighteenth and nineteenth centuries, the seduction of a pure and rarefied female was more of a socio-political conceit, contrived by poets, artists and social critics who sought to embarrass bourgeois values by spinning melodramatic tales of the seduction and downfall of the "virtuous" girl.

Today, the love story seeks to redress an imbalance in the masculine and feminine psyches. Unlike Eastern cultures, where this balance is achieved by going *inward,* in the west, we are taught to seek self-individuation and "wholeness" by coupling with a "significant other." The result is a nation of lovesick lonelyhearts, greeting card love-junkies and rampant co-dependency. Alas, as absurd as any Harlequin novel, the myth of romantic love is the stuff of pure fiction when it fails to represent our deeper, more spiritual yearnings.

However slow we are to learn it, we know that no one lives "happily ever after." The ecstatic fairy tale ending has moved into oblivion. The once commonplace epiphany of marriage, after an adventure as a kind of reward, is no longer that but is now often represented as a type of living death—a future we can only assume will descend into routine, stagnation, heartbreak, disillusionment, and, potentially, divorce. Today, the storyteller replaces "happily ever after" with a metaphorical or actual death and spiritual rebirth, where one or both of the amorous couple must die or be reborn, and their frustrated union is achieved in the hereafter. Since the audience knows that a perfect union is not achievable here on earth, we create stories where the couple must be "spiritualized" to obtain their goal:

Heathcliff and Kathy on the moors in Emily Brontë's *Wuthering Heights,* Patrick Swayze and Demi Moore in *Ghost,* "The love you shared here on earth, you take with you." Or in *Truly, Madly, Deeply* (referred to as the thinking man's *Ghost*), where the lesson about moving on in life and death is so poignantly proven.

*The English Patient,* far more than a mere love story, is really about identity and the self-serving superficial ways we misjudge the character of others. The only way we can ever really know someone, the writer says, is to experience how deeply they loved and how much they sacrificed to achieve it.

In many ways we are back to where we started, where love stories are more of a metaphor for the union of matter and spirit (Agape), as told in the Greek myth of *Cupid and Psyche.* Audiences still yearn for great love stories, but the screenwriter makes a grave mistake in contriving tales that cater only to the baser aspects without understanding the deeper aspirations of the genre.

In constructing a modern love story, the opponent/antagonist often serves as the romantic interest as well. In *Moonstruck,* the best of the modern examples of this genre, Loretta is driven to wrong conclusions about her life and seeks to abandon her true nature in favor of ritual and superstition. Ronny Cammareri then, is her perfect opponent, because he is emotional, passionate, untamed and unconventional. What we seek in their union is a "spiritual" release for both. The ending should be felt not as a reward, but as a personal epiphany, or as transcendence from suffering (*Sleepless in Seattle, The Truth about Cats and Dogs, If Lucy Fell, The Perez Family*).

## DETECTIVE STORIES/THRILLERS

The reason for the continuing popularity of this genre, and the eternal resuscitation of the detective/cop as hero, is not, in spite of contrary evidence, due to a national obsession with law enforcement officials. We regard detectives and policemen as heroes because they are seekers of the truth by their very vocation. Our fascination with them is very similar to the way the heroes of old once captured our imaginations. They leave a conventional world to journey through a murky underworld where they attempt to solve a personal and overarching mystery. In the detective story the hero's quest for a personal destiny is replaced with the solution of a mystery.

In *Vertigo* (written by Alec Coppel and Samuel Taylor, based on the novel *D'entre Les Morts* by Pierre Boileau and Thomas Narcejac), James Stewart's retired detective sets out to trail an old pal's philandering wife and winds up confronting his own dark obsessions and deeply flawed motivations.

In *Chinatown*, Jack Nicholson's emotionally blighted private eye sets out to solve the Water Commissioner's murder and winds up confronting his oldest nemesis: himself.

In *Witness*, John Book sets out to protect an eyewitness and solve the murder of an undercover police officer; he ends up confronting his own glaring self-righteousness.

In *The Silence of the Lambs*, Clarice Starling sets out to interview the infamous psychiatrist/sociopath Hannibal Lecter and comes face to face with her most hidden flaw: her own repressed femininity.

In *In the Line of Fire*, Horgan sets out to track down a would-be presidential assassin and winds up confronting his gravest fear—does he have the right stuff to throw himself in the line of fire?

In *True Lies*, secret-agent Harry Tasker sets out to spy on his wife, whom he believes is cheating on him, and ends up confronting his own duplicitous behavior.

In *Seven* (written by Andrew Kevin Walker), Brad Pitt, as the impetuous and ambitious Detective David Mills, sets out to solve a bizarre series of murders based on the seven deadly sins only to find himself guilty of the deadliest sin of all—wrath.

In *The Big Easy* (written by Daniel Petrie, Jr.), Louisiana good ol' boy Lieutenant Remy McSwain (Dennis Quaid) sets out to solve a heroin scam and finds his family and himself at the center of years of entrenched departmental graft.

In *Angel Heart* (written by Alan Parker, based on the novel by William Hjortsberg), Mickey Rourke's Harry Angel is hired by the mysterious Louis Cyphre (Robert De Niro) to track down a "welcher" who dabbled in the occult, only to find that it is his own soul, in fact, that owes the devil his due.

In the detective mysteries of a recurring nature, like Sherlock Holmes, James Bond, Batman, Hercule Poirot, Ace Ventura or even Inspector Clouseau, the heroes are endowed with glam-

DETECTIVE FILMS/THRILLERS/MYSTERIES

*Above Suspicion, The Adventures of Sherlock Holmes, All the President's Men, Atlantic City, Basic Instinct, The Believers, Bellman and True, The Big Easy, The Big Sleep, Blow Out, Body Double, The Boys From Brazil, Cape Fear, Charade, The China Syndrome, Consenting Adults, The Crying Game, The Day of the Jackal, Dead Calm, The Dead Pool, Diablolique, Experiment in Terror; Farewell, My Lovely; In the Heat of the Night, Shadow of a Doubt, The Third Man, The Untouchables, Vertigo, The Wicker Man, Z*

orous, abnormal, ingenious, comical or even superhuman qualities in order to solve their crimes. Our interest lies in either seeing these powers challenged to the nth degree, or by watching them succeed in spite of themselves.

Detective stories are divided into three plot variations:

1. The detective knows who committed the crime, but cannot prove it. (*Witness*)
2. The detective does not know who the criminal is. (*The Silence of the Lambs, Chinatown, Seven*)
3. The audience knows who the criminal is but the detective doesn't. (*In the Line of Fire*)

## HORROR: A shuddering feeling of abhorrence; a painful emotion excited by something frightful or shocking

Horror is one of my favorite genres, as the best ones seem to strike a central psychological chord in all of us. Horror films are at their best when attacking man's more grandiose schemes or uncovering our deepest, most hidden psychological terrors. Alfred Hitchcock once explained his obsession with the macabre as stemming from a terrified childhood—his films were a way of expressing and exorcising those childhood fears.

When choosing a topic that frightens you, be mindful of why you are attracted to the material in the first place. If you can find the psychological reason behind your terror, you may find something disturbingly true about yourself. If it truly frightens you, then there is a good chance it will scare others as well.

When I was adapting the Lizzie Borden murders for the screen, initially I thought it was because of my youthful fascination with the folktale limerick:

> *Lizzie Borden took an ax*
> *gave her mother forty whacks*
> *when the job was neatly done*
> *she gave her father forty one!*

Captured in popular song by the Chad Mitchell Trio during the sixties, I remember hours of delight while listening to it. Later while researching the original case, I sought nothing more than indulging this childhood whim, while finding a "hook" that would terrify today's audiences. I read everything about the case, and found that there are as many conspiracy theories surrounding it as there are about the Kennedy assassination. All of these were informative, even plausible, but my interest remained in mining the riches of cinematic gold.

Then, when I read Victoria Lincoln's *A Very Private Affair*, and Ann Tyler's *Women Who Kill*, my nostalgic and mischievous musings melted away into sheer terror. While the conspiracy theories were well-documented and even fanciful, compared to Lincoln's and Tyler's real accounts, they collapse in the sheer light of truth. In spite of her acquittal, Lizzie actually did it! And of this there can be no doubt. But what is even more terrifying than the brutality of the murders and the fact she got away with it, is the psychological reasoning behind what she did. For dear, spoiled little daddy's girl, Miss Lizbeth Borden of Fall River, Massachusetts, literally cut off her father's face so that he could neither witness or shame her for hacking her stepmother to death.

This profoundly humanizing detail evoked both sympathy and horror, while unsettling something troubling lurking deep within my own psyche. I started being "visited" by a menacing, ax-wielding banshee at the periphery of my sleeping state. Lizzie started appearing before me nightly as this maniacal crone with frizzy mane and raging eyes. I could no longer sleep, or if I managed to doze off I would awaken drenched in sweat. This went on for weeks and months as I researched the story. No doubt I had found something at the very core of my own fear. The task now was to find out what.

Through Lizzie Borden came my own day of reckoning. While visiting a friend's remote cabin in the mountains near Taos, New Mexico, and browsing through her library, I came upon a book that practically leapt into my hand. The book, *Meeting the Madwoman*, by psychologist Linda Schierse Leonard, is a collection of case histories from artists, writers and professional

HORROR FILMS
*The Abominable Dr. Phibes, Arachnophobia, Audrey Rose, The Birds, Candyman, Carrie, Cat People, Creepshow, Dawn of the Dead, Dr. Jekyll and Mr. Hyde, Dracula, The Exorcist, Frankenstein, Friday the 13th, Ghost Story, Godzilla, Halloween, Hellraiser, The Hitcher, The Howling, The Island of Dr. Moreau, Jacob's Ladder, The Lost Boys, Murders in the Rue Morgue, Nightmare on Elm Street, Night of the Living Dead, Nosferatu, The Omen, Phantom of the Opera, Piranha, The Pit and the Pendulum, Poltergeist, Psycho, The Raven, Rosemary's Baby, Scream, The Sentinel, The Shining, The Texas Chainsaw Massacre, Wolfen*

women, who had all suppressed their creative, intuitive and "feminine" sides with the common apparition of a "madwoman" appearing before them to rage against such internal oppression. Leonard maintains that the figure of the enraged anima appears in all cultures, mythologies and cosmologies. Whether it is the goddess Kali of India, Inanna from Sumer or Medusa and Medea from Greek mythology, the role of the oppressed, vengeful and wrathful female has long been a powerful archetype of suppressed creativity and authenticity.

As I delved deeper and deeper into my personal terror, I started remembering this shadowy obstreperous "wraith" as the single most constant subject of my earliest childhood fears: The broomstick-riding witch in my Child Craft nursery tales, the closeted hag on roller skates in *House on Haunted Hill*, the knife-wielding "Mother" in *Psycho*, the meat cleaver-brandishing Olivia de Havilland in *Hush, Hush, Sweet Charlotte* and later with the relentless antics of Glenn Close in *Fatal Attraction*. For me these spectacularly terrifying "madwomen" embodied more heart-stopping horror than all the Frankensteins, werewolves, vampires, mummies and malformed extra-terrestrials in the universe.

Lizzie Borden emerged from folkloric novelty to haunt my most rigidly maintained "masculine" imprints. Oh sure, I lost plenty of sleep and spent thousands in therapy, but the result was not only finding the "hook" to my proposed film, but an alarming personal awakening. Since then, my female characters have become much more sympathetic, realistic, well-defined and less stereotypical. The "madwoman" with her axes and blood-drenched garland of skulls is still out there lurking, but I've made my peace with her, and am severely chastened should I ever fail to pay her due respect again.

ACTION/ADVENTURE: A relation of all the parts and
elements of a work constituting a harmonious whole
and producing the single general effect of action; one
of the three principles of plot construction: unity of
time, unity of place and unity of action

Some screenwriting theorists maintain that the action feature is
the purest form of cinema—no dialogue, no music, no character—just unadulterated edge-of-your seat suspense: Harold Lloyd
hanging from the hands of a clock tower; a tightrope walker over
Niagara Falls; Pauline tied to the railroad tracks with an oncom-
ing train racing toward her—and indeed, these are wonderful
cinematic examples of pure action. Watching silent movies can
teach you a lot about action sequencing, in lieu of this, finding
your favorite action film and turning off the sound, observing
both the onrush of images and your own reactions to it, can be
very enlightening.

George Lucas best defined the essentials of the action genre as
being *speed* and *clarity*. This imperative drives *Star Wars, The
Empire Strikes Back, Return of the Jedi* and *Raiders of the Lost Ark*.
While some critics and industry peers find limitations in Lucas's
imperative, there can be little doubt that it works.

The action movie must be fundamentally action-oriented right
from the beginning, and build dynamically to the final conclusion. Rather than undergo personal change, the action hero
effects change on the world of story. So a good way of structuring
your action story is to determine the specific points in your out-
line normally reserved for your protagonists personal revelations—then reverse them to the external world. This allows you
hero to become an agent for change rather than an example of
change.

The eight elements of the action plot are:
1. A protagonist who can fight.
2. An opponent who is worthy.
3. The hero and opponent wage a physical struggle based on
   each one's objective purpose, so that the emphasis is on ability, skill and ingenuity rather than character traits.
4. A protagonist who clearly wins in the end.

5.  An antagonist who clearly loses in the end (but can be miraculously resurrected for the sequel).
6.  Three to four physical conflicts between the hero and opponent, including the final climax, and the obligatory scene of the hero at the mercy of the opponent.
7.  The hero defeats his opponent and extricates himself from his difficulties.
8.  The novelty and invention of the setting for the final conflict.

This does not mean that in all action stories the hero does not change, but rather that the scope of his internal growth is limited. It is limited because there is not enough time—within the course of a two-hour movie—to reasonably expect both. The sheer demands of the genre require that one be sacrificed in direct proportion to the other. We sacrifice deep, meaningful personal change for clear, concise and rapid changes in the world of story. *The action story is more akin to the outlaw structure in that the action hero has one single focused goal and a limited range of virtues, devices, chances, and skills to achieve it.*

In *Star Wars*, the Rebel Alliance is under attack by Darth Vader and his minions, compelling Princess Leia to dispatch her personal androids with a holographic S.O.S. addressed to Obi-Wan Kenobi. The speed and clarity of this running start sets the central plotline of rescuing her and destroying the Death Star rolling. When Luke Skywalker intercepts the message, he becomes personally involved in the quest and his destiny is set. All that is needed to send him irreversibly on his way is to find the only home he has ever known burned to the ground and his aunt and uncle brutally murdered.

In *The Terminator*, man and machine export their war of the future into modern Los Angeles, where their quest to seek out, save and/or destroy Sara Connor sets up the film's opening and builds relentlessly to the end. The speed and clarity with which these events unfold is so powerful it created two riveting motion pictures out of one ingenious plotline.

In *Lethal Weapon*, Mel Gibson plays a suicidal detective whose obsession with dying makes him fearless, unpredictable and nearly invulnerable, especially to those who would use this threat of death against him.

In *Deliverance*, the homosexual rape of one of their own pits a group of culturally civilized men against a feral human species while trying to survive the grueling trek of a whitewater river expedition.

In *Raiders of the Lost Ark*, the international race to uncover archeological wonders pits the forces of science and knowledge against the prospect of world domination by the Nazis.

In *The Wages of Fear* (written by Henri-Georges Clouzot and Jerome Geronimi, based on the novel by Georges Arnaud), the lust for money and greed sets four scurrilous expatriates on a mission to drive a shipment of nitroglycerin through an intense jungle terrain. Edge of your seat suspense abounds with every rut, oil pit and stomach-churning cliffhanger along the way.

In *Predator* (written by Jim Thomas and John Thomas), an elite combat unit on a rescue mission in the South American jungle is pitted against a stealth "alien" hunter who mercilessly stalks and slaughters them, one by one.

In *Executive Decision* (written by Jim and John Thomas), an egg-head intelligence analyst teams up with elite commando unit to thwart a jumbo jet overrun with Arab terrorists headed for Washington, D.C., with a payload of chemical weaponry.

In *The Hunt for Red October* (written by Larry Ferguson and Donald Stewart, based on the novel by Tom Clancy), a virtually undetectable Soviet nuclear submarine is headed for the West. While "hawks" and "doves" scramble to determine whether its intent is nuclear war or defection.

In *Independence Day*, an alien invasion spurs a desk-jockey President, a Jewish scientist and a black paratrooper to work together to combat overwhelming odds and save the earth.

The simplicity of the action genre relies upon the intense nature of conflict established at the very core of the film's objective storyline and premise. All subtle detailing of personal character

ACTION/
ADVENTURE FILMS
*Apollo 13,
Avalanche,
Backdraft, The
Bear, Billy Jack,
Blind Fury,
Caravans, Code of
Silence, Conan the
Barbarian, Death
Wish, Deliverance,
Die Hard, Double
Impact, The Eiger
Sanction, Firefox,
First Blood; For
Your Eyes Only, The
Fugitive,
Goldfinger, Gone in
Sixty Seconds,
High Road to
China, Indiana
Jones and the
Temple of
Doom, Jaws,
License to Kill, The
Lost World,
Magnum Force,
Moby Dick, Never
Say Never Again,
Papillion, The
Professionals,
Robinson
Crusoe, The
Running Man,
Seven, Tarzan, Top
Gun, The Towering
Inferno, Two Years
Before the Mast,
White Fang, The
Wind and the Lion,
You Only Live
Twice, Zulu Dawn*

growth takes a secondary position to the overt ones of confrontation and opposition.

## WESTERNS

Three excellent source books exist to assist you in interpreting the structure of the Western genre: Lord Raglan's 1936 publication of *The Hero*, Professor Will Wright's *Six Guns in Society* and Larry McMurtry's *Film Flam* in which the master gives an-all-too brief summation of the other two. All three, though out-of-print, are extremely worth the times spent to find them; especially the latter, as it is a telling journal of McMurtry's own experiences as a novelist and screenwriter (*Terms of Endearment, The Last Picture Show, Lonesome Dove, Texasville, Hud*).

(The following is my "cheat sheet" synthesis of Professor Wright's breakdown of sixty Western plots filmed between 1930 and 1972.)

### *1. Classic Western Plot*

In these Westerns the hero is endowed with extraordinary qualities and enters the provincial world from the outside. The hero is not completely accepted by the people of the provincial world at first, but as the population is threatened by powerful antagonistic forces, they turn to him for assistance. Gradually the hero is drawn into the fray, usually when his own sense of values is called into question. He joins the fight, defeats the villain and ensures the safety of the provincial world for good. In the end he is accepted into their society and retires his outsider status for all time. (*Cimarron, Dodge City, San Antonio, Yellow Sky, Vera Cruz, Saskatchewan, Shane* and *Hombre*)

### *2. The Vengeance Plot*

In the classical plot, the hero enters the fight because of his extraordinary abilities and the provincial world's inability to fend for itself. In the vengeance plot, the hero abandons the provincial world because of his personal disdain for its timidity and hypocrisy. He views the provincial world as compromised by the villainous forces that oppress them and is determined to do something about it. At this point, he leaves the provincial world and goes it alone to rid the society of the threat, whereby he returns with the moral authority to forge a better world. (*Stagecoach, Red River, Winchester '73, The Man from Laramie, The Searchers, One-Eyed Jacks, Nevada Smith*)

### 3. The Transition Plot

Here the hero is a member of a very progressive community that refuses to take a stance either for the hero or against the forces of villainy that oppose him. They view the ensuing conflict as the hero's responsibility alone and see no reason to support him. This puts him at odds with both external forces and the internal will of his own people. The romantic interest tries to reconcile the hero with the provincial world, but this proves futile, and ultimately she too, must go it alone. Though he is personally vindicated in the end, he cannot remain in a place of such moral ambivalence and decides to leave for good. (*Broken Arrow, Johnny Guitar, High Noon*)

### 4. The Professional Western

In these plots the provincial world is under the threat of great villainy from outside the community. As a result, they hire a group of professionals with extraordinary capabilities to rid themselves of the problem. The group is comprised of a rag-tag set of misfits and rugged individuals, each of which possesses a unique set of virtues and skills. As hired professionals, they feel no moral allegiance to either side; only for the reward they'll earn at the end of the ordeal. In the ensuing conflict, the prize ultimately becomes less important as each member must decide whether to disband or stay and fight against overwhelming odds. (*Three Amigos, The Magnificent Seven, The Professionals, The Wild Bunch, Young Guns*)

## SCIENCE FICTION

I maintain there is no reason to project into the future or revisit the past unless you can find strong underlying thematic relevance to modern issues. While there is great production value in the worlds of the future—and with the advancement of special effects technology the ability to create these locales can be both awe-inspiring and intensely realistic—the central core of these stories should be of contemporary interest and importance. *Star Wars* draws its power from the time-honored hero tales of the past, while *Alien, Blade Runner, Close Encounters of the Third Kind, E.T.* and *Independence Day* play on our on-going speculation about extra-terrestrial life forms. Their plausibility and success in suspending our disbelief comes from masterful manipulation of very basic human emotions: fear, heroism, interspecies prejudice, racism, classicism, slavery, dehumanization and the ability to survive in extraordinary situations.

With the overwhelming popularity of the science fiction genre recently invigorated by the success of Tim Burton's *Planet of the Apes* and the reissue of the *Star Wars* trilogy, we are about to be inundated once again. When tackling science fiction, it is important to find a central hook to the film that is universally and immediately comprehensible. In lieu of instantaneous identification, one should carefully determine the underlying genres involved. Is it science fiction horror? Science fiction myth? Science fiction action adventure? Science fiction romance? Comedy? War? What genre are you working with?

As science fiction is the raison d'etre for many devoted fans (e.g. Trekkies), specialized talents and towering intellects, one should only enter the field with great trepidation and a heightened awareness of what is current in other mediums (such as television, literature, fan magazines and contemporary science). Your special take on a science fiction subject may be unique to you, but it won't do you any good if it's old hat to devoted fans of other mediums.

## WAR

Historian Jacques Barzun, the author of From *Dawn to Decadence: 500 Years of Western Culture,* defines the very nature of decadence as an appalling and prevalent lack of new ideas. Director John Milius gave voice to this viewpoint rather poignantly when he stated, "We started out wanting to change the world with our films, but I'm not so sure we've succeeded in doing anything more than making bigger bangs!"

Intermittent war stories such as *Apocalypse Now, Missing, Platoon, Born on the Fourth of July, Heaven and Earth, Salvador, A Clear and Present Danger* and *Schindler's List* crop up from time to time to focus on modern themes and situations that pique our current interest (the absurdity of war, the role of women in combat, the travesty of Vietnam, the political injustice of backing the wrong side, etc.). These searing examinations can be exceedingly worthwhile from an historic, political and sociological point of view.

When war is used as a backdrop it can enhance the immediacy, danger and polarity of the issues in any given story. *The English Patient* is an excellent example of using the background of war to further explore the ease with which we politicize and wrongfully impugn a man's character—without really knowing the depth, passion and personal sacrifice they may have undergone in their lives. In this particular case the inhumanity of war serves to counterbalance our deepest humanity—to love. Likewise, *Casablanca* uses the backdrop of war to focus on the insignificance of our romantic yearnings in the face of overwhelming global disorder.

"Love is selfish and doesn't amount to a hill of beans in the whole universal picture," Rick reminds Ilsa, summoning up his heroic, self-sacrificing leanings. "Besides, we'll always have Paris."

War for war's sake, without the examination and contrast to deeper, more humanistic values such as heroism, bravery, sacrifice, love or enslavement, quickly descends into exploitation and racism. As a result, these gratuitous tales serve to contribute to the problem rather than its solution. Aside from their moral deficiencies, they rely on little more than comic book titillation to command an audience (*Top Gun, Navy SEALS, Rambo, G.I. Jane, Pearl Harbor*).

While attending the premier of *The Last Unicorn* in Munich, Germany, I found myself deeply ambivalent about my visit. On the one hand, these people had embraced my film with overwhelming appreciation and grace, on the other hand I couldn't get over being in a land responsible for twelve million horror stories. Everywhere I went I envisaged the terror of Krystalnacht, the roar of marching storm troopers, the unexpected, rapid-fire knocks on the door in the middle of the night, the devastation of whole families, the murderous gas chambers, torture racks and crematoriums. A billion war stories fevered my brain. Being of Jewish heritage, I was in the land of my enemy and comported myself throughout my stay with clenched teeth and glaring cynicism. Every where I looked, it seemed there were Nazis in the nasturtiums.

One night, while sitting in a hotel lobby writing letters home, I struck up a conversation with a well-dressed and slightly intoxicated German businessman. He seemed to have a personal stake in approaching me, almost as if he could sense my moral dilemma (either that, or he had previously decided to impose his views on the next unsuspecting American he chanced upon).

"I've never believed that one race is superior to another!" He began, "Even though I attended war college in my youth."

Which made him the correct age for goose-stepping right along with a million others of his generation. Immediately, I began to picture this very tall, proud and demanding businessman in Nazi uniform.

"You know what is war college? Not where you learn to hate, but where you study military strategy. You have such colleges in the U.S., no? West Point, yes?"

"Yes" I replied, "we have many such schools."

"Ja. But even at war college, I've always believed mankind is equal. We are one race of people. Do you also believe this?"

" Yes, of course, I do." How could I not?

"Well then" And here came the catch. "If you believe that, then my Hitler is also your Hitler. No?"

**WAR FILMS**
*Apocalypse Now, Bataan, The Boys in Company C, Braveheart, A Bridge Too Far, Catch-22, Days of Glory, The Deer Hunter, The Dirty Dozen, Dr. Strangelove, Exodus, Farewell to the King, Force Ten from Navarone, Full Metal Jacket, Gallipoli, The Green Berets, Hamburger Hill, Hope and Glory, It Happened Here, Les Miserables, Memphis Belle, A Midnight Clear, Orders to Kill, Paris after Dark, Paths of Glory, Platoon, Pork Chop Hill, The Red Badge of Courage, The Road to Glory, Sahara, Sands of Iwo Jima, The Sea Wolves, Spartacus; Tora, Tora, Tora; Triumph of the Will, The Wings of Eagles, Yanks, The Young Lions*

Okay, I was set up. But I couldn't help but follow his logic. Every race on earth is guilty of one atrocity on another: the white man upon the Native American. The Dutch upon the African, the Spaniard upon the Aztec, the Caribe and the Arawak, the Jew upon the Palestinian, the Arab upon the Jew, the Serb upon the Bosnian.

Germany is not exclusive to this barbarism, no matter how efficiently it carried it out. If I could accept the equality of all humanity, then I would also have to also accept humankind's inhumanity as well. No race is immune to the act of genocide. And by attributing evil to one specific race or another, I was guilty of the same intolerance, the same moralizing and rationale that ultimately sent millions of people to their deaths. It was time for me to move on. This powerful revelation put me at ease and I could now start to forgive and enjoy the rest of my stay in an otherwise extraordinary country.

The point here is that for war stories to have relevance in today's movie-going climate, it must transcend the genocidal motivation of previous wars—and attempt to elevate the enemy to one of universal threat.

# THE TENTH STAGE
## Research

One of the most uncanny developments I've experienced as a writer is in the way that certain information—books, articles, insights or clues—seem to appear "magically" whenever I need them. Everyone has experienced this from time to time. You're reading something and chance upon a word or expression you've never heard before and then for the next three weeks you see examples of it everywhere. This is the power of intuitive awareness. It is one of our most sadly underdeveloped instincts and tools. Sharpening one's intuitive instincts is a fundamental task for the aspiring writer, as it will add to the immense reservoir of understanding you will require as a professional mythmaker.

Dreams, too, are powerful tools of prescience and consciousness that can tap into our most repressed emotions and fears to indicate aspects of ourselves that require our attention. Most people dismiss them as little more than bizarre or pleasant interludes in the night. The fact is that your dreams are more purely aligned with the real you than any other single factor of your existence. The writer, artist or visionary forms a relationship with the inner self—the whole manifestation of art becomes an attempt to integrate the wellspring of the subconscious with practical everyday conscious existence.

When they say, "Write what you know," it does not mean simply indulging areas of personal erudition. It means, write from your gut, from your intuition, from who you really are. The ultimate purpose of any art form is to access the bottomless reservoir of your entire being.

> *"Write what you do not know, because you will find that there is some part of you that does know. It teaches you something you knew that you didn't know you knew, There's always that sense of discovery, personal discovery.*
> —Bill Whitliff

Colin Wilson, in his ingenious book *The Occult*, names our natural intuitive powers Faculty X, and defines them metaphorically as if we were all living in this magnificent cathedral of super consciousness, with most of us never venturing out of the confessional. The artist, writer, hero uses art to leave the confessional and explore the vast edifice beyond and, in effect, shout back to the rest of us—"come on out, it's incredible!"

Research is an excellent way to tap further and further into your subconscious self. When the writer is in tune with his intuitive self, the research process is every bit as enlightening and informative as the writing process. To research a topic solely to gather facts is a mistake; fact is not really the predominant goal of fiction or drama. While it always important to educate an audience with specific details and the authority of your writing skills, the emphasis should be on suspending their disbelief and intelligently involving them in the plight, training and obstacles of your hero. Untested writers are often so heavily burdened by the particular facts of their story that they neglect the real goal, which is to gain personal insight into their character's psychological makeup and worldview. Facts can be a distraction to the real work of forming a personal insight into what the story is really about.

The movies of Oliver Stone are extremely controversial, with many critics deriding him for his freewheeling approach to the "facts." But Oliver Stone knows that the facts can be interpreted a thousand ways by a thousand different individuals. As an artist and filmmaker, Stone is more concerned with his own truth, and the passionate conveyance of that truth, forcing "the facts" to take a secondary role to his own personal insights. This is the inherent right of the artist. While Stone's films can be aggravating, controversial and even infuriating at times, they are always remarkable motion picture experiences. In a day and age of mind-numbing political correctness, moral ambiguity and conformity, it is much more exhilarating to see an artist challenge our pre-set societal notions and penetrate to the heart of the matter, even if they are disastrously askew of "the facts."

In *The English Patient*, the historical Count Almazy is far different from the character Ralph Fiennes portrays in the film. First of all, there is evidence that the real Count was homosexual, which would have negated the whole force of this romantic epic. To better prove the writer and director's theme about identity and harsh social judgment, the reality of this brooding, self-serving and mysterious personage was required to take a back seat to his movie-formulated persona. For a thoroughly entertaining and informative examination of historical facts versus motion picture "revisionism," I suggest reading George Macdonald Frasier's excellent *The Hollywood History of the World*.

If you are driven with a passion for the "facts," then it is possible that narrative fiction is not your particular bailiwick. In which case one might be better served in exploring the demanding field of documentary filmmaking.

## DISCIPLINE

I organize my day into six phases:
- Writing
- Personal
- Book Research
- Business
- Film Research
- Reading

4:00 AM to 12:00 noon is devoted purely to writing. This is a holdover from the time I lived in India, where the whole country awakens for Brahma Mahurta, the "birth" of the morning. It is a time when universal energy is on the rise. It is also the most peaceful part of the day, and relatively free of phone calls and nagging interruptions. As a single parent, I need this tranquil time away from household chores and parental duties in order to collect my thoughts and tap into my deeper creative instincts. I do not turn on the radio, read the newspaper or do anything else to interfere with the thoughts, musings and problem-solving I may have done during the night. I try as best as I can to avoid conversing with anyone, as I find this an annoying distraction as well. Those who insist upon calling me at 5:00 A.M. for idle chitchat— "I knew you'd be up!"—constantly astonish me. Most acquaintances who aren't writers cannot fathom the need for lengthy, uninterrupted contemplation.

I spend the first two hours of every morning rereading and rewriting the pages I put down the day before. This helps me "get into character" and immerse myself further into the characters, world, conflict, meaning and narrative voice of my story. I spend the next six hours writing; sometimes I manage ten pages on a good day, or two pages on a more ponderous one. If I am having difficulty, I take this as a call for further research and development to let the story "cook" some more. If problems crop up, I'll make a note and try to address them in my research later in the working day.

12:00 to 1:30 PM—I exercise, shower and walk to the library (a brisk thirty minutes from the house).

2:00 to 4:00 PM—At the library, I will attack some of the problems that arose in my morning session, while perusing and selecting various related subject matter for the images, vocations, language, history and cultural backgrounds of my story. The information I gather will determine the important details required in shaping the visual, factual, metaphorical, attitudinal and authentic nature of my script. Sometimes I will "freestyle" through books, shelves and articles of interest. I am constantly amazed at what I can turn up in wholly unrelated areas. This is the power of allowing your intuitive self to work as your guide. The books that strike me as pertinent or that convey a positive feeling, I take home to review and make notations.

5:00 to 7:30 PM is devoted to work-related, personal and familial matters before dinner. As California is an hour ahead of my time zone, this affords me an opportunity to catch up on business affairs on the West Coast.

7:30 to 9:30—Movie time. I either watch a current video release or a film that I've selected as relevant to what I'm writing about. If I have more than one film to watch, I take the time from my research schedule.

9:30 to 10:30 is spent reading the books and articles I've brought home in order to inspire my subconscious problem-solving while I sleep. I have found that the most insurmountable plot holes, structure development and character problems can all be solved with a good night's rest. (For more on this, I suggest reading Naomi Eppel's excellent book: *Writer's Dreaming*.)

This schedule was adapted from my old days at an ashram and does not allow for much socializing during the week. If you choose to live a more integrated lifestyle, I recommend slowly building a daily writing time for yourself in the morning or late evenings. This exclusive block of time should be strictly adhered to with the appropriate explanations and apologies to loved one made in advance.

The basic requirements of time, solitude and "creative space" are unique and not widely understood in today's externally addicted world, so you will probably have to defend your boundaries often. Be tough, patient and compassionate. In the end, even the most persistent ninny will eventually get the hint and leave you alone.


## SEX AND VIOLENCE

Sex and violence can be exhilarating and important tools for furthering the screenwriter's goal of conflict, drama and suspense. Both have a way of shocking us out of our complacency and playing on raw nerves. In a civilized society where we rarely have the opportunity to live life on such a visceral level, it is an important, cathartic and sometimes transcendent experience for the audience at large.

Intelligent writers and directors will try to find a way to use sex or violence to keep us on edge so the emotions we feel are both stirring and honest. When sex and violence are used with an intelligent, thematic and artistic approach, the audience is riveted and the story is enhanced. If the approach is hackneyed and gratuitous, we are left empty, disgusted and cheated. These misguided efforts and failures ultimately play into the hands of those ever-righteous moral authorities who stake their political careers on Hollywood bashing and censorship. The way to stop this is by each artist personally determining to be a part of the solution, rather than contributing to the problem.

## MORALITY AND IMMORALITY

*"Whereas the artist is concerned with the order of morality, the Nazi is consumed by the morality of order."*
—Rollo May, *The Courage to Create*

I feel one of the most "moral" films ever made is Leni Reifenstahl's famous propaganda piece, *Triumph of the Will.* Here, we are saturated with images of Hitler as the great father, descending from the clouds with millions cheering and waving him on. Looking at the adoring faces of the idolatrous crowd, and the fervor with which they greet their beloved Führer, one can only compare such an event to the return of the Messiah himself. What makes this film so ultimately immoral is the depravity and horror it conceals behind the facade.

I am forever reminded of the artistic truism espoused by Woody Allen's ruminating playwright (played by John Cusack) in *Bullets Over Broadway,* as he wrings his hands and declares, "an artist must be free to determine his own morality!" This is one of the greatest artistic mandates ever pronounced. Questioning society's morality and daring to define your own as apart, is one of the most courageous acts you can do as a screenwriter, or as a human being.

In *Cabaret*, we see the self-same thematic juxtaposition of morality and immorality as Germany descends from decadence into fascism. In one of the most powerful sequences in modern cinema, we see a beautiful young man appear in a country beer garden, singing nostalgically of a purity of time, place and people. Very soon the crowd is swept up by his sweet and simple song. One by one others are compelled to join in and take up the young man's verse, "Tomorrow belongs to me." The scene then turns darkly ominous as we pull back to reveal he is a Hitler Jugend, and his moralistic rallying cry will lead to one of the darkest and immoral periods in the history of mankind. The subtle and thematic treatment of "immoral" decadence serves to punctuate an even greater immorality: The "moral" rise of Adolph Hitler and the subsequent devastation of twelve million human souls.

The use of immorality to present a higher moral understanding, or the use of morality to indicate an even greater immorality, is the underpinning and goal of the screenwriter's art.

James Cameron's *Terminator II* was highly criticized for its violence, yet Cameron protested, and rightfully so, that his tale was deeply moral and thematically nonviolent. The moral violence of his story attacks the greater immorality of technology ruling over humanity—so the violence is justifiable and moral in its teaching.

In *Pulp Fiction*, we are laid bare to the emotional bone by the murderous banality of outlaws who seem to operate in a world without recrimination, or the slightest threat of police intervention. This shatters our general sensibilities and naïve expectations for society. We are taught to trust that our governmental agencies will protect us from unsavory criminals, when, more often than not, this is simply untrue. Though criticized and condemned for its seemingly wanton immorality, I found *Pulp Fiction* to be highly moral—in that the violence within the film serves to intensify the anti-heroic quests of Butch and Jules as they struggle with their personal virtues and effect their escapes to a better life outside of outlaw society.

In *Unforgiven*, a brilliant thesis on mankind's need to rationalize his need for violence leads to murder and mayhem when an irrational killer is brought into the picture. In this instance, the

violence is used to highlight a more important moral imperative—that all violence is irrational, no matter how we seek to
rationalize it.

In *Blade Runner*, the violent imperative of Rick Deckard only
serves to underline the hero's need to understand the humanity of
all living things. In this case the violence is subservient to a higher moral lesson—the sanctity of all life, regardless of its origin.

*The People vs. Larry Flynt* (written by Acott Alexander and
Larry Karaszewski) uses the "immorality" of *Hustler* magazine to
punctuate an even greater immorality of censorship and the
sacred right of all Americans to express themselves.

In *The Unbearable Lightness of Being* (written by Jean-Claude
Carriere and Phillip Kaufman, based on the novel by Milan
Kundera) as well as *Henry and June* (written by Phillip Kaufman
and Rose Kaufman, based on the novel by Anaïs Nin), the sexuality and passion of the on-screen characters serves the greater
moral imperative of illustrating, through their explicit sexuality
and intimacy, an intensified human experience.

Alternatively, *The Last Tango in Paris* (written by Bernardo
Bertolucci and Franco Arcalli, based on a story by Bertolucci) and
*9 1/2 Weeks* (written by Sarah Kernochan, Zalman King and
Patricia Louisiana Knop, based on the novel by Elizabeth
McNeill), take a dark look at the violence, exploitation and self-
destruction inherent in the shadow side of human passion. In
these instances the violent endings serve a higher morality of
showing the abuse of male/female sexuality.

In *Un Couer en Hiver* (written by Jacques Fieschi, Claude Sautet
and Jerome Tonnerre), a Geppetto-like master craftsman of vio-
lins seduces a promising young virtuoso whose repressed sexuality and passion are hindering her career. Rather than loving her,
he psychologically brutalizes her, not out of cruelty, but in
attempt to free her emotions. In effect, he does what only a fine
craftsman can do: he breaks the instrument in order to repair it.
His so-called immoral behavior serves the greater morality of
freeing her art.

# THE ELEVENTH STAGE

## Image Systems

*"The most important frame of any film is the opening image."*
—Robert Zemeckis

Determining the image system of a film is one of the most exciting aspects of movie watching and screenwriting. Peter Weir, Robert Zemeckis, Werner Herzog, Jonathan Demme, Sydney Lumet, Norman Jewison, Jean Cocteau, David Fincher, Robert Redford, Robert Benton, Francis Ford Coppola, Phillip Kaufman and Lawrence Kasdan are all especially creative, original and subtle in their design of visual metaphors. Of course, some themes lend themselves more readily to symbolic representation than others, but it is always refreshing to see the work of writers and directors who have a special flare for the image itself.

In *Forrest Gump*, Robert Zemeckis opens and closes on a feather floating in the wind. Why? Well, for a story that has a great deal to say about simplicity, love, loyalty, heroism and one simpleton's success in achieving all of them, the feather becomes a metaphor for the honest and unassuming way we all might live our lives. It is an important feature of this story that Jenny and Captain Dan, both of whom have very clear goals for their lives, both fail miserably in obtaining them. Whereas Forrest, who is too simple to have any glaring ambition, succeeds in winning all of life's great bounties. He becomes a football star, a war hero, a multi-millionaire, a spiritual leader, visionary and loving father—not through any self-serving enterprise, but by staying true to himself and his friends, and by remaining open to the serendipitous turns and twists that life presents to him. Gump lives his life like the proverbial feather in the wind, or as another of the film's metaphors implies "...like a box of chocolates; you never know what you're going to get."

In *Moonstruck*, the image systems of the moon; the music of Dean Martin, Vicki Carr and Puccini's *La Boheme*; funeral parlors, florist shops, "Sweetheart Liquors," the old man pulled by a herd of dogs, a bakery (bread is life), and constant references to death in dialogue, music and locale, go a long way in reinforcing the film's theme of choosing life over death. It is a complete symphony of ideas, emotions, music, dialogue and image in masterful use through the screenwriter's craft.

In *Witness*, a film whose very title infers the "act of seeing and knowing through experience," an astonishing array of close-ups of the players' eyes are used. One can only speculate that Peter Weir cast Kelly McGillis (her debut), Lukas Haas (his debut) and Alexander Godunov (his film debut) entirely for their doe-like countenances. Watch the early scenes of Lukas Haas on the train, or when Alexander Godunov bids him farewell with, "You'll see so many things." Follow the boy through the train station as he observes the sights, images and oddities of this new strange land. Go back and look at the shots of Harrison Ford, whose range of acting techniques through his eyes alone are some of the most expressive of his prolific career.

In *The Verdict*, a film that focuses on one attorney's need to reconnect with his integrity as he uncovers the "whole truth" about a case, the use of arches and other architectural symbols reinforces the thematic notion that we are not "seeing" the complete picture—an apt metaphor for the judicial edict. "the whole truth and nothing but the truth." Frank Galvin's office offers a partitioned arch window in the background. The court building, hospital and corridors are shot with fresh and inventive angles of divided windows and obscured arches. What is an arch, if not an incomplete circle? And if a circle represents a whole, then these arches convey a sense of half truth or imperfect knowledge.

Another example of one of *The Verdict's* most ingenious image systems is the developing Polaroid in Galvin's hands as he is awakened to his moral responsibility as an attorney. This revelation becomes crystal clear with the developing photo when he stops looking at his comatose client as a paycheck and realizes the tragic injustice done to her by her physicians. A nurse happens by at the exact moment and says, "I'm sorry sir, but you can't be in here." Galvin, falters, stricken by the awesome nature of his job, and replies as if comprehending it for the first time, "It's all right, I'm her attorney."

In *The Silence of the Lambs*, Ted Tally and Jonathan Demme use a brilliant array of visual metaphors around death, transformation, metamorphoses and gender confusion with recurring images and dialogue bites referring to butterflies, Death's Head moths and characters struggling with masculine/feminine issues. Note too, how all the key locations are shot in the basement of either the FBI, the mental asylum or and Buffalo Bill's chamber of horrors—all thematically derived from Lecter's cold-blooded temperament. The recurring visual placement of cold and damp brick takes on startling relevance when Dr. Chilton describes Lecter's pulse as never raising above 85, even when tearing out a nurse's tongue. Once again, the inspired translation of themes into visual metaphor is just one of the elements that made this an Academy Award®-winning screenplay and one of the finest motion pictures ever made.

*The Big Chill* (written by Barbara Benedek and Lawrence Kasdan) examines the changing attitudes and ideals from the sixties to the eighties, and uses an incredible soundtrack from both periods, as well as wide variety of "yuppie" appliances (such as espresso machines, video equipment and high-tech stereos) to further punctuate the changing values of these individuals and their times.

In *Chinatown*, the image system of both positive and shadow aspects of water is masterfully reinforced throughout the story. "In the middle of a drought, the water commissioner drowns." Later, Roman Polanski's character says, "You stick your nose out and I'll cut it off and feed it to the goldfish." And yet another, when we hear the Japanese gardener say, "Bad for glass," indicating the salt water that has mysteriously found its way into Evelyn Mulwray's pond. Here we see symphonic support of images through dialogue and numerous plot points and visual references surrounding water. Yet the most powerful image system of all remains the title itself, which not only represents the Jake Gittes shadowy past, but the thematic resolve of the entire motion picture—Chinatown.

The intelligent perception and the creation of themes and their correlated imagery is the real art of cinema, and the joy of the screenwriter's craft.

# THE TWELFTH STAGE

## Break the Story Down Scene by Scene

This last stage of development can prove to be the most difficult, and may even seem redundant and self-defeating at times. Very few accomplished screenwriters will actually go through this step unless forced to, and many even bypass the treatment stage altogether. This is because professional screenwriters have already internalized their best development methods through trial, error and experience. The aspiring screenwriter must advance to this stage and often work tirelessly to achieve it. To bypass or forego this internalizing stage in the beginning is to cheat yourself of the desirable, educating and exacting process that is the hallmark of professional screenwriting.

A screenplay might range anywhere between sixty to a hundred and sixty scenes. Every one of them is necessary for a wide variety of purposes: establishing the world of story; the main character, his relationships, desires, shadow, flaws, objectives, and plot complications; conflict (both internal and external), growth, outcome and the final impact of his actions. The opening scenes of the first act will be longer than the acts that follow, because there will be less and less exposition to deal with. The way we pace a story is by determining the length of scenes from beginning to end.

It is good discipline to limit a scene's length to about five pages in the first and second acts. Then, as you approach the middle of your story, start shrinking the scenes incrementally as you build to the latter half of the second and third acts. The method of shortening the length of your scenes allows you to quicken the action and pick up the pace. To gain an objective look at how your story is paced, and how it is unfolding from one scene to the next, try hanging a bulletin board or corkboard near your workspace. Make sure it is of sufficient size to accommodate at least a hundred or so three by five index cards laid out in connecting columns of ten each. You may not need the whole board for plotting your master scenes, but you can use the remaining space to list images, auxiliary worlds, facts, dialogue bites and pertinent details as they come up.

Now, like a painter, you can visualize your story unfolding on a much larger canvas, almost like the forty-foot images that will appear on-screen in your local movie theater. This helps broaden your perspective and measure how your story will appear on the screen.

When you tire of writing, or hit a particular snag in your development, return to the breakdown board and start playing with your cards. Write down the most salient aspects of each scene and try to determine their underlying value—either positive or negative. This will help you monitor the particular tone of a story, so if you have a run-on sequence of negative scenes, you may need to break them up with some more positive ones. Or, if your breakdown indicates a run-on sequence of positive values, you may need to introduce some twists and turns to keep the tone balanced and the story moving forward.

In detailing each scene, try to use as few words as possible. You need not be too descriptive here because the goal is to prompt ideas, narrative flow, pacing, tone and plot. The aim is to enhance your writing process, not turn it into something laborious and redundant.

If you are the impetuous sort (as most beginning writers are), and want to get on with the script, use the story breakdown board as a play period to further stimulate your creativity as you write. Sometimes merely glancing at your breakdown board can be more productive and less distracting than staring out your workplace window.

# TROUBLESHOOTING AND REWRITING

At a very early age, I unexpectedly became an enthusiast of personal mechanics and do-it-yourself auto repair. One of the first jobs I ever had was assisting John Muir in the preparation and testing of his classic do-it-yourself guide, *How to Keep your Volkswagen Alive and Happy*. True to this grand literary tradition, what follows is a quick glance of the problems that often arise in writing your first screenplay. I've broken the section down into three sections, according to the problems that may arise with each act.

## THE FIRST ACT

### *I've written thirty pages of my script and I'm stymied, where do I go from here?*

This is a clear indication that you did not follow the twelve stages of development. STOP! Go back and rework your premise. The second and third acts should directly result from your first act set-up and lead to confrontation and resolution. It is futile to write a story without having clearly established these. The ability to anticipate your ending provides you with an internal map of where you are headed; without it you will become lost. Don't think that you can create the ending when you come to it, because you will never get there.

If you're the stubborn type and decide to tough it out, fine. Use the hard work you've done as practice. Remember that in writing nothing is ever really wasted; the mistakes you make will turn you into a better writer down the line. If you give up now it's because you're trying to cheat the process and win the lottery, in which case you're only fooling yourself.

### I have a great second and third act, but I don't know where to begin.

Go back to your theme. What's the story really about? Now go to the end value. With the end value clearly established, how do you get there from Point A? What dramatic events can you create to set the hero on his journey of confrontation and resolve? Or, try to create a thematic image that imparts a stunning metaphor for what the film is about. Look at the chapter on image systems and try to determine an appropriate visual to resolve your thematic problem.

What is the world of story? What is your hero's connection to that world? Does he rise from within it, or does he leave it? Look at your external structure. Is it a myth, inverted myth, fairy tale or drama?

Then follow the stages of internal development: What is your main character's problem? How is he affecting others? What is his immediate desire? Look at your character's shadow—is it worth showing up front, or is it better suited to a gradual unraveling?

Reexamine and evaluate your inciting incident—does it compel your character out of a provincial world and into a journey? Or does it settle on your main character and drag the story down?

Rework your premise and ask yourself the question, *When*? Does your story immediately begin unfolding towards a dramatic incident?

### My first act is boring, too long, and uneventful.

Chances are that you've begun your story in the backstory and are not starting the film as late as possible. Try to begin with a running start: An event, conflict or character flaw that will create a compelling opener—an audience grabber. Then pull back and build towards the inciting incident.

Examine your scene lengths: Do they top off at five pages or are they spilling over into seven and eight pages or more? Try reducing them down to four pages if necessary. Give yourself less time to get in and out of a scene. Make sure your scene segues and sequencing flow from one into the next seamlessly.

Try structuring the end of one scene as a question and then answering it with the beginning of the next scene. Look at *The Silence of the Lambs,* and watch how Ted Tally segues from Jack Crawford's office to that of Dr. Chilton's at the mental hospital.

> Crawford: Believe me, Agent Starling, you don't want a
>   man like Lecter inside your head.
> Starling: Why is that Sir?
> Dr. Chilton (V.O.) Oh, he's a monster!

Another example is *Beauty and the Beast.* Listen to how David Ogden Stiers' brilliant narrative ends on a question—only to be answered with the film's first song and Belle's introduction.

> Narrator: "...for who could ever learn to love a Beast?"
> Opening shot: Belle carrying a basket of flowers, singing, "Little town, it's a quiet village..."

This is scene sequencing and segueing at its best.

### My hero's problems are getting in the way of his "likeability." He comes off as mean and self-serving rather than appropriately flawed.

This is a toughie. Just as most beginners make their characters too one-dimensional favoring a main character's good qualities, a common over-correction is to make the hero too flawed and unappealing. This ventures into the terrain of the anti-hero, which can be effective, but it may greatly impair the selling of your script. Hollywood likes its heroes to be clear cut and will tolerate some inner deficiency only as long as it doesn't destroy their overall heroic nature.

Likewise, some movie stars do not wish to portray deeply flawed characters, or to be shown in a less than positive light. If your anti-hero is too problematic, it may hinder the casting of a star who can get the picture made. This is an unfortunate occupational hazard. Rather than drastically alter a character for the sake of the marketplace, you may want to rethink this strategy on your next script.

**My first act reads too technically and my scene headings seem so abrupt that they're disconcerting. In short, it's a terrible read.**
You're underwriting or overwriting, which is a clear indication of lack of clarity in character development and emotion. Practice writing maximum emotion, action, character motivation and location using minimal words. Try to segue from exterior locales to interior locales through powerful, inventive and creative methods rather that the staid EXT. or INT. Write with flow, flair and inventiveness. Use your words like the camera—revealing images exactly as they would unfold on-screen. Don't let your writing deficiencies and self-doubt get in the way of your reader's involvement.

**My story is a good one, but it takes too long to set up and never really gets going until the second act.**
You're probably giving us too much information in the beginning, which is a sign of poor development. Early on in a writing career, the tendency is to spill all the beans up front, which leaves you nowhere to go. Remember: only impart as much information as the audience needs. This will mean finding ways to get to the nuts and bolts of your story—overarching desire, objectives and conflicts—and then, if we need more information, try to find a way to bring it in future acts on a strictly need-to-know basis.

**My dialogue is sing-songy and on-the-nose. It's either too talky or trips on the tongue when read aloud.**
I contend that all dialogue starts out badly, no matter how much you're in love with it when you write it. Dialogue, more than anything else, requires constant rewriting, cutting and revision.

Movie language tends to be short and concise, and either direct or indirect. Snappy repartee can also be very intoxicating and lull you into thinking you're the next Preston Sturges. You're not. (Not yet, at least!) The best safeguard against bad dialogue is avoiding it in the first place. Chances are that you're just writing it because it's easy and fun. It may be fun, but it's not at all easy. The best fail-safe method is to rewrite, rewrite and rewrite again, no matter how good you think it is. If you're still wincing, it is better to err on the side of discretion and brevity. Let the images, actions and subtext do the talking, rather than your characters.

If you need to exposit information through dialogue, a good trick is to let it come out through conflicting characters, although even this tried and true method can become tiresome and grating if abused. Poor usage of conflicting exposition is rampant in the film *Bad Boys* (written by Michael Barrie, Jim Mulholland and Doug Richardson, based on a story by George Gallo) starring Martin Lawrence and Will Smith. Here, the tiresome, screeching, vulgar, incessant argumentation has the effect of nails across a chalkboard and sent me catapulting from the theater looking for the next Zen monastery.

Another cause of runaway dialogue is insufficient plotting and thematic development. If your theme is rich and well-formed you will have a thousand alternatives to mere dialogue. Go back and watch *Witness*, and see for yourself how little dialogue is required to tell a compelling motion picture story.

### My inciting incident comes on like a steamroller crushing an ant. It's too abrupt, too forced and seems to come from out of nowhere.

Though inciting incidents generally happen within the first thirty pages, it is a mistake to believe that it is the first event of the film. Most stories need a tickler before then. Try subtle foreshadowing of the inciting incident, so the steamroller doesn't come as such a surprise. You might also try building up to it over several scenes rather than just laying it on your audience all at once.

Look at the movie *Vertigo*, which has an excellent first act, an action-packed opening and a slow methodical build up to the inciting incident. The main character's flaw is established through his shadow with even the promise of a romantic interest early on.

Look to your selected genre. If it is action, begin with action. If you're writing a comedy, then begin with a big comedic moment. Above all, be sure and pace your best stuff with what will come later—this will inevitably lead you in the right direction.

## THE SECOND ACT

*My hero seems more of a victim to events rather than a proactive agent for change.*
Try reworking the hero's desire and objective. With a clear objective, the hero has something to strive for, rather than just letting events fall into place. When the protagonist's objective is clear, this will indicate a means for how his opponent obstructs him, and this will in turn determine how your hero combats his obstruction, pursue his objective and achieve his overarching desire.

Go back to the chapter on internal structure and redefine your hero's overarching desire and objective. Then map out a way for him to clash with his opponent in a proactive way.

*I love my first act, but the beginning of the second act is troublesome. If can get over this hump, I'm home free.*
You will need to create a reversal, or plot complication, for page forty-five. Right now you should be introducing the characters who will obstruct your hero's objective and overarching desire. Remember, as your hero's immediate desire changes to an overarching one, a whole new series of dynamics, obstacles and relationship will be introduced.

*My second act begins just fine, but slumps in the middle like a sway-back horse.*
Imagine the middle of your second act like the convergence of hot and cold fronts in a thunderstorm. This is the start of your hero's thematic conflict with his opponent—two converging forces

clashing by page sixty—the middle of your 120-page script. The events that transpire here will thrust your character towards the end of the film.

If your middle is sagging (which is a common problem in screenplays), you need to look at your opponent's thematic construction and make sure there is enough development there to bring about a series of confrontations.

Once again, look at *Witness*—in the middle of the movie we already know who the criminals are, but now John Book is battling with his own inner flaw; his partner has just been killed, and this incites his rage. When a group of local troublemakers begin harassing the Amish, Book is compelled to intervene through his old (flawed) ways of self-righteous violence. Eli Lapp warns him, "No, Book, it is not our way!" And Book responds, "No, but it's mine!"

He strikes out violently, and this flawed decision reveals his whereabouts to his enemies and brings the forces of corruption down around the people he most wants to protect.

### *I have a dynamic story right through to the middle, but I'm having difficulty bridging it with the third act.*

At this point, your characters should be headed for extreme conflict as the mid-act climax forges into a full on confrontation between hero and opponent. The next clash should be near page seventy-five. This will leave your hero near defeat and prove to be a major setback towards his objective. This reversal will force him to correct his inner flaw. He will spend the next fifteen pages (75-90) resolving it before launching into the final conflict of the third act.

### *My second act is too long and seems to plod along. How can I quicken its pace?*

You might try combining scenes through action sequencing in order to move the story along through rapid plot progression. In this case, you will want to determine the end value and purpose of the sequence and then rapidly build towards conflict, emotional release or a personal complication that will send your hero into the third act with an obsessive drive.

Look how *The Verdict* twists and turns and sends Frank Galvin nearly back to the beginning point of his character arc. His need to win conflicts with his greater need to reconnect with his integrity. This plot progression moves rapidly as he:

A.  Sees the mail being delivered along with the phone bill.
B.  Rifles through an obstinate witness' mailbox, and steals the bill to obtain the whereabouts of another witness.
C.  Calls the New York phone directory, and tracks down the missing witness.
D.  Catches a plane to New York.
E.  Confronts the key witness and pleads, "Will you help me?"

All in fewer than three pages of screen action.

Conversely, the movie, *Vertigo* overuses a series of action sequences to bridge the middle of the second act to the third with seemingly endless and tiresome scenes of James Stewart trailing Kim Novak. While it does reveal the main character's obsession, it has a dulling effect after a while. One suspects that the script fell disastrously short in the middle and the director tried to compensate for it in the camera. Only Hitchcock could get away with it.

### My second act is too short!

Usually this is due to insufficient development of the opponent. One has to bridge the middle of the second act with the third by clearly establishing the opponent's theme, objective and how he attacks the hero's objective and inner flaw.

Another reason for a short middle act is that your main character's shadow has not been fully developed. A good way to "up the stakes" for your hero, and to intensify the second act, is to bring your hero's shadow into the picture for the first time. If you've already revealed the shadow, you may want to rethink its earlier placement and reveal it here.

A common mistake is to have revealed too much in the beginning, which now comes back to haunt you. Try paring down the information you've been so liberal with in the beginning and see if you can hold something back to reveal it in the middle. If you ever have need of a flashback it is now, but instead of yielding to that temptation, try to find a more novel way to bring in your main character's shadow and backstory.

In *In the Line of Fire* Frank Horgan's aging reflexes and shadowy past are placed in the hands of his opponent in the second act, and this intensifies Horgan's drive to save the current President of the United States.

*Mr. Holland's Opus* tries to hide its second act deficiencies through montage and action sequencing, with both good and bad effects. The writer needed to convey a character's growth over a large block of years, so it was perfectly sound thinking, however, one suspects that it's the heavy reliance on montage is because the second act was too short. Watch out for using an action sequence or montage in lieu of good plotting and character development. Very often it can be used as filler and this will only serve to highlight structural deficiencies.


## THE THIRD ACT

### *My third act isn't big enough for the movies.*

Big problem. Either you've used up your big events too early or you're now facing the results of having started a screenplay without an ending in mind. Go back to the first stage and start again. If your situation is hopeless, maybe it's time to start a new screenplay. This time, don't begin to work until you have an ending that is big enough and clear enough in mind. Try not to fool yourself into thinking your ending is big enough if it really isn't. You cannot bluff your way through until you have sufficient years of experience and many finished screenplays behind you.

Avoid pat endings. At this point all the clichés, mistakes and problems of your story will confront you. Here is where you will need to be most inventive and creative. The solution in early Greek dramas was to lower an all-powerful god down on to the stage, effectively getting the character (and the writer) out of his mess. This was called *Deus ex Machina*, or literally, "God on a Machine." Writing a great ending to your film is difficult because you've worked very hard to get there. You're anxious to finish and you want your reward *now*! Unfortunately, there is no prize to be had if you throw your ending away without sufficient development. Here is where you will have to face your most glaring shortcomings. Do not despair—if nothing else, you will have learned a valuable lesson and your work will improve with your continuing efforts. A good ending should expand from your original theme, and prove itself as startling and revelatory for you as it is for your hero and audience; it should smack them straight between the eyes and make their hearts race. Don't be frustrated if you're not there yet. Rewriting and rethinking your script can help you solve the problem, either with future drafts, or in your next screenplay.

### My ending is a good one, but arrives too soon.

Try to put off your hero's fulfillment of his objective until the very end. Between page ninety and one hundred and twenty, there are at least five important turning points: page 90, page 105, page 110, page 115 and the final impact on the world of story, page 120. So, if by page seventy-five your hero has resolved his inner flaw, then by page ninety he is confronting his opponent with renewed vigor. But the opponent attacks again with surprising alacrity and the hero falters (page 105). He picks himself up again, but this time with the right balance required, so that by page 115 he has finally changed sufficiently to defeat his opponent. The remaining five pages can be devoted to showing the hero obtain or not obtain his objective and the impact this has on the world of story.

If your third act still seems anti-climactic, you may want to look for ways to foreshadow events in earlier acts. By now you will have a hyper-awareness of the details of your story, so you can go back and layer in this information into earlier acts. This will give you some last minute details to pay off in the concluding moments of the film.

Try to remember that you probably won't write a great script every time you sit down. Some, if not most of them, will fall disastrously short of the mark. True art, as well as true genius, is rarely achieved and can most often be attributed to a gradual process of plying one's craft over the course of years. While we are all dazzled by the success of a Callie Khouri—who wrote *Thelma & Louise*, won an Academy Award® for it and earned millions of dollars with her first effort—the seasoned writer knows that this can be as much a curse as anything else. The problem with such success stories is that you can easily be persuaded into thinking you have the answers, but now you face all the same burdens as the unsold screenwriter, only you must now shoulder the extra weight of success. Every screenplay that follows your triumph will be judged against that mega-star breakout hit.

Everyone bombs, whether you're James Cameron or Jane Austen. While it is easy to say, "I told you so," or look back on another's work in hindsight (which I realize I've done to a great extent in this book), it is very hard to determine who is to be faulted or who is to be credited with the final success or failure of a film.

- George Lucas had his *Howard the Duck.*
- Sydney Pollack had his *Havana.*
- Steven Spielberg had his *Always.*
- Barry Levinson had his *Sleepers* and *Toys.*
- Quentin Tarantino had his *Four Rooms* and *From Dusk till Dawn.*
- Joe Ezterhaus had his *Showgirls.*
- Francis Ford Coppola had his *One from the Heart.*
- William Goldman had his *The Last Action Hero.*
- Rob Riener had his *North.*

"It is just as hard to write a bad novel as a good one."

–Ken Kesey

Are they any less worthy, talented, or ingenious individuals? Decidedly not, they're human with problems, desires and ambitions every bit as complicated as your own. The one thing we know about every one of them, is that they are all very serious about their craft. Their dedication and commitment to their craft and personal visions will inspire film-goers to both watch and learn from their failures and successes until the last light in the last movie theater goes out for good.

## PERSONAL ADVICE

*Do not squander your creative energy,* or cast thy pearls before swine. If you have an extroverted personality and wish to cultivate a more somber creative voice, my advice is to restrain the tendency to spew your mental musings to anyone willing to listen. Do not be so eager to impress, enthrall or win the heart of everyone you meet with the film you're writing. In the end, you may be a hit at cocktail parties, but find yourself depleted and empty when it comes to finishing your project.

*Eschew collaboration in the beginning.* The beginner turns to writing partners as a way of easing the loneliness of the craft. You may think you don't have sufficient discipline, talent or craft to write a full-length screenplay—even if this is initially true—if you dilute the process by taking on a partner, you only put off the invaluable experience of learning it for yourself. A large part of the writer's personal journey is slaying the demons of self-doubt. If you stall, share or procrastinate, you are only avoiding the inevitable.

*Learn to distinguish between your creative voice and your editorial voice.* While both are important and require cultivation, the editorial "you" will sound-off more strongly in the beginning. It usually chimes in with harsh criticism, second guesses and general discouragement. The determined writer turns this negativity into a constructive and exacting tool. Like everything else, the editorial voice needs to be trained and focused, rather than be allowed to oppress your creativity and inspiration. It has an important job to fill, but it needs to be put in perspective as well. The only thing that separates the professional from the amateur is the persistence and perseverance to endure through their mistakes. Writers write; non-writers try and then give up. Keep Einstein's equation in mind: Genius is 90 percent perspiration and 10 percent inspiration.

*Do not gossip.* Gossip is soul-deadening; it wastes the mind and destroys your truth-telling. Most gossip is based on lies and half-truths born out of conformity and a misguided desire to better your opinion of yourself at someone else's expense. As Mark Twain once observed, "It takes a friend and a foe working together to hurt you to the quick: one to slander you and the other to bring you the news!" As life progresses you will find that some of the most reviled outcasts of society are usually those with the most unusual and invaluable gifts to offer.

*Be wary of entertainment shows and trade papers.* Like the tabloids, their allure is to promote lottery fever. They feed off the miraculous and the misfortunate, often without understanding the real facts behind either. They tend to offer up soothing pablum and pseudo-solutions regardless of the real circumstances involved. The truth is that behind every success, no matter how menial or "overnight" it may seem—there probably was a great deal of courage, hard work, sacrifice and ingenuity behind it. I believe this wholeheartedly and do not try to relegate anyone's achievement to mere luck. Someone else's misfortune can lure you into feeling good about yourself. But the fact is that every misfortune is a blessing as well. If you are cavalier about someone else's downturns, you are not paying enough attention to your own.

> "In Hollywood, it is not enough that you should succeed, but your friends must fail as well."
>
> –F. Scott Fitzgerald

*Avoid the co-dependent and the needy.* The writer's first and primary relationship is with the craft. So, it is only logical that others will become jealous of your time. They will want you for themselves. Nietzche once observed that a healthy person has more to fear from a sick person than from another healthy person. Sick, needy and co-dependent people will drain your creativity, time and vitality. They are the vampires, addicts, game players, energy-sumps and power-mongers whose spiritual emptiness is so complete, their fulfillment can only come from sucking your vitality and self- sufficiency.

*Use a computer or word processor and appropriate screenwriting software.* The screenwriting format is an exact and time-honored tradition. While it constantly changes and evolves, there are certain requirements that assist the writer's quest for a professionally crafted story. I firmly believe that with the advent of the computer we will hear from exciting, original and previously muted voices; voices that may lack the literary mastery and discipline previously required of their predecessors.

It is foolish to even attempt to write a screenplay in longhand. It only creates more work and defers the creative process to office staff and typists. Writing is best served when it *serves you*. The computer assists the novice writer by granting freedom from the daunting mechanical requirements of cutting, pasting, editing and rearranging sentence and scene structure—all devices which prove to better a story. The ease with which these meticulous tasks are accomplished via computer allows the writer to focus on the power and effect of the words, rather than the convention of how they are assembled.

The conventions of the spoken word are different than words applied to paper. Chances are that you have a lot of practice speaking, but very little in writing. In speech, our ideas usually come forth in a flow of ideas, with particular emphasis on the beginning and ending of each sentence. When you write them down there is a tendency to invert the last idea with the first one, and this creates a confusion in logic and sequencing for the reader. In a screenplay, the words unfold on paper exactly as they would on-screen, so it is necessary to develop the kind of unique sentence logic and mental discipline the lends itself to the flow of moving images.

For instance, when you're panning a room, your mind conjures up the end result of the pan but when you write it down, your focus is on the end object or person. So you write that first rather than showing how the end point came to be—through the slow, exacting pan. The tendency is to detail the person or object before the action has taken place, which creates a jumble of screen logic. This is natural to freestyle writing and will require going back and rewriting the sequence so that it unfolds sequentially. This requires mental and intellectual discipline. A large part of your rewriting chores will be clearing up the flow of freestyle writing and organizing it to follow a logical sequence of action.

*Write every day—It is how God speaks to you.* By writing every day, you remove the twaddle and clutter of your sleeping state and wake the divine genius within. You are probably not the person you have told yourself you are, but much, much more. Writing, like dreaming will reveal the real you. The writer is not male, female, Black, White, Democrat, Jew, Christian or any physical designation. The writer is, as Heraclitus once said, a tool for the mind of God. A good way to become so pure and worthy a vessel is to write, write and write! When the vessel is empty of pollutants it can be filled with divine insight. The way to further the process of purification is to write.

*Read the classics!* Limit your time spent on mental junk food such as magazines, newspapers and popular fiction. If you have only so much time during the day and reading is difficult, you need to prioritize your input schedule. The idea is to develop an original mind. The works of the masters reveal the "encounter of the intensely conscious souls with their world," whereas most media is engineered to soothe the sleeping, robotic state of the unconscious masses.

*Don't believe everything you think.* The mind is a tool designed to feed back what you pour into it. Garbage in, garbage out. The mind is trained to operate on a binary system of duality. Good/Bad, Pleasure/Pain, Loss/Gain, and so on. Above the mind however, is the intellect and somewhere beyond that, if you search hard enough, is your own genius—your own personal cathedral of intense knowing and experience. It's time to venture outside of the confessional and explore the unbound dimensions of your own being.

# More Screenwriting Books from IFILMPublishing

## HOW NOT TO WRITE A SCREENPLAY
*101 Common Mistakes Most Screenwriters Make*
by Denny Martin Flinn

There is no shortage of experts telling you how to write a screenplay, but *How Not to Write a Screenplay* is the writer's secret weapon. After all the work you've put into your screenplay, the last thing you want to do is give the reader an excuse to put it down. Learn to avoid the pitfalls of bad screenwriting. **ISBN 1-58065-015-5**
$16.95 (+$4.50 shipping)

## ELEMENTS OF STYLE FOR SCREENWRITERS
*The Essential Manual for Writers of Screenplays*
by Paul Argentini

The ultimate quick-reference guide. Clear and concise instruction on screenwriting format, structure and style. Includes a chapter on playwriting and an updated list of literary-agent contacts. **ISBN 1-58065-003-1**
$11.95 (+$4.50 shipping)

## THE COMPLETE WRITER'S GUIDE TO HEROES & HEROINES
*Sixteen Master Archetypes*
by Tami D. Cowden, Caro LaFever, Sue Viders

Create extraordinary characters and elevate your writing. Follow the guidelines of the archetypes presented in this comprehensive guide. With examples from great literature and classic films, *The Complete Writer's Guide to Heroes & Heroines* will help you create truly unforgettable characters. **ISBN 1-58065-024-4**
$17.95 (+$4.50 shipping)

## THIS BUSINESS OF SCREENWRITING
*How to Protect Yourself as a Screenwriter*
by Ron Suppa

Practical tips for the writer, with advice on crafting marketable treatments, pitches, spec screenplays and adaptations. Plus important information on how to protect your work, get representation, make deals and more! Suppa helps writers survive and thrive in the sometimes messy collision of art and business. **ISBN 1-58065-016-3**
$19.95 (+$4.50 shipping)

## To order, call 323.308.3490 or visit www.hcdonline.com

# More Filmmaking Books
# from IFILMPublishing

## DIGITAL BABYLON

*Hollywood, Indiewood and Dogme 95*

by Shari Roman

In an exploration of the influence of Dogme 95 style filmmaking and the new technologies that have brought film and video making within reach of the layman, Shari Roman has created an entertaining and clear-sighted account with *Digital Babylon: Hollywood, Indiewood and Dogme 95*. Exclusive, in-depth discussions with maverick filmmakers Lars von Trier, Mike Figgis, Wim Wenders, Harmony Korine, Rick Linklater, and Gus Van Sant. **ISBN 1-58065-036-8**
$19.95 (+$4.50 shipping)

## THE INDIE PRODUCER'S HANDBOOK

*Creative Producing from A to Z*

by Myrl A. Schreibman

Myrl Schreibman has written a straightforward, insightful, and articulate account of what it takes to make a successful feature film. Filled with engaging and useful anecdotes, Schreibman provides a superlative introduction and overview to all of the key elements in producing feature films. Useful to film students and filmmakers as a theoretical and practical guide to understanding the filmmaking process. **ISBN 1-58065-037-6**
$21.95 (+$4.50 shipping)

## THE IFILM DIGITAL VIDEO FILMMAKER'S HANDBOOK

by Maxie D. Collier

Maxie D. Collier's book covers the creative and technical aspects of digital shooting and is designed to provide detailed, practical information on DV filmmaking. Collier delves into the mechanics and craft of creating personal films and introduces the reader to the essential terminology, concepts, equipment, and services required to produce a quality DV feature film. Includes DVD. **ISBN 1-58065-031-7**
$24.95 (+$4.50 shipping)

## THE ULTIMATE FILM FESTIVAL SURVIVAL GUIDE, 2ND EDITION

by Chris Gore

Learn the secrets of successfully marketing and selling your film at over 600 film festivals worldwide. Author Chris Gore reveals how to get a film accepted and what to do after acceptance, from putting together a press kit to putting on a great party to actually closing a deal. Gore includes an expanded directory section, new interviews as well as a new chapter that details a case study of the most successful independent film to date, *The Blair Witch Project.* **ISBN 1-58065-032-5**
$19.95 (+$4.50 shipping)

# To order, call 323.308.3490 or
# visit www.hcdonline.com